Illegal Immigration

Recent Titles in the
CONTEMPORARY WORLD ISSUES
Series

Books in the **Contemporary World Issues** series address vital issues in today's society such as genetic engineering, pollution, and biodiversity. Written by professional writers, scholars, and nonacademic experts, these books are authoritative, clearly written, up-to-date, and objective. They provide a good starting point for research by high school and college students, scholars, and general readers as well as by legislators, businesspeople, activists, and others.

Each book, carefully organized and easy to use, contains an overview of the subject, a detailed chronology, biographical sketches, facts and data and/or documents and other primary source material, a forum of authoritative perspective essays, annotated lists of print and nonprint resources, and an index. Readers of books in the Contemporary World Issues series will find the information they need to have a better understanding of the social, political, environmental, and economic issues facing the world today.

Illegal Immigration

A REFERENCE HANDBOOK

Second Edition

Michael C. LeMay

 ABC-CLIO™

An Imprint of ABC-CLIO, LLC
Santa Barbara, California • Denver, Colorado

Library of Congress Cataloging-in-Publication Data

LeMay, Michael C., 1941–
  Illegal immigration : a reference handbook / Michael C. LeMay. — Second edition.
     pages cm. — (Contemporary world issues)
  Includes bibliographical references and index.
  ISBN 978-1-4408-4012-8 (acid-free paper) — ISBN 978-1-4408-4013-5 (ebook)   1. Illegal aliens—United States.   2. Illegal aliens—Government policy—United States.   3. United States—Emigration and immigration—Government policy.   I. Title.
  JV6483.L46 2015
  325.73—dc23   2015019015

ISBN: 978-1-4408-4012-8
EISBN: 978-1-4408-4013-5

19 18 17 16 15   1 2 3 4 5

This book is also available on the World Wide Web as an eBook. Visit www.abc-clio.com for details.

ABC-CLIO
An Imprint of ABC-CLIO, LLC

ABC-CLIO, LLC
130 Cremona Drive, P.O. Box 1911
Santa Barbara, California 93116–1911

This book is printed on acid-free paper ∞

Manufactured in the United States of America

Illegal Immigration: A Reference Handbook, Second Edition, defines the concept and analyzes the flow of unauthorized immigration to the United States since 1970. It focuses on why illegal immigration and the reform of immigration policy regarding it continue to be such a vexing political problem—what is well described as a policy conundrum. What makes good (that is, popular) politics on the issue often results in bad policy (that is, inefficient or ineffective policy). The gaps and failures as well as unanticipated consequences of provisions in legal immigration contribute significantly to the illegal immigration flow. It demonstrates the extent of the problem of unauthorized immigration—its causes and effects. This second edition adds a chapter comprising original essays that offer various perspectives on the issue. It adds a significant discussion of the groups who lobby or agitate politically to either reform immigration policy or oppose such reform, several of whom have arisen since the election of President Barack Obama in 2008. Still other groups had been politically active but until recent years had not entered the political fray over immigration policy reform. These pro and con groups struggle to determine the nature and content of illegal immigration policy that has resulted in the current stalemate on the issue in the U.S. Congress. Moreover, it recognizes that immigration policy regarding both legal and unauthorized immigration is inherently *intermestic policy*—one that involves both domestic and international concerns. Immigration policy has significant political consequences for and across a number of related policy areas. Whatever the Congress does on immigration law, whatever executive actions the president takes on the matter, and whatever court decisions have been rendered on cases involving the issue have implications for U.S. international relations. And often what other nation-states do or fail to do in their policy profoundly affects the illegal immigration flow. Developments on the international scene, moreover, are in constant flux and contribute to the flow of migration across national boundaries. Unauthorized immigration waxes and wanes in response to such events, which serve as push factors in the flow. This makes the problem increasingly difficult in complexity and scope, thereby making policy responses all the more difficult.

The unauthorized immigration issue has been on the national political and policy agenda, largely unabated, since 1970. Sometimes the issue is on the front-burner of American political discourse; and sometimes it is on the back-burner. But it is nearly always on the agenda of government and politics at one or several levels of government in the federal system. It is an issue that is substantive in its importance and timely in its impact on the culture, economy, and politics of American society. The undocumented immigration flow, largely across the nation's southern border, moreover, contributes to a collective perception of national identity—a sense of peoplehood—often in ways that engender fear and resistance to change among a significant portion of the population. In recent years threats from international terrorism and from epidemic diseases that become pandemic in nature have fueled xenophobia and increased calls for restrictions in immigration. Since 2001, a sense of "Fortress America" has permeated the political debate and policy making on the issue. Immigration policy regarding both the legal and, especially, the unauthorized flow has become an important element in our homeland security and defense policy making.

The United States is one of the leading and, in absolute numbers of persons entering, *the* leading immigration-reception nation in the world. Its population now includes significant numbers of permanent residents who come from nearly 200 nations of origin. Since the United States began counting them, legal immigrants have exceeded 75 million. Added to those numbers are an estimated 11–12 million unauthorized immigrants. The decade 2000–2010 has seen exceptionally high levels of immigration. The recession of 2009–2013, the nation's most severe economic downturn since the Great Depression of the 1930s, was politically all the more stressful as a result of the issue and illegal immigration flow.

Today, American politics struggles with heightened fears that unauthorized immigration overburdens public education, health care, prison, public health, and welfare systems, especially at state and local government levels. There have been significant increases in fears that the unauthorized immigrant flow contributes to terrorist cells or brings in with it the newly emerging "hot virus" disease epidemics. Such fears suggest that the current era of immigration policy making may well be described as the "storm-door era."

This second edition concentrates on those trends and policy developments since 2000. It offers answers to essential questions about illegal immigration to the United States and inherently connected issues that are accessible to high school students, undergraduate students, general readers, and individuals who are interested in topics such as immigration, border security, and human rights issues. It examines the history of illegal immigration in the United States, describing in detail its key issues and events. It explores the myriad of problems and controversies that are linked to the issue of illegal immigration, and explains how politicians, policy makers, and policy implementers have tried, and continue to grapple with, efforts to solve them. It surveys the complex history of illegal immigration in a manner that helps the reader identify the key issues in an easy-to-understand fashion. The perspectives chapter allows a broad range of voices, from all sides of the issue, to be heard. These voices add crucial and diverse perspectives to that of the author's expertise.

The economic and political instability in Mexico and Central American countries such as El Salvador, Guatemala, and Honduras has led to a huge influx of unauthorized immigration. Other nations have contributed to the spike in both legal and illegal immigrants, particularly those from China, India, the Philippines, and the Dominican Republic. These new migrants often experience very perilous journeys through hostile environments, risking their lives and expending precious and extensive resources in an effort to find a better life. A significant portion of the American populous, however, is outraged by the illegal immigration flow and by the immigrants' very presence. They label illegal immigrants criminals. Such critics cite vexing problems like poverty, unemployment, crime, security, and public health risks that are exacerbated by the illegal immigration influx. They feel those problems must be addressed and seriously mitigated before the nation attempts to care for those entering the borders illegally. Other Americans feel sympathy for illegal immigrants, especially the children who come unaccompanied by adults, citing the dangerous circumstances in their home countries from which they are escaping. They hold the position that, given those circumstances, aiding those children and other unauthorized entrants is a humanitarian issue.

This second edition addresses a host of questions with respect to illegal immigration. Who is coming illegally and why? How does one become illegal? What events created the economic disparities that compel them to leave their nation of origin? Does the United States have any responsibility for taking care of the more than 11 million persons unauthorized to be here? Are illegal immigrants a benefit or a burden? Do they help or harm the economy and infrastructure of the United States? Should and can the United States secure its borders, as is called for by many politicians, especially those on the "right" of the political spectrum? Should the United States be more lenient and allow for "earned legalization" of the millions of persons here illegally? Should we adhere to our long-standing tradition of being a "country of immigrants" and a place of asylum for refugees?

Is there really a difference between amnesty and earned legalization? Are illegal immigrants criminals by the very fact of their illegal status? Is it ethical to demand more deportations? Should the United States maintain its current immigration policy position of preference for family unification? Or, should it tilt immigration law in the direction of aiding the economy? What, if anything, can the government do to pass immigration reform? Will such reforms actually help, or will they simply serve as an incentive, drawing still more illegal migration?

Chapter 1 discusses the background and history of illegal immigration to the United States. It provides a thorough examination of the economic, political, and social contexts surrounding the phenomenon, and discusses key moments along the timeline of the flow. It examines the development of public policy aimed at coping with immigration more broadly, providing the context to better understand current events. It shows why the topic of illegal immigration matters, and demonstrates the importance of the issue. Information in the chapter provides insights from current works and studies of the issue. It is synthesized and presented in a manner both comprehensive and unbiased for the reader's consumption, better enabling them to form their own judgments on the issues.

Chapter 2 outlines the most problematic situations related to illegal immigration, and why the issue poses such a policy conundrum. It addresses the efforts taken by governments at all levels and branches of government to cope with these problems, detailing the specific actions taken. Finally, it discusses proposed solutions to the problems on the agenda of government, particularly at the national level.

Chapter 3 comprises eight essays by scholars and other individuals who are involved in the issue. It brings together key voices from diverse disciplinary contexts. These voices represent various positions on all sides of the matter and enrich the perspective that the author is able to provide.

Chapter 4 describes the key individuals and organizations involved in the illegal immigration discourse. The chapter profiles nongovernmental actors and organizations that advocate for or against the various policy proposals to resolve the policy conundrum of illegal immigration. They are the "stakeholders" in the policy debates on the issue who must be involved in any solutions to the problems.

Chapter 5 offers data and documents gathered from the illegal immigration debate. Examination of these data helps to answer the following questions: Who is entering the country undocumented, and from where are they coming? How do persons who enter with documents become unauthorized and thereby illegal immigrants, and from where do they come? How many such immigrants establish successful lives here? How many estimated deaths have occurred in failed attempts to cross the border? How many people are being deported, and what are the effects of those deportations? How much money is being spent to care for illegal immigrants? How are those costs borne differentially by the levels of government in the U.S. federal system? How much money is flushed into the U.S. economy by illegal immigrants? Do they benefit the Social Security system? What are the economic impacts of the illegal immigration flow on border towns and regions, as well as on the United States as a whole?

Chapter 6 is a resource chapter, presenting an annotated bibliography of print and electronic resources especially relevant to the issue. The primary resources are books and Internet sources, but other items useful for further research by the reader include magazines, government reports and statistics, and other print and nonprint resources.

A chronology of the key moments in the history of illegal immigration is then provided.

Finally, a glossary provides easy access to definitions of the key terms used in the illegal immigration debate. The glossary is followed by a comprehensive index. The book closes with a brief "About the Author" page indicating the author's bona fides for writing the book.

Illegal Immigration

Introduction: The Scope and Nature of Unauthorized Immigration

More than 75 million legal immigrants (also known as authorized immigrants or permanent resident aliens) have entered the United States since the country began keeping count in 1820. Since 1970, an estimated 10 to 15 million persons have entered or have become unauthorized immigrants (also known as illegal immigrants). Current estimates of illegal immigrants in the United States place their number at about 11.5 million (Pew Hispanic Research Center 2014a). The presence of so many immigrants who remain in the shadows of the population has revived decades-old concern about the ability of the United States to control the borders. The issue of illegal immigration is once again at the forefront of American politics and on the agenda of the national government and even some state governments as a serious problem needing to be addressed. There is widespread consensus that the immigration system is broken.

To better understand the nature and scope of the problem a few terms need clarification. A person may become an unauthorized, or illegal, immigrant in several ways. *Undocumented immigrants* are those who enter the country without paperwork, a visa

A Mexican migratory laborer, employed under the Bracero Program, harvests tomatoes in southern California. The Bracero workers who came for nine months during the Bracero programs' years of operation, 1942–1964, established the chain migration networks that influenced the illegal immigration flow from 1970 to date. (AP Photo)

3

or legal authorization. They are commonly referred to as illegal aliens. They enter the country from both its northern and southern borders. They are often pejoratively referred to as *wetbacks*, a slang term deriving from the fact that so many of them came across the southern border and the Rio Grande River. Another way to become unauthorized is by becoming a visa-overstayer. These are migrants who enter the United States with paperwork, a temporary visa of some sort, like a tourist visa or student visa, and who subsequently stay in the country after the visa has expired. Migrants can also become unauthorized when they enter with a conditional visa and then break the conditions of the visa. A good example is a person who enters on a student visa and then fails to attend school, or who takes a job, which he or she is not allowed to do with a student visa. Still another way to become an unauthorized or illegal immigrant is by entering with fraudulent papers. Finally, a person can become an unauthorized or illegal immigrant by committing a crime after entry, thereby being subject to deportation, and then failing to depart (Information Plus 2014). Among the approximately 11 million unauthorized immigrants, roughly 60 percent are undocumented entrants, while the remaining 40 percent are overstayers, fraudulent entrants, or persons failing to depart when under orders to do so (Pew Hispanic Research Center 2014b).

Two further terms useful to the discussion of policies aimed at the illegal immigration problem refer to why persons become international migrants who intentionally seek permanent residence in a country other than their nation of birth or origin. These terms distinguish between factors influencing their decisions to migrate. *Push factors* are those reasons that compel persons to emigrate from their nation of origin (LeMay 2013a: 5). Push factors include events such as wars, widespread epidemic diseases, extreme and widespread poverty in a country with a failed economy, or ethnic, racial, or religious persecution. Push factors may lead individuals to conclude they must emigrate or face death. *Pull factors* are reasons that draw millions of migrating persons to a particular country, like the United States. Pull factors are exemplified by subsidized travel, an abundance of

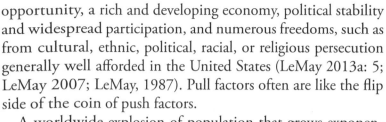

opportunity, a rich and developing economy, political stability and widespread participation, and numerous freedoms, such as from cultural, ethnic, political, racial, or religious persecution generally well afforded in the United States (LeMay 2013a: 5; LeMay 2007; LeMay, 1987). Pull factors often are like the flip side of the coin of push factors.

A worldwide explosion of population that grows exponentially, coupled with enormous poverty and extremely high levels of unemployment and political turmoil experienced by many so-called Third World nations, drives ethnic and religious tensions. Natural disasters are another push factor compelling international migration. The United Nations estimates that there are more than 15 million refugees worldwide (www.unhcr.org/51c071816.html, accessed February 7, 2015).

This distinction between push and pull factors is significant analytically precisely because policy makers in the receiving nation (like the United States) can do little if anything in their public policy that will directly affect push factors, other than raising or lowering refugee rates. Most policies that can affect international migration driven by push factors must be by multinational organizations, such as the United Nations, the World Health Organization, UNICEF, the World Bank, and so on. However, their policies can only recommend actions to receiving countries; they cannot compel agreement or compliance. Illegal immigration to the United States is an especially vexing problem because the United States is a First World economy that shares a porous, 2,000-mile border with the Third World country of Mexico. Mexico has a deeply troubled economy. It, too, experiences a significant flow of illegal migration across its southern border by persons fleeing Central American nations like El Salvador, Guatemala, and Honduras, the vast majority of whom are intentionally just passing through Mexico on their way seeking to enter the United States (LeMay 1994; Hammermesh and Bean, 1996; Kiser and Kiser, 1979).

This chapter will discuss the background and history of the issue, focusing particularly on the trend toward increasing

numbers of illegal entries since 2000, and on the greater dispersion in recent years of the unauthorized immigrant population.
No longer are most unauthorized immigrants clustered in just
a handful of border states, nor even the 10 states that have been
characterized as gateway states (Zuniga and Hernandez-Leon
2005; LeMay, 1987). Illegal immigration is no longer a
border-states problem, as today some 30 states have significant
and growing percentages of their population in unauthorized
status. It is now truly a national problem. This chapter will
summarize and explain the trend, covering different points of
view as to the nature and impact of unauthorized immigration,
and will touch upon possible solutions—some tried with little
success, and others proposed but not yet enacted.

The Roots of the Problem

Unfortunately, illegal immigration arises out of problems in
the legal immigration system and policy enacted for its implementation. Moreover, it is the result, more often, of push factors than of pull factors. Current legal immigration policy is
established by the act of October 3, 1965, the Immigration and
Naturalization Act of 1965 (79 Stat. 911).

Gaps, flaws, and unanticipated consequences with current
legal immigration law and policies form the basis for the nature
and scope of the illegal flow. In a very real sense, one cannot
grasp the development of the unauthorized immigration flow
without first understanding the impact of the Bracero Program
and its demise in 1964.

Unauthorized immigration to the United States increased
exponentially after 1970. The Bracero Program was a temporary worker program that allowed U.S. employers—mostly
agriculture producers and the railroads—to import workers
from Mexico on a nine-month basis in a given year. It began
in 1942, during World War II, as a measure to cope with the
severe labor shortage in agriculture when millions of workers
left the farms for the high-wage wartime production jobs in

metropolitan areas. Other workers left to serve in the armed forces, which grew to millions in uniform. Then, the rapidly expanding postwar economy continued the need for and even expansion of the Bracero Program. Congress passed the Agricultural Act of 1949, which codified the program (63 Stat. 1051), and the influx peaked in the mid-1960s with annual totals around 350,000. The program ended in 1964, when it was stopped as part of an agreement to pass the Immigration and Naturalization Act of 1965 (LeMay 2004: 266; Calavita 1992; Craig 1971; Information Plus 2006). Organized labor and various patriotic and restrictionist groups argued that the program was getting out of hand. Their lobbying on the issue resulted in the program's termination in 1964. The controlled entry of temporary farm and railroad workers was replaced by the flow of undocumented immigrants, especially from Mexico, who were essentially the same workers who had participated in the Bracero Program (Muller and Espanshade 1985; LeMay and Barkan 1999; LeMay 2007; LeMay 1987).

Numerous studies noted the importance of Mexican immigration patterns established during the Bracero period, which essentially set up *chain migration* flows that persisted long after the end of the Bracero Program (Andreas 2000; Bustamente 1981; Calavita 1992; Chiswick 1982; Crockroft 1986; Conover 1987; Craig 1971; Kiser and Kiser 1979; Kirstein 1977; Massey et al. 1990; Nevins 2002). These undocumented immigrants filled a niche in the economic-wage structure of the U.S. economy. Their wages were low enough to allow the employer to make a profit. Faced with the end of this cheap labor flow, employers had few options. They could move operations overseas or across the border, replace their workers with machines, hire illegal immigrants, or go out of business. With the demise of the program, in California only lettuce and citrus growers raised wages to attract domestic workers. Tomato growers switched to mechanical harvesters. Asparagus growers moved to Mexico, and marginal growers in all crops simply closed down and sold their farms. When the 1965 immigration law imposed a new preference system with a 20,000 per country limit, hundreds of thousands of workers who had been coming to work for nine months simply continued to come but without documentation. Their numbers quickly grew to an estimated half-million per year. These workers knew where to find work and places to live. Former Bracero workers passed on that knowledge to kinfolk and village compatriots.

Likewise, employers who had legally hired workers through the Bracero Program continued to hire them after it ended. From 1965 until the enactment of the Immigration Reform and Control Act of 1986 (IRCA), it was illegal for workers to come to the United States without documents—a civil law—but it was not illegal for employers to hire them. A provision known as the "Texas Proviso" in the 1952 McCarran-Walter Act exempted employers of illegal aliens from the harboring provisions of the law, then using the quota system (Glazer 1985: 52–53; LeMay 1994: 10). Employers knew and valued the former Bracero workers and accepted their recommendations for hiring their compatriots. The undocumented flow simply replaced those entering under the temporary worker provision, except they did not return to Mexico after nine months of seasonal work. Increasingly after 1970, they came and remained permanently as unauthorized immigrants (LeMay 1994: 26–27; Suro 2015).

The consistency of the flow from Mexico to a few specific states, termed "gateway states," showed a clear pattern of state of residence from 1940 to 2000, as is their gradual dispersion to nongateway states after enactment of IRCA in 1986.

The undocumented flow exacerbated the job and income problems of blacks, legal residents of Hispanic origin, and other secondary job market workers by reducing the number of such jobs available to them, depressing wages for those jobs they did hold, and impacting working conditions (Papademetriou and Miller 1984; Phillips and Massey 1999; Zuniga and Hernandez-Leon 2005; Hammermesch and Bean, 1996; Kiser and Kiser, 1979; LeMay, 1987).

Push factors propelled the rising flow. As noted in the Final Report of the Select Commission on Immigration and Refugee Policy (SCIRP):

One of the greatest pressures for international migration is and will be the world population growth. Projections of this growth show more than a 50 percent increase from 1975 to the year 2000, from 4 billion to 6.35 billion. It has been estimated that 92 percent of this growth will take place in countries whose resources are least able to accommodate the needs of new population. . . . World economic and political instability would be threatened by the sudden, large-scale population moves which could result from widespread political or economic chaos in developing nations. (1981: 19–20)

Rising push factors induced waves of migration that had long-term impact and were more powerful than any other factors—especially pull factors. The changing flow of legal and unauthorized immigration resulted in a growing concern in the news media, in public opinion polls, and within government of the inadequacy of immigration laws to meet the new challenges and to "control the borders" (SCIRP 1981: 10; Bean and Sullivan 1985: 67–73; LeMay 1989: 8–10).

More immigrants, legal and unauthorized, entered the United States between 2000 and 2005 than in any other five-year period in U.S. history—an estimated 8 million. Nearly half, 3.7 million, entered illegally, according to Census Bureau data reviewed by the Center for Immigration Studies. In 2005, Arizona and New Mexico declared states of emergency in an effort to cope with problems of crime and financial exigencies that their respective governors (both Democrats) linked to massive illegal immigration. The immigrant population set a record at 35.2 million in March 2005, greater than those of the immigrant wave of 1910. Immigrants today comprise about 12 percent of the total U.S. population. Chapter 5 presents tables and figures detailing the number of immigrants by state, ranked by their share of the population of that state, and numbers arriving after 2000.

Changes in Legal Immigration: Setting the Stage for Illegal Immigration

The Immigration and Naturalization Act of 1965 changed legal immigration from the quota system to a preference system. Whereas the quota system reflected the racism of the 1920s, the 1965 act reflected the changed attitude that was more open to immigration as national policy makers struggled with reevaluating many national laws in the civil rights era, immigration law included. The post–World War II need to modify the quota system, exemplified in the use of special acts, nonquota immigration policies, and refugee/escapee laws, amply demonstrated the need for comprehensive reform of immigration policy. Healthy economic conditions in the early 1960s enabled even organized labor to favor a more liberal immigration policy. The 1965 act replaced the quota system with a seven-category preference system that allocated visas for each foreign state on a first-come, first-served basis with a cap of 20,000 visas per year. The categories were:

1. First preference: unmarried sons and daughters of U.S. citizens
2. Second preference: spouse and unmarried sons and daughters of permanent resident aliens
3. Third preference: members of the professions and scientists and artists of exceptional ability
4. Fourth preference: married sons and daughters of U.S. citizens
5. Fifth preference: brothers and sisters of U.S. citizens
6. Sixth preference: skilled and unskilled workers in short supply
7. Seventh preference: refugees

Worldwide events soon outstripped the ability of the law to accommodate refugees and its annual limit of 20,000 visas per country was also applied to immigrants from the Western Hemisphere nations, which previously had none. These provisions resulted in enormous pressures for immigrants to arrive in the United States "through the back door." Long waiting lists for legal visas began to backlog into scores of years, prompting many to come as undocumented immigrants. The number of undocumented border crossings soon swelled to what began to be called a flood of illegal immigrants.

In 1970 the Immigration and Naturalization Service (INS), within which the Border Patrol agency was housed, apprehended about a quarter-million undocumented persons attempting to cross the porous, 2,000-mile southern border. By 1986 that number had risen to nearly 2 million. SCIRP estimated the total unauthorized immigrant population as of 1978 at between 3.5 and 6 million. Hispanics, especially those from Mexico, and then from Central America, made up the bulk of the undocumented. Roughly two-thirds of the undocumented were Mexicans driven north by grinding poverty and enormous unemployment at home. Many were former Bracero workers or relatives of those who had come in the period of the program, 1942–1964.

Mexican immigrants, who made up about 60 percent of Hispanic immigrants, especially the undocumented ones, came from rural and small-town areas, fleeing dire poverty. They often exhibited a "sojourner" attitude since they resided close to their native areas. They frequently returned to their place of origin, thereby keeping strong family, social, and cultural ties. Whereas earlier immigrant waves were eager to naturalize, having come expecting to remain permanently, and often having cut off formal ties with their countries of origin, Mexicans, and particularly the undocumented, considered the border a mere nuisance rather than a barrier. They moved back and forth, retaining strong ties with their homeland and slowing their rate of naturalization.

Estimates of the number of illegal immigrants at any time vary considerably and are best viewed as "guestimates," since persons of illegal status do not identify themselves for fear of deportation. The numbers vary, too, seasonally. Figure 5.1 shows the estimated number of unauthorized immigrants in the United States from 1986 to 2014, based on estimates from several sources. Thus, the total number of illegal immigrants rose from about 3.2 million in 1986 to 9.3 million in 2002, to 11.2 million in 2012. In 2000, about two-thirds of the unauthorized immigrants resided in six so-called gateway states: California (with 27 percent), Texas (13 percent), New York (8 percent), Florida (7 percent), Illinois (6 percent), and New Jersey (4 percent) (Information Plus 2006). The Pew Hispanic Research Center estimated that by 2009 the total number had risen to 11.3 million and then fell to 11.2 million in 2012 (Pew Hispanic Research Center 2014a).

The Crisis of Border Control: Illegal Immigration and Enactment of IRCA

Rising levels of unauthorized immigration and apprehensions of undocumented persons attempting to cross the borders led to a growing sense that the United States had lost control of its borders. Widespread dissatisfaction with the INS was soon registered in the news media and general public opinion polls, and within government at all levels of the federal system. During the Iranian hostage crisis, which lasted nearly two years during the Carter administration, the nation was shocked to learn that the INS did not even know how many Iranian students were living in the country, let alone how many were doing so illegally (by overstaying their visas or by accepting employment while on student visa status). Many Iranians whom the INS was able to identify as being subject to deportation failed to attend deportation hearings or to leave when ordered to do so. Several hundreds of thousands were estimated to overstay their visas annually (SCIRP 1981: 8–9).

Organized labor agitated to deal with what they viewed as a threat from illegal aliens during the mid- to late 1970s, a period when the economy was mired in stagflation: increasing unemployment, rising cost of living, and a recession that hit lower-wage jobs particularly hard. Rep. Peter Rodino (D-NJ), from a state hard-hit by the recession, was convinced by the American Federation of Labor–Congress of Industrial Organizations (AFL-CIO), the International Garment Workers Union, and by the National Association for the Advancement of Colored People (NAACP), which viewed illegal immigration as especially threatening to the status and jobs of urban blacks, to propose an employer sanctions amendment to the Immigration and Naturalization Act of 1965, eliminating the Texas Proviso (Perotti 1989: 83–84; LeMay 1994: 29–34). The Texas Proviso had favored growers of agricultural crops and employers of unauthorized immigrants by exempting them from criminal action for hiring undocumented workers, although it was still a breach of civil law for workers themselves to immigrate without documents.

Sen. Edward Kennedy (D-MA), Rep. Peter Rodino, and Rep. Joshua Eilberg (D-PA) linked employer sanctions with limited legalization (an amnesty provision) and antidiscrimination provisions. However, Sen. James Eastland (D-MS), a leading advocate in the Senate of the interests of growers, opposed the employer sanctions approach. With support of such lobbying groups as the National Council of Agricultural Employers and the American Farm Bureau Federation, Eastland insisted that any reform of immigration law that did not have a foreign workers (also known as "guest-workers") program would make it unacceptable to growers and other employers. Essentially, this coalition of political forces wanted to replace the illegal immigrant labor force with guest-workers in an expanded H-2 temporary workers program. At the time, Senator Eastland was the powerful chairman of both the Senate Judiciary Committee and of its subcommittee on immigration and naturalization. He effectively killed the Kennedy-Rodino-Eilberg-sponsored bill by stalling it in committee.

In 1977, the Carter administration became involved. President Carter appointed as his new Secretary of Labor, F. Ray Marshall, an economist at the University of Texas, who had long been interested in the issue. The Carter administration, however, was somewhat split on the question, as was the Congress. Secretary Marshall and U.S. Attorney General Griffin Bell favored limited amnesty and development of a tamper-proof worker-eligibility card. The commissioner of the INS, Leonel J. Castillo, and various White House aides led the fight for a generous amnesty program but deplored the civil-liberty implications of a worker-eligibility card.

Rodino was frustrated that, despite the recommendations of two presidential commissions (one appointed by President Ford and one by President Carter) for an approach similar to his (that is, blending employer sanctions, legalization, and strong border enforcement measures), nothing would pass the Senate over the intransigent opposition of Senator Eastland. President Carter and the U.S. Congress established a joint presidential-congressional commission, the Select Commission on Immigration and Refugee Policy (SCIRP). Sen. Edward Kennedy, then made chairman of the judiciary committee, viewed SCIRP as the means to carve out a pivotal role in any legislation on immigration reform. SCIRP studied the issue thoroughly and issued its final report in 1981, which ran more than 450 pages, and its supplemental staff report, in excess of 900 pages. The commission's recommendations covered the full spectrum of issues involving the illegal immigration debates.

SCIRP recommended closing the back door to undocumented immigration while opening slightly the front door to accommodate more legal immigration. The final report stressed the need to define immigration goals more sharply, and to set forth procedures to ensure fair and efficient adjudication and administration of U.S. immigration law aimed at increasing legal and reducing unauthorized immigration. The report maintained that continued immigration was in the best national interest while recognizing the limited ability to absorb effectively large numbers of immigrants. It emphasized that the first priority was to bring unauthorized immigration under control. It recommended modest increases in legal immigration by expediting clearance of the huge backlogs, which would ease family reunification pressures. It recommended an increase in annual legal immigration from 270,000 to 350,000. It stressed enforcement of existing law by imposing an employer sanctions provision and by increasing the size of the Border Patrol, and coupled those with an amnesty program and a restructuring of the immigration bureaucracy and procedures of legal immigration. Each of its recommendations had been articulated in prior immigration reform discourse. SCIRP, by linking them together, legitimized the duality of the employer sanctions/legalization approach. It said, in essence, that one could not work without the other. Employer sanctions would "demagnetize" the pull of the U.S. economy. Amnesty would bring the current undocumented immigrant population out of the shadows. SCIRP's final report set the agenda for all subsequent discussions of and proposals to reform immigration law, adding its weight to proposals that previously had been stymied in committee.

SCIRP's emphasis on the problem of undocumented immigration as "the most pressing problem" shaped and limited the debates in Congress and much of the news media over immigration policy reform. It stated flatly: "Most U.S. citizens believe that the half-open door of undocumented/illegal immigration should be closed" (SCIRP 1981: 104).

The Reagan administration, which had just assumed office, responded to the SCIRP report by establishing its own Task Force on Immigration and Refugee Policy in March 1981. Headed by Attorney General William French Smith, it soon made its recommendations to the new president:

1. *Amnesty.* It recommended aliens living in the United States illegally since January 1, 1980, be permitted to remain, becoming eligible for resident-alien status after having been

in the country for 10 years, at which time they could seek naturalization. It estimated the number of such immigrants at 5 million.

2. *Guest-worker program.* It recommended allowing 50,000 Mexicans to enter the United States annually to work temporarily and, over the course of several years, to increase the number gradually up to hundreds of thousands annually.

3. *Employer sanctions.* It recommended that employers who "knowingly" hire more than four illegal aliens be fined up to $1,000 per violation.

4. *Enforcement.* It recommended a 50 percent increase in the INS budget and recommended the addition of 1,500 new officers to the Border Patrol to enhance enforcement of immigration and labor laws.

5. *Boat people.* In response to a wave of "economic refugees" from Haiti, it recommended that boats carrying Haitians be intercepted and that detention camps be set up to hold as many as 6,000 people, pending their deportation hearings.

6. *Legal immigration limits.* It recommended increasing the annual limit for legal immigration to 610,000, with special preference to those from Canada and Mexico (LeMay 2004: 14–15; LeMay and Barkan 1999: 278–279).

By fall of 1981, the House and Senate judiciary subcommittees on immigration, chaired respectively by Rep. Romano Mazzoli (D-KY) and Sen. Alan Simpson (R-WY), had crafted the recommendations of the SCIRP report and the Reagan administration's Task Force into legislative proposals they considered essential as incentives to cooperation among the many groups competing over the illegal immigration reform issue. The measures were introduced to their respective chambers in March 1982. After committee hearings, the bills were reported out in mid-May. The Senate passed the Simpson bill by 81 to 19 in August 1982. The House bill, saddled with several critical amendments, required introduction of a clean version, sponsored by Rep. Romano Mazzoli and Rep. Hamilton Fish Jr. (R-NY). After passage of the Senate version, the full House Judiciary Committee approved the Mazzoli–Fish version in mid-September.

Since the House and Senate versions differed, Speaker of the House, Tip O'Neill (D-MA), referred the House bill sequentially to four committees: Education and Labor, Agriculture, Ways and Means, and Energy and Commerce. The bill finally reached the Rules Committee in December, during the lame-duck session of the 97th Congress. When it finally reached the House floor, 300 amendments had been filed. It died on the floor.

In 1983, Simpson and Mazzoli renewed their efforts to craft a compromise, reintroducing versions of bills nearly identical to those passed in 1982. Agricultural interests, led by the Farm Labor Alliance and advocated by Fish, developed a guest worker program. Rep. Edward Roybal (D-CA), a leading member of the Congressional Hispanic Caucus, introduced an alternative bill emphasizing tough enforcement of existing labor laws and minimum wage laws to clamp down on the hiring of unauthorized immigrants as a substitute for the employer sanctions approach.

These bills moved slowly through their respective chambers. Once again, the Senate progressed more rapidly, with senators Simpson and Kennedy working out compromises on key provisions. In the House, the Mazzoli bill again moved sequentially through four committee referrals. Representatives Mazzoli and Rodino, with the support of the Reagan administration and House Republican leadership, pressed for quick floor action. However, political complications from the pending 1984 elections led to obstructive amendments, and the bill did not pass until June 1984, and then by a slim margin (216–211). Since its provisions differed from the Senate version, the bills were sent to a House-Senate conference committee, where it failed to achieve an acceptable compromise and died.

In May 1985 Simpson introduced a new version of his bill, without the sponsorship in the House by Mazzoli. Rodino introduced a bill similar to the version that died in conference committee. The two chambers again passed differing versions. The Reagan White House, naturally, supported the Senate version sponsored by Senator Simpson. The Senate Judiciary Committee rejected all attempts by Senate Democrats to make the Senate version more like the House version. After the conference committee again appeared to be stymied, the bill seemed to be a corpse on its way to the morgue. But a small group of legislators involved in the illegal immigration reform battles refused to let it die. In October 1986 they fashioned some key compromises enabling passage. Rep. Charles Schumer (D-NY) met with Representatives Fish and Hamilton, Rep. Howard Berman (D-CA), Rep. Leon Panetta (D-CA), and Rep. Dan Lungren (R-CA). They fine-tuned key provisions and led House members to agree on a package of provisions, including numerous points designed to protect the rights of temporary workers. They secured Senator Simpson's approval of the compromises, and after a decade of dealing with the issue, Congress finally passed the measure. By the time, the Mexican economy had deteriorated further and push factors have led to 1.8 million border apprehensions by the INS—a historic high. With the midterm elections over, and in view of the growing conservative political mood of the nation, opponents of the measure concluded that continued resistance might lead to an even more restrictive bill in 1987. The Hispanic Caucus split on the bill—and voted five for and six against passage. That split by the Hispanic Caucus members enabled the Congressional Black Caucus to split on the bill as well: ten for and eight opposed (LeMay 1994).

The House passed the compromise conference bill by a vote of 238 to 172 on October 15, 1986. The Senate approved it 63 to 24 on October 17, 1986. President Reagan signed it into law on November 6, 1986, as the Immigration Reform and Control Act of 1986 (IRCA). The long and bumpy road to enactment was followed by an equally bumpy road to implementation of a complex law whose very compromises crafted to ensure its passage led to complications and unintended consequences. Employer sanctions proved ineffective in demagnetizing the pull of the U.S. economy. IRCA allowed for 14 documents to be accepted as valid proof of a person's eligibility to work. This fact simply fueled a phony-document industry, enabling illegal aliens to continue coming and employers to continue hiring them without fear of legal penalty for "knowingly hiring" unauthorized workers. Enforcement problems by the INS, coupled with massive use of counterfeit documents, resulted in a decline in undocumented aliens successfully crossing the border that lasted but a very brief period. Within a year after its passage, illegal immigration was back up to pre-IRCA levels.

Although IRCA authorized a 50 percent increase in Border Patrol staff, actual increases fell far short due to difficulties in recruiting and expanding training staff and facilities. Moreover, as the Border Patrol increased in size, so too did its duties. After 1986, the interdiction of illicit drug traffic across the borders became a prime focus (in response to the 1986 Omnibus Anti-Drug Law). Border Patrol agents shifted their emphasis from alien apprehension and smuggling to work with the Drug Enforcement Agency on Operation Alliance. The Border Patrol also reallocated the number of staff being used to guard refugee camps and to identify, prosecute, and deport alien criminals (Bean, Vernez, and Keely 1989: 44).

Annual alien apprehensions climbed from the tens of thousands in the late 1960s to nearly a half-million by 1970, to three-quarters of a million by 1985. By the time IRCA was passed, the number was approaching 2 million annually (Figures 5.1 and 5.2). Legal immigration rose as well. The 1980 census enumerated 5.6 million foreign-born persons who had entered during the 1970s. That number, of course, does not include persons who came but were not counted in the census. An estimate of 1 million uncounted is realistic. Thus, the net immigration during the 1970s totaled 6.6 million, exceeding the total immigration of the decade beginning in 1910, which had only been about 4.3 million. It is likely the net flow from 1970 to 1980 was the highest level for any period in the twentieth century (LeMay 1994: 22–23).

As the tide of illegal aliens increased to what was perceived as a "flood-level," interest groups traditionally involved as well as new groups entered the battle over policy to restrict illegal immigration. State governments entered the arena, placing new pressures on Congress to respond and to "fix the problem" of illegal immigration and border control. States receiving the bulk of illegal immigrants (Arizona, California, Colorado, Florida, Illinois, New Jersey, New Mexico, New York, and Texas) pressured Congress. Three states, California, Florida, and Texas, sued the federal government in their respective district courts for the estimated billions of dollars that states had to bear for costs related to illegal immigrants and their children. They claimed enormous expenditures in education, health care, prisons, and welfare caused by illegal immigrant residents. They argued that the federal government, by failing to control the borders, was responsible for the increased costs borne by the states. In 1994, California attempted to reduce the draw of its economy and services to illegal immigration by passing an anti-immigration measure known as Proposition 187. Using its initiative process, California voters passed the measure, officially entitled the "Save Our State Initiative," by 60 percent. It required state and local agencies to report to the INS any persons suspected of being illegal, and to prevent illegal aliens from receiving benefits or public services in the state of California. It set off a trend of "devolution" of immigration policy to state and local agencies (Suro 2015; Motomura 2014; Rodriguez 2008, 2014).

The authors of Proposition 187 anticipated a federal court challenge to its constitutionality and were correct in their anticipation. It was immediately brought to court by the League of United Latin American Citizens (LULAC), and the federal district court ruled that many of its provisions were unconstitutional (*LULAC et al. vs. Wilson et al.* 908 F. Supp. 755 C.D. Cal. 1995: 787–791). The court so ruled as many of its provisions were held to constitute state infringement on the federal government's sole authority to enact immigration law, or were state actions preempting existing federal law. Despite the court's actions, however, Congress did get the message sent by Proposition 187. It addressed yet again the illegal immigration problem.

In 1996, Congress passed and President Bill Clinton signed into law two measures enacting the major provisions of Proposition 187. Congress passed a welfare reform act that contained several provisions aimed at illegal immigrants. Still other of the proposition's provisions were folded into the omnibus fiscal 1997 spending bill (Illegal Immigration Reform and Immigrant Responsibility Act of 1996, the IIRIRA, H.R. 3610, P.L. 104–208), which President Clinton signed into law on September 30, 1996.

As noted, the number of illegal immigrants entering the United States dipped slightly after the passage of IRCA, but then climbed again to reach and eventually exceed pre-IRCA levels. The number of unauthorized immigrants, estimated at 3.2 million in 1986, rose to 9.3 million by 2002. The region of origin of these unauthorized residents shifted in significant ways during this period as well. In 1986, a Congressional Research Service study found that among the 3.2 million unauthorized residents, 69 percent were from Mexico, 23 percent were from Canada and South America, 6 percent were from Asia, and 2 percent were from Europe (these include both undocumented entrants and visa overstayers). By 2002 the estimated 9.3 million unauthorized residents comprised 57 percent from Mexico, 23 percent from other Latin American countries, 10 percent from Asia, 5 percent from Canada and Europe, and another 5 percent from all other sources.

The Pew Hispanic Research Center estimated that between 2000 and 2004 another 3.1 million arrived, bringing the total of unauthorized residents to 10.3 million (see Camarota 2006). The center also estimated that, in 1990, 88 percent of all unauthorized residents lived in the six gateway states: California (45 percent of the total), New York (15 percent), Texas (11 percent), Florida (9 percent), Illinois (4 percent), and New Jersey

(4 percent). The remaining 12 percent resided in all the other states. By 2004, the estimated 10.3 million were even more dispersed: 62 percent resided in the big six states, with California at 24 percent, New York at 7 percent, Texas at 14 percent, Florida at 9 percent, and Illinois and New Jersey each at 4 percent. The number residing in the remaining states had risen to 39 percent. Between 2009 and 2012, the unauthorized populations changed in 21 states but remained relatively stable overall. Moreover, for the first time on record, more non-Mexicans than Mexicans were apprehended at U.S. borders in 2014 by the Border Patrol, according to a Pew Research Center analysis of more than 60 years of Border Patrol data (http://www.cbp.gov/sites/default/files/documents). PEW data show that unauthorized immigrants from Mexico are crossing significantly less often than they did before the Great Recession.

Other studies estimated that in 2004 as many as 5 million workers were being paid "off-the-books," comprising a "stealth workforce" that distorted official government economic statistics and projections, understating job growth, inflating U.S. productivity, and shortchanging tax revenues by an estimated $35 billion per year (Justich and Ng, in Information Plus 2006: 74).

In part to address these issues, Congress passed, in June 2000, the Immigration and Naturalization Service Data Management Improvement Act (PL. 206–215). This law amended the IIRIRA of 1996. The 2000 amendment required an electronic system to be developed to integrate and provide access to the data on all arrivals and departures and to use such data to identify lawfully admitted nonimmigrants who might have overstayed their visits. A deadline of December 31, 2003, was set for all airports and seaports to have the system in place. Fifty land border ports, selected by the attorney general as having the highest numbers of arrivals and departures, were given until December 31, 2004, to have such an operating system by December 2005 (Ibid.).

As will be seen more fully later, the events of the terror attacks of September 11, 2001, and subsequent disbanding of the INS and the creation of the DHS changed the implementation of the act of 2000.

Border Security and Antiterrorism Concerns

The attacks on the World Trade Center in New York City and the Pentagon in Washington, D.C., on September 11, 2001, resulted in sweeping changes in the law, changes aimed at combating international and domestic terrorism, but with significant implications for immigration policy directed at the illegal immigration problem. Enactment of these laws demarcate what we well might call the "storm-door era" of U.S. immigration policy and signal the erection of what has been called Fortress America. The disarray at the INS was made apparent by the 9/11 attacks and sped up the process. Attorney General John Ashcroft ordered the INS to strictly enforce the rule requiring foreign visitors to file change-of-address forms that the national government was supposed to use to keep track of visitors. The INS had an existing backlog of some 2 million paper documents (its record-keeping not yet made electronic), piled up in boxes and stored in a warehouse in Kansas City. The attorney general's directive resulted in the INS receiving 30,000 change-of-address forms per day, and the backlog quickly rose to 4 million documents. An INS report indicated an estimated 4 million foreigners were in the country with expired visas. Adding to its misery and its reputation for utter ineptitude, the press soon revealed that the INS had sent letters to a Florida flight school approving the student visas for two of the 9/11 attackers, six months after the attacks! A government report on overall management in the Government Executive's 2002 Federal Performance Report, which had ranked the U.S. Coast Guard at an A, gave the INS a D. Border Patrol officers were quitting faster than they could be replaced. INS investigators were rated as undertrained, overworked, and overstressed, and the information management of INS was assessed as abysmal. Many in Congress concluded that drastic restructuring was needed.

Less than a month after the attacks, on October 8, 2001, President Bush issued Executive Order 13228. It established the Office of Homeland Security within the Executive Office of the President (Relyea 2003). In Congress, Sen. Joseph Lieberman (D-CT) introduced a bill (S. 1534) to establish the DHS as a cabinet-level department. He and Rep. Mac Thornberry (R-TX) later introduced a more elaborate version, in May 2002 (S. 2452, and H.B. 4660). President Bush responded to political pressure to do more than what E.O. 13228 could accomplish. A team from the administration drafted an alternative to Senator Lieberman's bill. Mitchell Daniels Jr., director of the Office of Management and Budget, Tom Ridge, appointed to head the Office of Homeland Security in the White House, Andrew Card Jr., the White House Chief of Staff, and Alberto Gonzales, the White House Counsel, met and drafted the president's departmental plan in late April. It was formally introduced as H.R. 5005 on June 24, 2002 (Relyea 2003: 617).

More than any other action, however, the USA Patriot Act and the law to establish the DHS most characterize the storm-door era and symbolize Fortress America. Within six weeks of the 9/11 attacks, a jittery Congress, then virtually exiled from their offices by an anthrax contamination incident and confronted by dire warnings of more terrorist attacks soon to come, responded to President Bush's demands for a new arsenal of antiterrorism measures, some directly linked to illegal immigration, which many feared was an avenue for international terrorist cells to infiltrate into the United States. For three weeks, from the initial outbreak of anthrax contamination on October 4, 2001, Congress and the public were unable to obtain clear information about the attack from the Centers for Disease Control and Prevention (CDC). Fear and threat exceeded actual damage. Despite vigorous objections from civil liberty organizations at both ends of the political spectrum, Congress overwhelmingly approved the USA Patriot Act, which stands for Uniting and Strengthening America by Providing Appropriate Tools Required to Intercept and

Obstruct Terrorism Act, by a vote of 356 to 66 in the House, and by 98 to 1 in the Senate. The hastily drafted, complex, and far-reaching law spans 342 pages but was passed with virtually no public hearing or debate, and was accompanied by neither a conference committee nor a committee report. On October 26, 2001, the act was signed into law by President George W. Bush (Torr 2004: 43–44).

The USA Patriot Act granted powers to the attorney general and the Justice Department that restricted the civil liberties of U.S. citizens, broadened the terrorism-related definitions in the 1965 Immigration and Naturalization Act, expanded the grounds of inadmissibility to include aliens who publicly endorsed terrorist activity, and gave the national government broad powers to monitor students and resident aliens and to detain and expedite the removal of noncitizens even suspected of having links to terrorist organizations. In short, the attorney general simply had to certify them as being threats to national security on whatever grounds. Critics charged that the law legalized racial profiling of Middle Easterners. (Parts of the act are excerpted in Chapter 5, Data and Documents.)

Advocates of the law argued that it was essential to catch terrorists and deter further acts of terrorism. Led by Vice President Dick Cheney, its proponents called for coercive interrogation of suspected terrorists to find and control enemy cells in our midst. They argued its sweeping new powers were essential to penetrate Al Qaeda. These included expanded surveillance, the use of informants, revisions of the search and seizure procedures, the use of secret wiretaps, and arrests and detention of suspected terrorists, uninhibited by the prior web of laws, judicial precedents, and administrative rules that its proponents argued had hamstrung law enforcement officials in dealing with the new terrorist threat. Soon after its enactment, the Department of Justice (DOJ) announced that it had broken up terrorist cells in Portland, Detroit, and Buffalo, and charged 17 individuals with terrorism-related activities. The DOJ targeted terrorist financing (Torr 2004: 29).

Critics of the law argued it was far too sweeping and a dangerous intrusion on civil liberty protections. They saw it as a threat to constitutional checks and balances, to open government, and to the rule of law. They viewed those threats as being greater than any posed by terrorists. "Not since the World War II internment of Japanese Americans have we locked up so many people for so long with so little explanation" (Chang, cited in Torr 2004: 16). They held that the Patriot Act evades the Fourth Amendment by enabling officials to conduct "sneak and peek" searches, covert searches of a person's home or office conducted without notice to the person. Mass arrests in secrecy and without judicial oversight outraged civil libertarians. The exercise of unilateral authority by the executive, establishing secret tribunals and breaching attorney-client communications without court order, was, in their eyes, a threat to patriotic dissent, a threat to liberty, and a threat to equality. And, in point of fact, nonterrorists who have been affected by the Patriot Act have mostly been immigrants. In the months after 9/11, some 1,200 immigrants, mostly Muslim, were rounded up by the police and the INS across the nation. Many were held for months without access to lawyers or even without charges brought against them before an immigration judge. Some were summarily deported for visa violations. Only a few were subsequently charged with any crime, and most were released months later as totally innocent, swept up in the postattack hysteria. The Patriot Act makes aliens deportable for wholly innocent association with a terrorist organization by defining a terrorist organization in such broad terms that any group that used or threatened to use violence could be so construed. The proscription on political association potentially encompasses every organization that has been involved in a civil war or a crime of violence, from a prolife group that threatened and sometimes killed abortion-clinic workers, to the African National Congress, the Irish Republican Army, or the Northern Alliance in Afghanistan (U.S. ally against the Taliban in Afghanistan). An estimated 1,500 to 2,000 persons were apprehended under the act, their identities still secret. Indeed, even their numbers can only be guessed at, as the government stopped issuing daily number counts after November 30, 2001, which was then at 1,182. No one of those detained was ever charged with any involvement in the 9/11 attacks. Most were cleared by the FBI of any involvement in terrorism (Etzioni and Marsh 2003: 37–38).

Creating the Department of Homeland Security: Dissolving the INS

On November 19, 2002, Congress passed the Homeland Security Act, establishing the Department of Homeland Security (DHS). It abolished the INS, restructuring its jurisdiction and functions into the new behemoth department composed of 22 agencies subsumed into it. Many the law's provisions dramatically changed the ways in which immigration policy was implemented, highlights of which are in Chapter 5, Data and Documents (LeMay 2004: 27–28).

The DHS launched the National Security Entry-Exit Registration System (NSEERS). It comprised three elements—point-of-entry registration, special registration, and exit/departure controls—aimed at preventing future 9/11-type attacks. The special registration component created a national registry for temporary foreign visitors (nonimmigrant aliens, such as tourists and international students) coming from 25 designated countries listed by the attorney general as supporters and exporters of international terrorism, and others who met a combination of intelligence-based criteria that identified them as potential security risks.

NSEERS addressed several security-related deficiencies in immigration policy and procedures. Beginning in 2003, all commercial carriers by air or sea were required to submit detailed passenger lists electronically before an aircraft or vessel arrived in or departed from the United States. Some of its provisions were suspended in December 2003, such as the need for aliens residing in the United States to register each year (the government had millions of such forms backlogged and stored, unprocessed, in warehouses in Kansas, and simply could not keep up with the paperwork). Other provisions of NSEERS remained in place, including requiring foreign nationals from Iran, Iraq, Libya, Syria, and Sudan to go through special registration at ports of entry and to report to immigration officials before departing the country; foreign nationals from other countries were registered if Customs and Border Protection officers (a new bureau within the DHS) warranted it necessary based on questioning upon arrival. Individuals from more than 160 countries had been registered in the NSEERS program by January 2005. The system provides detailed information about the background and purpose of the individual's visit to the United States, as well as departure confirmation (Information Plus 2006: 75).

In April 2002 the Justice Department issued a report on visa overstays, substantiating the fact that between 40 and 50 percent of unauthorized immigrants were not persons who had crossed the borders without documentation, but rather were persons who entered with proper documents as temporary visitors and then failed to depart when required to do so. The report set the nonimmigrant overstayer population as growing by at least 125,000 per year (Department of Justice 2002).

The Immigration and Customs Enforcement (ICE) bureau of the DHS is responsible for collecting documents from incoming travelers, but airline and shipping lines are responsible for collecting departure forms and sending such forms to ICE. Departure forms may have gone unrecorded, either because they were not collected or they were collected by the airlines and shipping lines but were not sent to ICE or the forms were sent to ICE but were incorrectly recorded. Such problems make an accurate assessment of the numbers of overstays difficult. In 2004 the General Accounting Office (GAO) reported that DHS estimated the number of visa overstays to be 2.3 million per year as of 2000. The GAO report noted that this figure did not account for an unknown number of short- and long-term overstays from Mexico and Canada, inasmuch as citizens from Canada admitted for up to six months and Mexican citizens with border-crossing cards entering the border in the Southwest for a stay of less than 72 hours are exempt from the visa admissions procedures. The GAO also faulted the tracking system that identified those who entered the country on visas but did not accurately track when, or if, those persons actually left the country (GAO-04-82, 2004).

Understandably, the tracking system is confronted by huge numbers. In 2003, the DHS reported 33 million arrivals at U.S. ports of entry. Those did not include Mexican and Canadian business or pleasure visitors. Of those nearly 33 million, an estimated 79 percent departed before their authorized stay had expired. There were no departure records for nearly 15 percent of all who arrived by land and sea (Information Plus 2006: 76). In the post 9/11 investigations, the GAO, in a report in May 2004, noted that of the six hijackers who flew the planes involved in the 9/11 attacks, two were overstays and one had violated a student visa by not attending school. In response, the DHS began an ongoing, multiagency effort it called Operation Tarmac, to identify unauthorized foreign nationals working in places vulnerable to terrorism, such as the baggage and security areas of airports.

The GAO report, Operation Tracking, found that as of 2004, a total of 195 airports had been investigated and nearly 6,000 businesses had been audited. In checks on employment eligibility forms (known as I-9 forms) of some 385,000 workers around the country, the DHS found nearly 5,000 unauthorized workers. Of more than 600 unauthorized workers arrested, 30 percent were overstays. Perhaps not surprisingly, but certainly ironically, one of the busiest ports of entry for such unauthorized workers was Houston's Bush International Airport. Ten unauthorized workers were from countries identified as "of special interest" under the NSEERS program, and five of those were overstays, according to the GAO report (GAO-04-82, 2004).

Alarmingly, the GAO noted many unauthorized workers had access to supposedly secure areas and were employed by the airports themselves, by airlines, or by support service companies in jobs such as aircraft maintenance, airline cabin service attendants, airplane fueling personnel, baggage handler, and predeparture screener. One was even working in the airport badge office. Such individuals used phony Social Security numbers and identity documents to obtain airport jobs and security badges. Operation Tarmac found unauthorized employees at critical infrastructure sites, such as nuclear plants, sensitive national landmarks, military installations, and the Alaska pipeline, and also at the 2002 Olympics in Salt Lake City and at the Super Bowl game. Seventy-nine unauthorized workers were arrested at the 2003 Super Bowl in San Diego, according to the GAO report. Of those, eight were overstays and twelve came from countries included in NSEERS special registration category.

On May 11, 2003, President Bush signed into law the measure passed by Congress by a vote of 308 to 58 in the House and 100 to 0 in the Senate, known as the Real ID Act of 2003 (Pub. 1, 109–13, 119 Stat. 302). This law set national standards that sought to insure the authentication and insurance procedures of state licenses, identification cards, and several related issues pertaining to applications for asylum and deportation for terrorism activity, and included provisions waiving laws that would interfere with the construction of physical barriers at the borders. It mandated states to comply with its provisions. By April 2008, however, all 50 states applied for extension of the May 11, 2008, date set for compliance. By October 2009, 25 states approved resolutions not to participate in the program. Many critics opposed the law as unnecessary intrusion of civil rights and a constitutional violation of the Tenth Amendment. The act remains controversial and several bills have been introduced since 2010 to amend it (LeMay 2013c: 13, 68). It prompted a period of state and local actions exemplifying a period of "cooperative federalism" to either cooperate with harsher federal enforcement of immigration policy or try to mitigate federal immigration policy, wherein states and localities work to integrate a system of policy making rather than claiming exclusive prerogatives (Rodriguez 2008, 2014; Illinois.gov 2005; Suro 2015; Tomas Rivera Policy Institute (TRPI) 2014). Between 2001 and 2011, as many as 16 states acted to mitigate the harsher aspects of the IIRIRA (National Conference of State Legislatures (NCSL) 2005, 2011).

The Intelligence Reform and Terrorism Prevention Act of 2004 (PL 108–458, 118 Stat. 3638) was passed in the House by a vote of 336–75, and in the Senate by 96–2, and signed into law by President Bush on December 17, 2004. A lengthy measure at 235 pages, it created a Director of National Intelligence and authorized 2,000 additional Border Patrol agents to the DHS per year for five years. It gave the federal government broader authority for surveillance of noncitizens, including the so-called lone wolf terrorists inspired by but not associated with radical Islamic terrorist groups like Al Qaeda, Al Qaeda in the Arabian Peninsula, or the Islamic State of Iraq and Syria (ISIS).

On October 26, 2006, President Bush signed the Secure Fence Act (Pub. L. 109–367). The bill had passed the House by a vote of 283–138, and the Senate by 90–18, mostly on partisan voting, with Republicans supporting the measure and Democrats opposing it. The act approved $1.2 billion to construct a 700-mile fence along the Mexican-United States border (none was suggested for the even longer northern border with Canada). Critics argued it would take $4.8 billion more to actually build the fence along the entire southern border and that it would strain U.S.-Mexican relations, disrupt the environment and wildlife, and increase the danger of immigrants trying to cross, and be ineffectual in stopping illegal immigration. By 2009, 613 miles of fencing were constructed spanning from California to Texas. In 2010, another bill was introduced to require the DHS to build another 353 miles, although that measure stalled in the Congress and the Great Recession and subsequent actions to drastically cut budget deficits have doomed its passage since then.

In March 2006, Congress enacted a law renewing, with minor amendments, the USA Patriot Act, commonly referred to as Patriot Act II. It changed regulations making it easier for DHS to remove aliens, increasing the number of aliens expelled or who voluntarily departed since 2002, due both to enforcement by the DHS and as a result of the Great Recession 2008–2009. Unauthorized immigration peaked nationally in 2007, at 12.2 million. It declined in 2008–2009, during the Great Recession, and has stabilized since 2009 at 11.2 million (http://www.pewhispa nic.org/2014/11/18/unauthorized-immigrant-total). The Great Recession demonstrated that events like severe economic recession work to "demagnetize" the draw of the U.S. economy far more effectively than does any legislation enacted to do so.

Progressives in Congress have been proposing annually since 2001 a bill for the enactment of what became known as the Dream Act (Development, Relief, and Education of Alien Minors). In May 2011, then Senate Majority Leader Harry Reid (D-NV) introduced the bill that had bipartisan support in the Senate but was staunchly opposed by House Republicans as an amnesty program. If passed, the bill would have granted conditional permanent residency to unauthorized alien students of good moral character who graduated from U.S. schools, having lived in the country for at least five years, and completed two years of military service or were enrolled in a two- or four-year institution of higher learning. The Congressional Budget Office (CBO) estimated the act would reduce deficits by $1.4 billion over the 2011–2020 period, and increase government revenues by a projected $2.3 billion over 10 years. A University of California Los Angeles (UCLA) study estimated that, if enacted, the Dream Act would generate between $1.4 trillion and $3.6 trillion in taxable income over a 40-year period (LeMay 2013c: 15–16). A number of groups made up a coalition to push for passage of the Dream Act, beginning with the Coalition of Humane Immigration Rights of Los Angeles and then the California Dream Network and expanding nationally into United We Dream.

In 2010 the state of Arizona, led by Governor Jane Brewer, passed a law mandating state and local police officers to demand anyone stopped who was suspected of being in the state illegally to show their papers certifying they were here legally. The law was immediately challenged, and the U.S. Supreme Court, in *Arizona v. United States* (132 S. Ct. 2492), struck down the law as unconstitutional.

Since 2008, the U.S. Congress has been stalemated over immigration reform, including comprehensive legal immigration reform and regarding the Dream Act and various bills introduced to "crack down at the border." When Congress refused to act on bills to amend the 287(g) program established by the IIRIRA, granting local law enforcement agencies for the first time the authority to screen people for their immigration status, President Obama used executive action two times, in 2009 and 2012, to mitigate aspects of the IIRIRA. Then, with respect to the Dream Act, President Obama issued executive actions in 2012 and 2014. In 2012 he issued the Deferred Action for Childhood Arrivals (DACA), which granted temporary, conditional legal residency status to students who complied with the conditions of the Dream Act proposals (Preston 2014). In November 2014, President Obama issued a new set of executive actions that broadened eligibility for DACA and created a new program—the Deferred Action for Parental Accountability (DAPA)—for parents of U.S. citizens and legal permanent resident aliens.

On June 27, 2013, the Senate passed S.744, a comprehensive immigration reform measure, by a vote of 68–32. Introduced by Sen. Charles Schumer (D-NY), it was a somewhat bipartisan approach (largely crafted by what became known as the Gang of Eight—four Democrat and four Republican senators long involved in immigration reform issues). The House had a similar Gang of Eight who sponsored a similar bill, but Speaker of the House John Boehner (R-OH) refused to bring the measure to a floor vote and the bill died in the House (htpp://www.immigrationpolicy.org; and http://www.politico. com/2013/immigration-bill-2013-senatepass).

Conclusion

The renewed high levels of illegal immigration since 1970 profoundly affected the United States in all manner of ways. Immigration policy reform, for both legal and illegal immigration matters, remains on the agenda of government at all levels of the federal system. Immigration control issues are particularly of concern to the U.S. Congress, although since 2008 partisan bickering has stymied adoption of further legislation, especially regarding comprehensive immigration reform. Proponents of that approach advocate a large-scale temporary worker program, increased beefing up of ICE and the DHS, some sort of earned legalization program, increased expedited removal, and better technology to track and control immigrants and visitors (LeMay 2013c: 16).

As this chapter has demonstrated, the politics of illegal immigration reform is complicated by the increasing spread of immigrants from the gateway states to more of the country and to more urban areas within 30 states. The shift in the composition of immigrants since 1970 from European nations of origin to those from Latin America and Asia has had profound effects on a host of related public policy areas (Daniels 1988, 2005; Motomura 2006; Navarro 2005; Reimers 1985; Yans-McLaughlin 1990).

The shift in the composition of preference immigrants has been both the result of and the cause for a series of changes in immigration law since 1970. Congressional enactments, court decisions, and executive actions have all shaped the immigration policy, each having intended and unintended consequences. Clearly, immigration policy will continue to impact the American economy, its culture and society, its politics, and a variety of related public policy issues, many of which are discussed further in Chapter 2, Problems, Controversies, and Solutions.

References

Andreas, Peter. 2000. *Border Games: Policing the U.S.-Mexican Divide*. Ithaca: Cornell University Press.

Bean, Frank D., and Teresa A. Sullivan. 1985. "Immigration and Its Consequences: Confronting the Problem." *Society* 22 (May/June): 67–73.

Bean, Frank D., George Vernez, and Charles B. Keely. 1989. *Opening and Closing the Doors*. Santa Monica, CA: Rand Corporation.

Bustamente, Antonio Rios, ed. 1981. *Mexican Immigrant Workers in the United States*. Los Angeles: UCLA, Chicano Studies Research Center.

Calavita, Kitty. 1992. *Inside the State: The Bracero Program, Immigration, and the INS*. New York: Routledge.

Camarota, Steven A. 2005. *Economy Slowed, but Immigration Didn't: The Foreign- Born Population, 2000–2004*. Washington, DC: Center for Immigration Studies.

Chiswick, Barry R., ed. 1982. *The Gateway: U.S. Immigration Issues and Policies*. Washington, DC: American Enterprise Institute.

Conover, Ted. 1987. *Coyotes: A Journey through the Secret World of America's Illegal Aliens*. New York: Vintage.

Craig, Richard B. 1971. *The Bracero Program: Interest Groups and Foreign Policy*. Austin: University of Texas Press.

Crockroft, James D. 1986. *Outlaws in the Promised Land: Mexican Immigrant Workers and America's Future*. New York: Grove.

Daniels, Roger. 1988. *Asian America: Chinese and Japanese in the United States*. Seattle: University of Washington Press.

Daniels, Roger. 2005. *Guarding the Golden Door: American Immigration Policy and Immigration since 1882*. New York: Hill and Wang.

Department of Justice. 2002. *Follow-up Report on INS Efforts to Improve the Control of Immigrant Overstays*. Report

No. 1–2002–006. Washington, DC: U.S. Government
Printing Office.

Etzioni, Amitai, and Jason H. Marsh, eds. 2003. *Rights v.
Public Safety after 9/11: America in the Age of Terrorism.*
Lanham, MD: Rowman & Littlefield.

General Accounting Office. 2004. *Overstay Tracking: A Key
Component of Homeland Security and a Layered Defense.*
GAO-04–82. Washington, DC: U.S. Government Printing
Office.

Glazer, Nathan, ed. 1985. *Clamor at the Gates: The New
American Immigration.* San Francisco: ICS.

Hammermesh, Daniel S., and Frank D. Bean, eds. 1996. *Help
or Hindrance? The Economic Implications of Immigration
for African Americans.* New York: Russell Sage. http://
www.cbp.gov/sites/default/files/document. www.politics.
com/2013/immigration-bill-2013-senate-pass. www.unhcr.
org/51/071816.html.

Illinois.gov.2005. "Gov. Blagojevich Announces Landmark
Immigration Policy." Springfield, IL: State of Illinois,
Office of the Governor.

Information Plus. 2006. *Immigration and Illegal Aliens:
Burden or Blessing?* Farmington Hills, MI: Thomson/Gale.

Information Plus. 2014. *American Immigration: An
Encyclopedia of Political, Social, and Cultural Changes.*
Farmington Hills, MI: Thomson/Gale.

Kirstein, Peter N. 1977. *Anglo over Bracero: A History of
the Mexican Workers in the United States from Roosevelt to
Nixon.* San Francisco: R and E.

Kiser, George C., and Martha W. Kiser. 1979. *Mexican Workers in
the United States.* Albuquerque: University of New Mexico Press.

LeMay, Michael C. 1987. *From Open Door to Dutch Door: An
Analysis of U.S. Immigration Policy since 1820.* New York:
Praeger Press.

LeMay, Michael C. 1989. *The Gatekeepers: Comparative Immigration Policies.* New York: Praeger Press.

LeMay, Michael C. 1994. *Anatomy of a Public Policy.* New York: Praeger Press.

LeMay, Michael C. 2004. *U.S. Immigration: A Reference Handbook.* Santa Barbara: ABC-CLIO.

LeMay, Michael C. 2007. *Illegal Immigration.* Santa Barbara: ABC-CLIO.

LeMay, Michael C., ed. 2013a. *Transforming America: Perspectives on Immigration, Vol. 1: The Making of a Nation of Nations, 1820–1865.* Santa Barbara: ABC-CLIO.

LeMay, Michael C., ed. 2013b. *Transforming America: Perspectives on Immigration, Vol. 2: The Transformation of a Nation of Nations, 1865–1945.* Santa Barbara: ABC-CLIO.

LeMay, Michael C., ed. 2013c. *Transforming America: Perspectives on Immigration, Vol. 3: Immigration and Superpower Status, 1945 to Present.* Santa Barbara: ABC-CLIO.

LeMay, Michael C., and Elliott Barkan, eds. 1999. *U.S. Immigration and Naturalization Laws and Issues: A Documentary History.* Westport, CT: Greenwood Press.

Massey, Douglas S., Rafael Alarcon, Jorge Durand, and Humberto Gonzalez. 1990. *Return to Aztlan: The Social Process of the International Migration from Western Mexico.* Berkeley: University of California Press.

Motomura, Hiroshi. 2006. *Americans in Waiting: The Lost Story of Immigration and Citizenship in the United States.* New York: Oxford University Press.

Motomura, Hiroshi. 2014. *Immigration outside the Law.* Oxford: Oxford University Press.

Muller, Thomas, and Thomas Espanshade. 1985. *The Fourth Wave.* Washington, DC: Urban Institute Press.

Navarro, Armando. 2005. *Mexican Political Experience in Occupied Aztlan.* Lanham: Alamira Press.

NCSL. 2001. "Presentation at the Conference on Illegal Immigration." Denver: National Conference of State Legislatures.

NCSL. 2011. "Undocumented Student Tuition: Federal Action." Denver: National Conference of State Legislatures.

NCSL. 2014. "Undocumented Student Tuition: State Action." Denver: National Conference of State Legislatures.

Nevins, Joseph. 2002. *Operation Gatekeeper: The Rise of the "Illegal Alien" and the Making of the U.S.-Mexico Boundary.* New York: Routledge.

Papademetriou, Demetrios, and Mark Miller, eds. 1984. *The Unavoidable Issue.* Philadelphia: Institute for the Study of Human Issues.

Perotti, Rosanna. 1989. "Beyond Logrolling: Integrative Bargaining in Congressional Policymaking." Paper presented at the American Political Science Association Meeting, August 31–September 3, Atlanta, GA.

Pew Hispanic Research Center. 2005. "Immigration and the States." A presentation by Roberto Suro, Director, Pew Hispanic Center, to the NCSL Regional Conference on Immigration and the States, Denver, CO, December 12.

Pew Hispanic Research Center. 2014a. "Unauthorized Immigrant Totals Rise in 7 States, Fall in 14." http://www.perhispanic.org/2014/11/18/unauthorized-immigrant-totals.

Pew Hispanic Research Center. 2014b. "U.S. Border Apprehensions of Mexicans Fall to Historic Lows." http://www.pewhispanic.org/2014/12/30/u-s-borderApprehensions.

Phillips, Julia A., and Douglas S. Massey. 1999. "The New Labor Market: Immigration and Wages after IRCA." *Demography* 36, no. 2: 233–246.

Preston, Julia. 2014. "Ailing Cities Extend Hand to Immigrants: National Desk." *New York Times*, October 7, A.18.

Reimers, David. 1985. *Still the Open Door: The Third World Comes to America.* New York: Columbia University Press.

Relyea, Harold. 2003. "Organizing for Homeland Security." *Presidential Studies Quarterly* 33, no. 3 (September): 602–624.

Rodriguez, Cristina M. 2008. "The Significance of the Local in Immigration Regulation." *Michigan Law Review* 106 (4): 567–642.

Rodriguez, Cristina M. 2014. "Negotiating Conflict through Federalism: Institutional and Popular Perspectives." *Yale Law Journal* 123 (6): 2094.

Select Commission on Immigration and Refugee Policy (SCIRP). 1981. *Final Report.* Washington, DC: U.S. Government Printing Office.

Suro, Roberto. 2015. "California Dreaming: The New Dynamism in Immigration Federalism and Opportunities for Inclusion on a Variegated Landscape." *Journal of Migration and Human Security* 3, no. 1: 1–25.

Torr, James D. 2004. *Homeland Security.* San Diego: Greenhaven Press.

TRPI. 2014. "New Laws Extend Privileges Regardless of Status." Los Angeles, CA: Tomas Rivera Policy Institute, University of Southern California.

Yans-McLaughlin, Virginia, ed. 1990. *Immigration Reconsidered: History, Sociology, and Politics.* New York: Oxford University Press.

Zuniga, Victor, and Ruben Hernandez-Leon. 2005. *New Destinations: Mexican Immigration to the United States.* New York: Russell Sage.

Introduction

Involved interest groups and legislators struggle over particular bills proposed for illegal immigration reform. They often describe the conflict as a battle to solve once and for all the immigration problem, or argue that the passage of a bill would result in a national calamity. However, conflict over illegal immigration reform is never really over, never fully won or lost, and never without unanticipated consequences.

Why is there a continuous struggle to achieve an immigration policy that satisfies national needs and effectively resolves an issue viewed as the most pressing problem? Why is a true resolution an illusion? Why does illegal immigration reform pose such a policy conundrum? The answer lies in the very "intermestic" nature of illegal immigration-related policy (Manning 1977). Conditions in the policy environment change. No sooner are some international problems or foreign policy considerations dealt with than the world system changes. National policy makers cannot resolve the world's international conflict

People from the San Diego side of the border touch their hands on the fence, above, as it separates a group on the Tijuana, Mexico side of the fence, during a cross-border Sunday religious service on July 13, 2013. As federal lawmakers thousands of miles away consider further sealing the border, many here on the ground are trying to blur the line and unite a region that was split apart by the security crackdown since the terrorist attacks on September 11, 2001. The fence has not stopped the illegal flow, but rather it has shifted the areas across which illegal immigrants flow. (AP Photo/ Gregory Bull) nor set policy for other sovereign nation-states. In a global environment, what other nations do or fail to do affects the dynamics of illegal immigration and worldwide immigration flows. The failure of a nation to achieve a sound economy pushes its citizens to migrate. Foreign civil wars and domestic strife generate mass refugee movements. National disasters and epidemics compel hundreds of thousands to migrate elsewhere. Conditions change globally and affect both legal and unauthorized immigration, modifying the size and origin of the immigration flows.

So, too, are domestic conditions in flux. Any balance achieved among the contending political forces and agreed-upon policy responses can quickly tip out of balance. Some groups decline in their relative political influence, while others rise. This process renews pressures to readdress the balance previously achieved. New problems are perceived. Old problems are viewed in new ways. Demands for a change in the balance are registered in public policy-making arenas. America's complex federal system is dynamic with respect to the interrelations and interplay among the levels and branches of government.

This chapter reviews current issues arising from illegal immigration in the domestic political arena. Soon after an immigration reform bill is passed, one hears calls for another new law. The implementation of yesterday's law generates demands for some new permutation. What, then, are the major concerns? This chapter examines several policy issues of domestic concerns over current illegal immigration problems.

Current Domestic-Policy Concern: Amnesty or Earned Legalization Issue of the Unauthorized

The steady arrival of unauthorized immigrants, or illegal aliens, renews calls for some sort of a legalization, or amnesty, program. Many see proposals to enact a guest-worker program as nothing more than a thinly disguised amnesty. Legislators and interest groups and their lobbyists adamantly oppose a guest-worker program that would allow many among the 11 million unauthorized immigrants a path to legalize their status as an unacceptable amnesty program that rewards lawbreakers.

A June 5–8, 2014, Gallup public opinion poll asked, "should immigration be kept at its present level, increased, or decreased?" The Gallup poll found 33 percent in favor of keeping it at the present level, 22 percent thought it should be increased, 43 percent favored it being decreased, and 4 percent had no opinion. When asked what should be the main focus of the U.S. government when dealing with the issue of illegal immigration, 40 percent favored halting the flow of illegal immigrants, 53 percent favored developing a plan to deal with those immigrants currently in the country illegally, and 6 percent had no opinion. When asked how important it was that the government take steps to deal with the issue of controlling U.S. borders to halt the flow of illegal immigrants into the United States, 43 percent thought it extremely important, 34 percent very important, 16 percent moderately important, and only 7 percent not that important. When asked about their approval or disapproval of President Obama's executive actions regarding illegal immigrants, 9 percent strongly approved, 32 percent approved, 28 percent disapproved, 23 percent strongly disapproved, and 8 percent had no opinion (Gallup 2014).

On the last major congressional action establishing an amnesty program (a provision in the Immigration Reform and Control Act of 1986 or IRCA), both Republicans and Democrats in Congress split their vote. Democrats voted 196 (55%) in favor of IRCA to 88 (45%) opposed. Republicans voted 105 (49%) in favor to 109 (51%) opposed (LeMay 1994: 53). The two major parties differ on how they see the immigration function being reorganized (Aleinikoff, 2000). Since 2010, Democratic legislators are more likely to sponsor "earned legalization" (their term for conditional amnesty measures). Republicans are more divided on the issue. "Establishment" Republican legislators favoring big businesses see a guest-worker program as essential to supplying needed and cheaper labor. Tea Party and other socially conservative Republicans advocate restrictionist immigration policy and object to anything resembling an amnesty program, including an expansion of the guest-worker program.

Democratic sponsors of earned legalization argue that it will bring unauthorized immigrants out of the shadow of an underground economy and into the light of accountability. They maintain it will aid in the fight against terrorism. They view it as decreasing illegal immigration and aiding homeland security by allowing law enforcement to concentrate on border security and tracking down criminals and potential terrorists rather than chasing after millions of ordinary undocumented aliens who are in the country simply to find work and be reunited with family members. Proponents contend the majority of the millions of unauthorized immigrants have done what was asked of them: they work hard, stay out of trouble, obey the laws (other than the civil laws relating to immigration, of course), help their families, and desire the opportunity to legalize their status. Proponents maintain that economic studies have shown the unauthorized are a net asset, taking menial jobs that U.S. workers will not and paying taxes. Proponents consider the very status of being illegal makes such workers all the more exploitable by unscrupulous employers. Interest groups supporting earned legalization provisions include LaRaza, the United Farm Workers, Mexicano Estudiente Chicano de Aztlan (MECHA), League of United Latin American Citizens (LULAC), and several national church groups. Proponents contend it will improve U.S. foreign relations with Mexico and Central American and other Latin American countries. The millions of Mexicans in the United States (both authorized and unauthorized) send billions of dollars back home, but, proponents say, it all comes back to the U.S. economy (Gotcham and Martinez 2005). These billions in remittances exceed foreign investment as Mexico's second most important source of revenue after oil. These billions of dollars return to the United States by way of Mexican purchases of U.S. goods by increasing the well-being of Mexico's poor and working classes, thereby enabling them to purchase consumer goods produced in the United States.

Opponents of legalization contend it simply sparks further illegal immigration, spurs U.S. population growth, further stresses economic development, and adds to already overcrowded schools and water shortage problems in the Southwest. They view illegal immigrants as coming to the United States to exploit its welfare and public health care systems (Feere 2010; Lee 2006). One critic noted: "We pick up the tab in many ways for the undocumented—from burying their dead, to delivery of their babies, to emergency medical and surgical care. There are 300,000 babies born to undocumented mothers annually at a cost of $5,000 a baby." He went on to assert that Medicaid for such babies in Colorado alone totaled $30 million annually, in California $79 million, in Texas $74 million, in Arizona $31 million, and in New Mexico $6 million. Some hospitals, clinics, and emergency rooms closed after being overrun by the uninsured and undocumented (Kamau 2005: B-7).

Groups like the Minutemen and the Heritage Foundation see illegal immigrants as criminals—for breaking U.S. laws regarding immigration—and often as criminals from their nation of origin who essentially import increased levels of crime, and overcrowd U.S. jails and prisons (Center for Immigration Studies 2014; Heritage Foundation 2014; Camarota 1999, 2012b).

In 2005, House Judiciary chairman Rep. Jim Sensenbrenner (R-WI) authored the law barring states from giving driver's licenses to illegal aliens (known as the Real ID Act of 2005, P.L. 109–12, 119 Stat. 302), arguing that because some of the September 11, 2001, terrorists gained access to aircraft using driver's licenses as identification, all illegal aliens should be denied them (LeMay 2013: 68). Proponents of the Real ID Act argued that it enacted recommendations of the 9/11 Commission and that it implements common sense reforms to strengthen border security by interrupting terrorist travel and closing loopholes in the asylum system ("House of Cards" 2005).

Opponents of the Real ID Act contend it has serious legal issues. It raises the bar for persons seeking asylum from religious and political persecution and grants the Secretary of Homeland Security excessive power to circumvent the judicial branch in matters pertaining to border security. They fear that rather than closing the back door to those who would exploit asylum to do harm, the law closes the door on real refugees fleeing persecution precisely when the United States needs allies in the war on international terrorism. The law, they maintain, makes the United States less popular and sympathetic in the world, which the United States can ill afford. Before its enactment, the Real ID Act was opposed, too, by the National Governors Association and the National Conference of State Legislatures because of its top-down approach and unfunded mandate. Section 202 of the act, "Alien Smuggling and Related Offenses," turns into felons anyone—employers, aid workers, Catholic nuns—who willingly help an undocumented person.

The Secure Fence Act of 2006 (P.L. 109–367) authorized construction of a fence along the U.S.-Mexican border, from south of San Diego to Texas, waiving a host of environmental hurdles. It approved a 700-mile-long fence (LeMay 2013: 68).

The impact of unauthorized immigrants on the economy is hotly debated, but is without question significant. Economic analysts estimate the shadow economy at about 10 percent of the goods and services produced by the legal economy ("Jobs, Impact Ample in Shadow Economy" 2005). Economists who have analyzed the costs and benefits have reached varying estimates, depending on how they measure costs and benefits (Chiswick, 1982, 2005; GAO 2000b, 2004; National Association of State Budget Officers 2005, Pew Hispanic Center 2006; Vernez and McCarthy 1996; Cato 2009a, 2009b; Camarota 1999; 2012b). However, there is no question that unauthorized immigrants impact the labor market, put strains on the social fabric, and tend to lower labor market wages. In a December 2007 report, the Congressional Budget Office reviewed 15 economic studies of the impact of unauthorized immigrants on the budgets of state and local governments. It found great variance in their timing and scope. The federal system of government and how the various levels of government collect their revenue results in state and local governments bearing more costs from services provided to the unauthorized than they receive back in revenues (Schuck 2009). However, it is probable that the national level of government receives more in revenue from the unauthorized than it pays out. The Internal Revenue Service estimates that about 6 million unauthorized immigrants file individual tax returns each year and an undetermined more use Social Security numbers obtained using false documents and who thereby pay Social Security withholding taxes, state and local income, and payroll taxes for employees (Congressional Budget Office 2007). The undocumented hold an estimated 15 million jobs and many such jobs are "off the books," meaning the government does not receive taxes on wages. Steven Camarota of the Center for Immigration Studies estimated that, in 2012, of the 11–12 million illegal immigrants in the United States, 7–8 million held jobs (Center for Immigration Studies 2012).

Analyses by both the Center for Immigration Studies and the Pew Hispanic Research Center show that illegal immigrants earn far less than the rest of the population, with an average income at $27,000, which is 40 percent below the legal immigrant or native family income level of $47,000 (Center for Immigration Studies 2004, 2006; Pew Hispanic Center 2005, "Jobs, Impact Ample in Shadow Economy" 2005). Pew estimates Mexican immigrants at about 6.3 million, of whom about 3.5 million hold jobs, roughly 20 percent of the nation's Hispanic workforce. Despite the fact that their earnings are about half that of legal U.S. workers, those wages are nonetheless nearly three to seven times the average weekly salaries they earned in Mexico. Nor are illegal immigrants randomly locating. They follow jobs into the suburbs and to states that previously had seen few unauthorized immigrants, and into job market areas where the population is growing, requiring more restaurants and grocery stores, and more construction work and retail outlets. And whereas in the 1990s legal immigrants outnumbered illegal ones, by 2005 more than half of the estimated 1.2 million people who arrived were unauthorized. Of the 11.3 million living in the United States in March 2013, about half of them had been in the country for at least 13 years. Among unauthorized immigrants, Pew estimates that, in 2012, 2.1 million, or 38 percent, of adults lived with their U.S. born children. And about three-quarters of them had lived in the United States for 10 or more years (Pew Hispanic Center 2014a).

Building fences does not substantially reduce the number of undocumented crossing the borders; it simply induces them to go around the fence and to cross elsewhere——through Arizona, Texas, and New Mexico, where the climate and terrain are more dangerous, leading to a number of deaths. In 2005, a notorious incident highlights that fact. An immigrant smuggler, known as a coyote, was bringing in 74 people across Texas in an 18-wheeler in back of his truck, when the truck's refrigeration system broke down and temperatures inside reached 173 degrees, which resulted in 19 deaths, including a 5-year-old boy. In 2004 a record 415 people died while attempting to cross illegally. A volunteer group, No More Deaths, set up camps along popular crossing routes to conduct daily patrols and transporting immigrants in need to local hospitals. Several of the volunteers were arrested for aiding and abetting. Another group, Humane Borders, calls the Border Patrol when it encounters illegal immigrants in dire medical need and secures approval in advance to transport them to the local hospital ("Border: Felony Case Questions Migrant Aid" 2006).

Estimates of the growth in unauthorized immigrants peaked in 2007, at 12.2 million, then declined and have remained steady until 2013. The Department of Homeland Security (DHS), the Department of Labor, and several think tanks on both sides of the issue (Pew, Center for Migration Studies, Center for Immigration Studies) all estimate that 60 percent of unauthorized immigrants come across the borders, mostly from Mexico, without proper papers (that is, undocumented), and that about 40 percent enter legally but overstay or otherwise break conditions of their temporary visas.

A 2014 Pew Research report found that U.S. border apprehensions of Mexicans fell to historic lows and that for the first time on record, more non-Mexicans than Mexicans were apprehended at U.S. borders by the Border Patrol. About 229,000 Mexicans were apprehended in 2014 compared to 257,000 non-Mexicans (see data from Congressional Budget Office 2007; and Pew Hispanic Center 2014b). The two strongest magnets pulling unauthorized immigrants to the United States are jobs and family reunion.

The typical undocumented Mexican worker earns about a tenth of what his North American counterpart earns and many U.S. businesses welcome and even rely on undocumented workers as cheap and compliant labor. Community networks among recently arrived legal immigrants help establish systems used by illegal immigrants by helping provide jobs, housing, and entry for their illegal relatives and countrymen (Camarota 2005). A 2006 study among day laborers found that 75 percent were in the United States illegally, 49 percent of whom were employed by homeowners and 43 percent of whom worked in construction, most frequently as laborers, landscapers, painters, roofers, and drywall installers. Among them, 59 percent were from Mexico, 28 percent from Central America, and only 7 percent were born in the United States. Also among them, 73 percent stated they were placed in hazardous working conditions ("Study on Day Laborers Tallies Woes of 117,600" 2006).

Census Bureau projections estimate that the U.S. population will soon exceed 400 million. The immigrant population is growing at a rate six-and-a-half times faster than the native-born population, accounting for about 42 percent of the total increase in population between 2000 and 2010 (U.S. Census Bureau, American Community Survey 2010).

After the passage of IRCA in 1986, there was a slight dip in apprehensions at the borders, but those numbers climbed again since 1988, reaching a peak in 2007, as noted earlier. In 2014, total apprehensions by the Border Patrol were 486,651 (Congressional Budget Office 2014).

Perceiving them as a "flood" of illegal immigrants, some citizens began to act as do-it-yourself immigration law enforcers.

A number of vigilante groups began to actively patrol the border for undocumented crossers. Groups like American Border Patrol, Ranch Rescue, the Minuteman Project, and the Colorado Minutemen comb the deserts of Texas, New Mexico, and Arizona to report immigrants to the Border Patrol, sometimes using high-tech equipment such as drones, sophisticated listening devices, and light aircraft (LeMay 2007: 38; see also Minuteman HQ 2015; Minuteman Project 2015; Pollack 2005). A proimmigrant group, Border Action Network, argues that this makes for an inherently dangerous mix of people (Border Action Network 2015).

Arizona has emerged as a main entry crossing point and vigilante groups patrol along the 350-mile Arizona-Mexico border. One vigilante group member stated he spent $1,500 during his time on patrol in the Arizona desert, including the price of night-vision equipment, a directional microphone, and body armor capable of withstanding a round from an AK 47 assault rifle ("Smuggling Deaths Net Conviction" 2005).

The situation in Arizona and New Mexico prompted their governors to declare states of emergencies in 2005. The then-governor of New Mexico Bill Richardson (D-NM) declared that four counties in the state were crippled by the effects of burgeoning unauthorized immigration and called for national reform. His executive order declared that the counties were "devastated by the ravages and terror of human smuggling, drug smuggling, kidnapping, murder, property destruction and death of livestock." He committed $750,000 in state emergency funding and pledged an extra $1 million in aid, a portion of which would fund to build and staff a field office for the New Mexico Office of Homeland Security. In 2004, 300,000 undocumented immigrants were apprehended near the city of Columbus, New Mexico. In July 2005, someone shot at the city's chief of police. Area ranchers witnessed attempted kidnapping of three female undocumented immigrants by masked and armed men on a New Mexico ranch. In a similar action, then Arizona governor Janet Napolitano (D-AZ) declared a state of emergency in Arizona's border counties, and pledged $1.5 million in aid for extra sheriff's deputies and other officers' overtime costs and upgraded equipment (LeMay 2007: 39). Richardson's voice added weight to the issue as he is a Hispanic, a Democrat, and was a candidate seeking the party's presidential nomination in 2008.

The Americans for Immigration Control (AIC) led a state-by-state campaign to enact state legislation to clamp down on illegal immigration, sponsoring public awareness campaigns in many states. In 2006, Colorado held a special session of the legislature to pass a measure imposing fines on employers of unauthorized immigrants and requiring them to check the legal status of all prospective employees and verifying their Social Security numbers, their citizenship status, or their legal right to work (commonly called a "green card"). The AIC uses surveys, talk radio, Fox TV interviews, newspaper columns, and ads across the country to increase support for an immigration moratorium of three to five years, maintaining such a moratorium is necessary to give the present immigration population time to assimilate and for the Border Patrol (Immigration and Customs Enforcement or ICE) to regain control of the borders. It further advocates cutting legal immigration to no more than 300,000 per year. AIC advocates enacting laws or even amending the constitution, if that is necessary, to end birthright citizenship for children born in the United States of illegal immigrant parents (Feere 2010; Lee 2006).

Since 9/11, the federal government has pressured state and local law enforcement to take a more active role in enforcing immigration laws. Only a few departments have obliged; many were reluctant to do so citing costs of unfunded mandates, fears of civil rights lawsuits, and the need for training of local officers. Some local departments have policies and procedures specifically prohibiting them from checking on the immigration status of persons they pull over in traffic violations, and local officers are concerned that they will be suspected of racial profiling. ICE officers are stretched thin and do not always show up if persons are detained and reported by local police. ICE agents not only enforce immigration policy for wide geographic sectors, but also are concerned with child pornography, money laundering, and narcotics smuggling. ICE is often stretched too thinly to respond to local police whose departments lack the funding and their officers the training, and lack detention facilities to hold suspected illegal immigrants for much longer than overnight. California, Florida, and Alabama have entered into agreements with ICE to train members of their state patrols to identify and detain undocumented drivers. However, the National League of Cities has lobbied against proposed bills to expand local police enforcement of immigration laws as unfunded mandates that would divert much needed local resources to enforce federal obligations (Crummy 2005; Suro 2015).

Incorporation of Illegal Immigrants and Their Children

A public policy concern closely related to the issue of earned legalization or amnesty is the incorporation of unauthorized immigrants and their children. Concern for the assimilation of immigrant children is particularly at the forefront of American politics today as legislators grapple with such issues as the Dreamers, the impact on families of the surge in deportation of illegal immigrant parents of citizen children, and the recent influx of thousands of children from Central America unaccompanied by adults. Historically, each successive wave of immigrants raised anxiety about their ability to assimilate and that pattern holds true for today. Since 1965, the source of immigration shifted from Northwestern European nations to Latin America and Asia. That change in the composition of the immigrant flow renewed concerns about the ability of the newcomers to incorporate into U.S. cultural, economic, political, and social systems. Critics of illegal immigration fear especially the trend toward increased immigration from Mexico, South and Central America, and Asia, which is projected to alter the racial makeup of the U.S. population. These critics fear that immigration is changing the very face of America. The Census Bureau projects that by 2050 white Americans will be in the numerical minority.

Such critics further maintain that the nature of today's flow makes more difficult efforts for their "Americanization." Illegal immigrants are still highly concentrated in urban areas and in the top 10 receiving states. They also argue that illegal immigrants are less varied than were immigrants from the past. More than 50 percent speak Spanish as their native language, which critics argue is a degree of ethnic concentration unprecedented in U.S. history.

Although immigration trends, of both legal and illegal immigrants, are undoubtedly reshaping the racial composition of the United States and indeed changing the very appearance of "Americans," are illegal immigrants any less able to incorporate into the United States than the legal immigrants of the past? By most measures available, such fears seem more xenophobic than real. In large measure, how quickly any immigrant assimilates into society is influenced by the person's age. The median age of unauthorized immigrants is 28 years. The influx of young people is particularly important because the U.S. population, with its relatively low birthrate among native-born citizens, is aging rapidly. By 2025, when more than 20 percent of the population will be over 65, more working people will be needed to support them and maintain the solvency of the Social Security system through their payroll taxes. Young people acquire fluency in English much faster than do their parents. They enter the workforce and learn job skills more quickly as well. The younger the person, the more he or she absorbs the culture of majority society. Critics fear the very massiveness of the flow hinders economic incorporation. Illegal immigrant wages are well below those of native workers, leading to a steady rise in overall immigrant poverty.

Finally, critics argue that illegal immigrants oppose assimilation. They contend that illegal immigrants undergo at best a superficial assimilation. For such critics, Americanization is more than learning English or getting a job. They see the development of a visceral, emotional attachment to the United States and its history as part of a "patriotic assimilation," which they fear is unlikely to occur when the schools and the general culture are skeptical, if not hostile, to patriotism, and when communication technology enables illegal immigrants to maintain strong psychological and even physical ties to their countries of origin (Francis 2001; Lamm and Imhoff 1985; Nevins 2001).

Carefully constructed social science studies clearly question the idea that today's immigrants and their children, no matter their status, are any less able to incorporate, or will be significantly slower to do so, than were the immigrants of an earlier era. The findings of several studies show that respondents turn conventional expectations on their head, a result that potentially has long-term political consequences. These studies offer a different theoretical view of the assimilation process than that traditionally held. In place of viewing assimilation as a homogeneous, linear process, these scholars argue that it is better seen as a highly segmented, nonlinear process that does not lead to "amalgamation." Biculturalism and pluralism are as evident as is traditional assimilation (Portes and Rumbaut 2001; Bean and Stevens 2003; LeMay 2001; Stevens 2001; Wolbrecht and Hero 2005).

Of concern to most such scholars is the language ability and adaptation of immigrants. A study among immigrants who arrived between 1987 and 1989, and who therefore had little time to learn English in the United States, found that half of those recently arrived spoke English well or very well (Jasso et al. 2000). There is, of course, considerable variation within and among immigrant groups depending on their native tongue and on the educational backgrounds and occupational categories of the immigrants—as was the case in the past. Post-1965 immigrants are less likely to have entered with high levels of proficiency in English (Stevens 2001). However, census data show the children of immigrant families quickly become the family's English translators, and that performing that function helps their own assimilation and self-image (Obsatz 2002a).

Since there is no national policy on incorporation to encourage their learning of English akin to the national "Americanization" campaigns of the 1920s, such efforts vary across local and state areas and across time. While 25 states have "Official English" laws, an equal number do not. This patchwork of public and political responses to the varying language skills of these newest immigrants reflects the difficulties and benefits of welcoming newcomers to a nation that prides itself as being a nation of immigrants, although not recognized in national policy as an English-speaking nation (Stevens 2001).

What about the incorporation of their children? Immigrant children and the U.S.-born children of immigrants, no matter their status, are the fastest growing segments of the child-age population. U.S.-born persons with at least one foreign-born parent now exceed 60 million in number. The Children of Immigrant Longitudinal Study (CILS) is a multifaceted study of the educational performance and the social, cultural, and psychological adaptation of children of immigrants. It is the largest study of its kind in the United States (Rumbaut 2000; Portes and Rumbaut 2001; Stevens 2001).

CILS found that while more than 90 percent of immigrant children lived in households in which a language other than English was spoken, 73 percent preferred to speak English rather than their parent's native tongue. And by three years later, those who preferred English rose to 88 percent. Even among the most mother-tongue retentive group, Mexican youth living in San Diego with its large Spanish-speaking population and many Spanish-language radio and television stations, the 32 percent originally preferring English rose to 61 percent after three years. Among Cuban youth in Miami, the shift was even more dramatic. There, 95 percent preferred English three years later (Rumbaut 2000). The study found a somewhat lower but similar shift in identity in the second generation as well, where the U.S.-born children of foreign-born parents were four times less likely to identify themselves by their parents' national origin than were the foreign-born children. The CILS found an overall picture of resilient ambition and noteworthy achievement (Rumbaut 2000: 242–257).

Yet another source of pressure for illegal immigration is the desire for family reunification, coupled with huge backlogs in the applications for legal immigration visas. Visa application processing delays run from a year for immediate relatives to more than two years in other cases. A Mexican adult son or daughter of a legal permanent resident faces a wait of eight and a half years, as do nationals from other high-source countries such as India or the Philippines. Such years-long backlogs increase pressures for illegal entry as children in backlog often face the problem of "aging out" of their preference category if the delays result in their passage from under 18 (minor children) to over 18 years (adult children). In 2000, the estimated number of visa-backlogged persons was over 3.5 million (CILS, cited in Portes and Rumbaut 2001).

Another processing and due process issue involves "expedited removal," which has soared in number during the Obama Administration's time in office. Expedited removals were at 978,000 in 2009, with interior deportations at 236,376 and criminal deportations, as of 2012, at 153,000 (Center for Immigration Studies 2015). According to a Pew study, expedited removals rose for 350,000 in 2008 to 419,000 in 2012 (Pew Hispanic Center 2014a). Provisions for expedited removal were in the Illegal Immigration Reform and Immigrant Responsibility Act of 1996 (IIRIRA), which emphasized asylum reform—preventing, defeating, or deterring the use of asylum by claimants who had destroyed or hidden their identity in order to get past border screening who then disappeared into the country. Expedited removal subjects clearly fraudulent violators to a more efficient removal order and imposes even more severe sanctions should such persons attempt illegal entry at a later date. ICE agents have swept up a record number of unauthorized immigrants whose sole violations are visa overstaying or entering undocumented. A majority of those deported were returned to Mexico, while most of the remainder were sent back to Central America, South America, or the Dominican Republic. ICE owns and operates a fleet of jets to annually make hundreds of flights to return those thousands of persons to their native countries. The recent surge in children unaccompanied by adults coming from Central America increases the pool of known persons by several thousands, since they routinely turn themselves in to ICE immediately on arrival. The DHS struggles to reduce the number of illegal aliens who have disobeyed orders to leave the country or who have failed to appear at deportation hearings. Estimates of those numbers remain at about 400,000 because new unauthorized immigrants continue to come, particularly along the southwestern border, and continue to defy orders to appear at deportation hearings. ICE agents also track noncitizens who are serving time for serious crimes and to bring their cases to an immigration judge, and if a judge order them deported, they can be sent back home upon release from prisons, as were the 153,000 in 2012 (Leinwand 2005; Center for Immigration Studies 2015).

Critics of the expedited removal process, such as human rights advocates, legal organizations, and refugee service organizations, argue that the increased use of expedited removal results in some individuals denied entry as refugees who may not make it through the "credible fear" interview (Martin 2000; Wolchock 2000). President Obama issued executive orders (DACA, DAPA) that may ease the use of expedited removal, but the process is likely to remain a contested issue for the foreseeable future.

Border Control and Management Issues

The perennial proposals for illegal immigration reform (numerous bills are introduced annually) speak to another ongoing concern. Does the United States have adequate control over its borders? The political struggles to control illegal immigration, now more than three decades long, reflect the view of many that the nation has, indeed, lost control of its borders. Concerns were heightened after the September 11, 2001, attacks, resulting in the USA Patriot Acts I and II, the Homeland Security Act of 2002, the Real ID Act of 2005, and the Fence Act of 2006. Border control is an enormous undertaking. The United States shares 5,525 miles of border with Canada and 1,989 miles with Mexico. Ocean borders include 95,000 miles of shoreline and a 3.4-million-mile exclusivity zone. Annually more than 500 million persons cross the borders, among which are some 350 million noncitizens. They enter through 350 official ports of entry. Managing the borders, securing transportation systems by sea and air, and controlling international airports and seaports are inseparable and monumental tasks.

The DHS, established in 2002, has four divisions: Border and Transportation Security; Emergency Preparedness and Response; Chemical, Biological, Radiological, and Nuclear Countermeasures; and Information Analysis and Infrastructure Protection. DHS Act restructured the INS by moving the Border Patrol from the DOJ (Department of Justice) to the DHS. The act reflected the political consensus that the system of border control was obviously broken and in need of a major overhaul. The tension in policy is between the need for control pitted against service. Greater control is opposed to civil liberties. Group interest, identity, and diversity are balanced against shared national goals. Trying to balance such zero-sum, no-win trade-offs of deeply ingrained values in fundamental constitutional principles results in a never-ending quest to achieve balance (Bach 2000).

ICE *daily* encounters, processes, and makes decisions about 1 million border crossers. With globalization, the world's economies, so closely tied to that of the United States, depend increasingly on border crossings for increased trade, business, mobility, and tourism. ICE remains the primary agency for control of the borders and for catching undocumented immigrants and visa overstayers. Its biggest problems are at the southwestern border, although others enter as stowaways on ships, or enter through airports.

Past attempts to beef up border control at problematic stations resulted in increased apprehensions followed by a shift in the flow of illegal traffic. Increases in Border Patrol staff in San Diego, California, and El Paso, Texas, saw a decline in the rate of apprehensions at those stations (33%), but the traffic relocated to Tucson, Arizona, and to Del Rio, Laredo, and McAllen, Texas. And actual staffing increases in the Border Patrol have proven to be problematic to implement. Congress approved, in 1996, the hiring of 1,000 agents a year for the next five years. While 1,148 agents were hired in 1998, fewer than 400 were hired in 2000 (Information Plus 2006).

IIRIRA required the attorney general to install additional physical barriers in high illegal-entry sectors. In San Diego, bollard-type fencing (using reinforced steel) was constructed, adding 32 miles to the prior 14. The Fence Act approved more than 300 miles of such fencing. However, fencing has failed to substantially slow down undocumented crossings. It has been tunneled under (hundreds of tunnels have been found since the fence was erected), or simply bypassed, with the flow moving to Arizona and New Mexico.

Human Rights Watch has been critical of abuses committed by the Border Patrol, including the use of excessive force. The Border Patrol counters that their agents come into contact with human and narcotics smugglers who are prepared to use all means, including violence, to enter the United States, and that smugglers are, in fact, better armed than are Border Patrol agents. Individual citizens, mostly ranchers whose land abuts the Mexican border, have formed vigilante groups, some lethally armed. These groups patrol border areas looking for human smugglers and bands of illegal crossers.

Airline companies are responsible for screening passengers and preventing those without proper documentation from boarding. ICE requires them to provide a list of all departing and arriving passengers. Airlines are held responsible if they bring in passengers without documents, whether or not such documents are verified before departure. They can be fined $3,000 per illegal passenger and bear the cost for alien detentions—the costs of which run to as much as $10 million annually. Delta Airlines, for example, maintains a motel exclusively for detainees near JFK Airport in NYC. At some high-risk airports, carriers duplicate visas and passports prior to departure, collect and hold documents, or take other precautions to screen out document flushers and to establish that the passenger is not a stowaway.

Border management is complicated by high volume. But increased security results in cross-border exchanges that are slow and rely on relatively primitive technology. Risk to public safety and the potential risk of law enforcement violation are high. Ports of entry sometimes pose no credible law enforcement risks to smugglers, and the ability of smugglers and traffickers to adapt their techniques and tactics at border crossings increases the law enforcement problem.

Better border patrol and management service requires improved enforcement that slows traffic. How do policy makers accomplish the contradictory aims of increased security yet speeding up the flow for economic trade reasons? Future innovations in technology are needed to alter the past zero-sum, either-or approach (Bach 2000; Broder 2002; Gerstle and Mollenkopf 2001; Kemp 2003; Krauss and Pacheco 2004). Since the establishment of the DHS, border management relies on new technology and better use of information. These include improved advanced passenger information systems at airports, dedicated commuter lanes at Canadian and Mexican borders, testing by ICE of an information system matching passenger arrivals and departures being used between several European airports of embarkation and some major U.S. airports of debarkation. Enhanced enforcement system at land borders using new technology such as drones, motion sensors, automated inspection activities in high-volume stations processing of documents relying on traveler's being pre-screened, using traveler's fingerprints, and visual eye-scanning and photographic profiling and scanning with facial recognition technologies are under development or in testing usage.

Another approach relies on improved preinspection and preclearance arrangements with the governments of Mexico and Canada, where the locus of inspection can do the most good and least harm. Such overseas inspection occurs when inspectors have greater time, where security is greater, and under conditions where the governments have the upper hand. A regional framework means a shared set of rules for cross-border activity (Bach 2000: 244–248).

Domestically, improved procedures involve the cooperation and coordination of agencies such as the FBI, Department of Energy, Department of Commerce, and the DHS. The independent Terrorist Threat Integration Center was established in 2003. It is a joint venture between the DHS and the CIA, housed in CIA headquarters. The merger of so many departments into the DHS makes its management of so many tasks more difficult to do so efficiently (Lehrer 2004; Kemp 2003; Crotty 2003; GAO 2004; Haynes 2004; Hyong 2003; O'Beirne 2002).

Obstacles to DHS efficiency include mission complexity, bureaucratic-cultural incompatibility among disparate bureaus and agencies (22) merged into a superdepartment, task obfuscation, and using symbolic versus real performance (Krauss 2003; Birkland 2004; Broder 2002; Halperin 2003; Jacobson 2003; Light 2002a).

Another policy impacting illegal immigration was the enactment of the Intelligence Reform and Terrorism Prevention Act (P.L. 108–458, 2004) establishing an "Intelligence Czar" by restructuring intelligence operations. Critics are skeptical of the "czar" approach (O'Hanlon 2005). Critics point out that the Director of National Intelligence (DNI) has ignored minority views on how analysis of information is handled, voiced, and heard. They argue that the CIA routinely ignored State Department analyses.

At the heart of homeland security is the concept of national sovereignty. A unilateral perception of national security arises out of the traditional definition of sovereignty, which sees the nation-state as having the power and rightful authority to govern its territory and secure its borders. That requires a delicate balancing act between the needs of security and the traditions of civil liberty. When confronted by international terrorist organizations like Al Qaeda, Al Qaeda in the Arabian Peninsula, and Islamic State of Iraq and Syria (ISIS), such balance is all the more difficult. Terrorist bombings in England, France, Spain, and the Netherlands as well as in the United States suggest that a more international, multinational approach to security is needed.

A particularly worrisome form of international terrorism involves the use of bioterrorism, where casualties are potentially very high (O'Hanlon 2005). An efficient bioterrorist attack using a pathogen of contagious agents such as Anthrax, cholera, Ebola, or even a modified smallpox virus is technically possible and raises fear of such attack to heightened levels. In part, the extra edge to such fear results from the realization that the incubation period of these dreaded and deadly diseases is often days to weeks. A suicide terrorist could be infected, then fly to the United States on a tourist visa. Because the incubation period is longer than the flight time, such an individual, while in a contagious stage, could then travel internally to airports and train and bus terminals, and attend events involving mass public attendance and thereby spread the contagion, which would be difficult to detect, control, or contain. The recent natural epidemic of measles, which spread from Disneyland in California to hundreds (more than 500 as of this writing) in more than 30 states, is an example of the potential danger, which would be far more deadly and likely with far higher morbidity rates than the measles outbreak.

Former INS commissioner Bach suggests four strategies to bring people together rather than pitting them against one another, such as does the employer-sanctions approach. Bach recommends four strategies: (1) target criminals who should be imprisoned and removed; (2) target smuggling operations and rally all interest groups against human trafficking; (3) target worksite enforcement with improved involvement of the Department of Labor, the Equal Opportunity Commission, and state labor law agencies to enforce labor laws against employers who are hiring and exploiting unauthorized workers; and (4) prioritize technology to cope with document and visa abuse and fraud, essential to providing better services (Bach 2000).

The Cost of Illegal Immigration

Controversy over immigration centers on whether immigration is of overall benefit to the nation or is a huge drain on resources. Public opinion polls registering opposition against illegal immigration emphasize its cost to public education, health, prisons and jails, the criminal justice and state and local court systems, and welfare services. These costs are seen as a net drain on state and local governments. Critics maintain that illegal immigrants take away jobs from native-born citizens, especially blacks and other Hispanics. State governments, especially those in states with large percentages of foreign-born in their populations, are concerned that federal laws impose huge financial burdens (Borjas 1994; Camarota 2005, 2012a; Gorman 2004; Huddle 1993; Information Plus 2006; Kamau 2005; Mosisa 2002; Simcox 1997).

However, other scholars and studies dispute the "burden" argument and the methods and manner in which the cost-benefit ratio is measured (Fix and Passel 2002; Gotcham and Martinez 2005; Information Plus 2006; McCarthy and Vernez 1997; Moore 1998; Fix and Passel 1994; Smith and Edmonston 1998; Singer 2004: Spencer 2005). Proimmigration advocates contend that the United States, in the long run, benefits economically, culturally, and socially from immigration. Immigration, whether legal or illegal, brings workers and workers create wealth. They point out the United States benefits from the "brain drain" wherein highly talented individuals with strong entrepreneurial spirits migrate from developing nations to the United States, bringing with them their talents and ethic of hard work. Immigrants add workers to the labor force and, with their higher birth rates, continue to add to the employee base upon which an increasingly aging native-born population depends for the solvency of the Social Security and the Medicare systems.

The cost debate first came to national attention in 1993, when economist Donald Huddle completed a report for the Carrying Capacity Network, an environmental group concerned over rapid population growth (Huddle 1993). Huddle calculated that for every 100 unskilled immigrants who were working, 25 unskilled U.S.-born workers were displaced from jobs. In 1992, he placed the net costs at $42.5 billion, and in 1997 estimated those costs had risen to $68 billion.

An Urban Institute study by Jeffrey Passel disputed Huddle's findings. Passel maintained that Huddle had failed to account for the positive impact of immigrant businesses and consumer spending. Passel argued Huddle had overstated costs and displacement effects. Passel calculated that immigrants paid more than $70 billion in taxes, $50 billion above Huddle's estimates (Passel 1994).

Because of different approaches to measuring the cost-benefit ratio and the use of different assumptions in their calculations, it is difficult to assess which is more accurate. Their estimates of economic gains and losses differ substantially. The General Accounting Office (1995) examined three national studies of costs and benefits associated with illegal aliens. All three of those studies concluded that undocumented immigrants (visa overstayer data were not included in any of the studies) cost more than they generated in revenues to federal, state, and local governments. The GAO report found net costs ranged from $2 billion (Urban Institute) to about $19 billion (Huddle's 1993 study). Illegal immigrants' primary fiscal benefits are on the positive impact on the Medicare and Social Security systems. A study by Steven Moore (1998) noted that while immigrants pay into those systems, their own parents are not collecting benefits. Illegal immigrants using fraudulent Social Security numbers pay in to the system through payroll withholding taxes collected, but since they are unauthorized, they cannot draw on those accounts when they reach age 65. This creates a one-generation windfall to the Social Security system that helps ease the financial hardship to the system by the baby-boom generation of about 40 million people who started collecting their retirement benefits in 2011. A Social Security Trust Fund Board of Trustees Report (1998) estimated that immigrants, over the next 25, 50, and 75 years, would contribute an average of $19.3 billion, $22.3 billion, and $25.8 billion, respectively, to the Social Security Trust Fund. Moore (1998) estimated that, in 1997, the total immigrant income was $390 billion, generating $133 billion in taxes.

By contrast, George Borjas, a Cuban immigrant and professor of public policy at the John F. Kennedy School of Government at Harvard University, argues immigration is detrimental, claiming immigrants' lower educational levels mean that they will remain at an economic disadvantage and in the long run will result in greater use of welfare. However, the National Research Council concluded immigration had little negative effect on wages and job opportunities of most native-born Americans, and concluded that estimates of the costs to state and local taxpayers had been inflated (Smith and Edmondson, *The New Americans* 1997). In another study, Walter Ewing concluded that immigrants, on average, paid $1,800 in taxes to local, state, and federal governments above what they cost in services and benefits received, but notes that costs to state and local governments are higher than to the federal level as they provide more of the total services and depend for a greater percentage of their revenues on property tax and sales tax, whereas the federal government receives a greater percentage of its revenues from income taxes collected to a greater extent through payroll withholding (Ewing 2005: 5).

Guest-Worker Issues

The policy of allowing for guest-workers has been a recurring issue since the Bracero Program ended in 1964. Guest-workers are temporary immigrants who are legally admitted to the United States for a specified time (e.g., the Bracero workers for nine months of a fiscal year). Historically, most guest-workers have been associated with agricultural work. U.S. growers import such workers through the H-2A program. Congressional members associated with growers have consistently sought to expand H-2A. The National Republican Party platform in 2012, for example, called for an expanded guest-worker program (Moffett 2015). IRCA, in 1986, expanded the guest-worker program by creating an H-2B category for nonagricultural workers. The number of H-2B visas allowed was expanded by the IMMACT (the Immigration Act of November 29, 1990) in reaction to a projected labor shortage that never occurred. It allowed for 65,000 temporary visas for up to six years for people in special occupations and tied to a specific employer-sponsor. Government audits have found it rife with abuse. The current system allows for considerable exploitation and unscrupulous employers can retaliate against guest-workers if they try to assert labor workplace rights (Nevins 2001). During the Clinton administration, then Labor Secretary Robert Reich testified against the H-2B visa program, stating that industry was using it to replace skilled U.S. workers with cheaper foreign workers. There is no annual limit on H-2A visas, and a 66,000 annual limit on H-2B visas (LeMay 1994: 37–40, 2007: 59). Since 1990, the computer, electronic, and related high-tech industries have lobbied for increased numbers in the annual allotment of H-1B visas for high- or special-skilled workers (referred to as the STEM program, standing for science, technology, engineering, and mathematics workforce). Guest-workers increased from 44,000 admitted in 1981, to 139,000 in 1990, to 227,000 in 1996, to 106,000 in 2011, the latest year for which data are available. In 2011, there were just over 55,000 H-2A visas issued, and just over 51,000 H-2B visas (Southern Poverty Law Center 2013; Camarota 2006). The National Guestworker Alliance is a New Orleans–based advocacy group that tries to organize such workers across the country and tries to combat their exploitation (Moffett 2015).

The American Competitiveness and Workforce Improvement Act of 1998 increased the number of H-1B visas available by 142,500 visas over the course of three years. It imposed two employer requirements for H-1B workers: that the employer must pay a $500 fee per applicant, the funds from which were to support scholarships for Americans studying computer and related technical fields; and that employers with 15 percent or more such workers in their workforce had to certify that U.S. workers were not laid off for H-1B workers 90 days before or after the H-1B workers arrive at the workplace. The H-1B visa is a nonimmigrant visa issued to employers who will employ guest-workers temporarily in a specialty occupation or field. H-1B visas are issued for a period of up to three years but may be renewed for up to six years. The number of H-1B visas is limited, but the cap has fluctuated throughout the program's existence. Alongside the H-1B visa is the L-visa, used for persons employed at managerial or executive level and issued for three years and renewable for a maximum of seven years. The L-1B visa is for intracompany transferees with specialized knowledge in the field, issued for up to three years and renewable for up to five years. L-2 visas are issued to spouses of L-1 visa beneficiaries, allowing them to reside and work in the United States for the duration of the L-1 visa. Finally, there is the Optional Practical Training visa, offering practical experience through optional temporary employment, to F-1 student visa holders for up to 12 months. Those in STEM fields are eligible for a 17-month extension at the end of one year, with the option of later applying for an H-1B visa (Department for Professional Employees 2013).

STEM and guest-worker trends show fluctuation. The Department of Labor estimates about 50,000 employers sought applications in 1999, and about 44 percent admitted were from India, most of whom were computer programmers (Martin 2001).

The U.S. Department of State issued 134,212 L-visas in fiscal year 2010–2011. Among those, 64,430 were L-1 visas and 71,782 were L-2 visas. They were issued in nearly 200 countries, although 29 percent went to guest-workers born in India. FY2012 saw a 3 percent decrease in approved H-1B petitions, from 269,653 in 2011 to 262,569 in FY2012. While approved petitions for initial employment increased 29 percent, approved petitions for continuing employment decreased 23 percent between FY2011 and FY2012. In FY2012, 154,859 (59%) of H-1B recipients were in computer-related occupations, 26,239 were in architecture and engineering, 4,820 in life sciences, and 4,969 in mathematics and physical sciences. Together, STEM fields totaled 190,987 workers, 73 percent of H-1B approvals in FY2012. Computer-related occupations accounted for 81 percent of STEM-related H-1B visas (Department for Professional Employees 2013).

In 2013, there were nearly 3.8 million workers in computer-related occupations, 11 percent of whom were not U.S. citizens. Among them, computer analysts were 19 percent, and software developers and applications and systems software personnel were 17 percent. The Department for Professional Employees of the AFL-CIO estimates that H-1B admissions were associated with a 5 to 6 percent drop in wages for those STEM workers. According to the Bureau of Labor Statistics, real wages for workers in computer and mathematics occupations were flat from 2004 to 2012, while employment grew by 23 percent ("Occupation Employment Statistics, Occupational Employment and Wages" 2004 and 2012. See also Salzman et al. 2013). The total number of H-1B visa beneficiaries working in the United States at any given time can only be estimated and does not account for those who have remained in the labor market after their visas expired. Estimates indicate 40 to 45 percent of immigrants have overstayed their legally obtained visas (Marshall 2009; DHS 2013a).

There are policy trade-offs inherent in the temporary worker approach. Which is more valuable to U.S. society, cheaper food or higher farm worker wages? How long should temporary workers be allowed to stay? Do STEM workers fill a vital niche in the global economy and global workforce? Ultimately, the answers to those questions are political. As a National Research Council—the principal operating arm of the National Academy of Sciences and the National Academy of Engineering—found, "the current size of the H-1B workforce relative to the overall number of IT professionals is large enough to keep wages from rising as fast as might be expected in a tight labor market . . . [and further found] no analytical basis on which to set the proper level of H-1B visas, and that decisions to reduce or increase the cap on such visas are fundamentally political" (NRC 2001: 187).

Restructuring the INS into the DHS

Many of the issues and controversies discussed in the previous sections involved criticism of the INS. Calls for its restructuring go back to legislative proposals that predate the enactment of IRCA. During the Iran-Embassy hostage crisis, when the INS could not establish even how many Iranian students were in the United States, many in Congress called for its restructuring. The 1990 IMMACT established a Commission on Immigration Reform (CIR). The commission issued a report in 1997 calling for a restructuring of the INS (Meissner 2000: 3; Gardner 2000: 7–8).

The Jordan Commission, as it became known, held hearings, consultations, and roundtable discussions. It defined four core functions of government in implementing immigration policy. It held that there were two systemic flaws in carrying out those functions: (1) mission overload and (2) fragmentation and diffusion of responsibility. Among its several recommendations was a call for a newly created independent agency for immigration review (Gardner 2000: 17–21).

After the Jordan Commission report, several representatives introduced, in 1998, variations to restructure the INS, but those measures were put on hold when the House Judiciary Committee undertook its impeachment referral. In 1999, a new bill was introduced by Representatives Mike Rogers (R-MI) and Silvestre Reyes (D-TX) and Rep. Lamar Smith (R-TX), chair of the House Subcommittee on Immigration and Claims. This measure called for creating two bureaus: a Bureau of Immigration Services and a Bureau of Immigration Enforcement. Had it passed, the bill would have transferred to the director of the Bureau of Immigration Enforcement all functions—personnel, infrastructure, and funding—in support of the following programs: the Border Patrol, the Detention and Deportation program, the Intelligence program, the Investigations program, and the Inspections program. It would also have established a chief financial officer within the bureau (Ries 2001). Another proposal to restructure INS came from the International Migration Policy Program of the Carnegie Endowment for International Peace (Papademetriou et al. 1999). There were several areas of consensus among these three proposals. All agreed that a dramatic structural change of the INS was needed. All agreed that a separation of law enforcement and service functions and chain of command was needed. All agreed on the need for drastic improvement in management. Finally, all agreed that the detention function, like asylum, needed to be separated (Aleinikoff 2001: 22–27).

The terrorist attacks of September 11, 2001, made the proposals moot. The failure of the INS to prevent the terrorists from entering the country, combined with the announcement of approval, some six months after the attack, of visa applications for several of the hijackers to come to the United States to attend flight training schools, raised the level of rhetoric and the political support for—indeed, the demand for—something to be done. The Bush administration developed and announced a plan to establish a new cabinet-level DHS. Its creation involved the most extensive reorganization of the executive branch in decades. On November 19, 2002, President Bush signed the law establishing the new DHS.

It moved 22 agencies and 190,000 employees into the new department, the most massive reorganization of the federal government since the creation of the Department of Defense after World War II. The Congressional Budget Office placed the number of affected workers at 225,000, among the federal civilian workforce of 1.7 million, and pegged the cost of creating the new department at $3 billion. That was the cost of the restructuring per se, not the increased cost of additional security technology and the like. Scholars at the Brookings Institution warned that with such a massive reorganization, the new department's top management would need considerable time to be concerned with the integration of the agencies into a new management and budget system (Light 2002a). The 22 agencies had varied financial management systems and 100 personnel systems, and the new department managers had to negotiate contracts with 18 labor unions. Some of the agencies moved to DHS were widely viewed as "worst-run agencies" (the Customs Service, the INS, and the Border Patrol, in particular). INS investigators and Border Patrol agents were notoriously undertrained, overworked, and overstressed. The information management system of the INS was considered to be abysmal (Light 2002b).

Congressional debate on the measure generally followed party lines, with a majority of House Democrats voicing concerns that the law gutted civil service protections for employees, seriously limited civil liberties, and gave companies involved in homeland security excessive protection from legal liability. They wanted airport security guards to be federal employees rather than private sector employees under contract with airport authorities or airline companies.

Among the 22 agencies moved to the new department were the Coast Guard, the Customs Service, the Border Patrol, the Secret Service, the Transportation Security Administration, and the Federal Emergency Management Agency. DHS separates the functions of visa processing, immigration services, and Border Patrol (called Border Security in the new department).

Immigration and Related Policy Issues

Several public policy areas have important linkages to the illegal immigration problem. The high numbers of illegal immigrants, which have been rising exponentially since 1980, resulted in a dramatic demographic shift. In 1900, there were approximately one-half million Hispanics among the then total population of about 76 million (or 0.006%). The Census Bureau estimates that, by 2020, nearly 11 million, or 25 percent of the projected population of 438 million, will claim Hispanic descent. That dramatic shift has been and will continue to be fueled by immigration from Mexico and Central and Latin America, and by their higher birth rates compared to those of the general population. According to the Census Bureau, 82 percent of the increase in the Hispanic population will be from immigration. The Pew Hispanic Center projects an even higher rise in the Hispanic population—to 47 percent of the total U.S. population by 2050. The Census Bureau projects the Asian population to triple by 2050 (Fawcett and Carino 1987).

Financial impact studies that focus on the long-term effects of such demographic shifts found that immigrants contribute as much as $10 billion to the U.S. economy (Smith and Edmondson 1997; Simon 1989; Perez 2006). Reports by both the conservative Cato Institute and the liberal Pew Hispanic Center found that the increasing levels of immigration add increases to the GDP over 10 years, but do not hurt employment prospects for American workers (Cato Institute 2009a; Pew Hispanic Center 2012).

As is the case with its economic impact, there has long been controversy about the social impact of illegal immigration. Nearly every new group and every new wave of immigration, whether legal or illegal, arouses fear that it could or should not assimilate or that it was adversely affecting American society. The two elections of President Barack Obama only added to such fears, and calls from his ardent critics to "take back America." One would not feel the need to "take back" something unless one felt it was changing, and negatively so. After 9/11, suspicions of immigrants of Middle Eastern origin, and especially of Muslims, rose dramatically. Tensions between Asians, Black Americans, and Hispanics in the past have engendered riots and interracial violence (Bodner 1985; Foner and Frederickson 2004; Portes and Rumbault 1990; Suarez-Orozco 1998; Zuniga and Hernandez-Leon 2005; Schultz 2000). The perceived slower rate at which Mexicans shed Spanish and acquire fluency in English, for example, makes some question their incorporation (Borjas 2000). However, in the long term, every new immigrant group has assimilated into American society by the second or third generation (LeMay 2004: 36–45).

There is controversy over the health care and welfare impacts of illegal immigrants (Suarez-Orozco 1998; Simon 1989; Smith and Edmondson 1997). Illegal immigrants are far less likely to be insured and therefore rely on emergency rooms for nonemergency care, and studies have found that disproportionately lower access to unpaid health care by illegal immigrants is adding to the cost of the public health care system (Kamau 2005), although that may change as the Affordable Care Act's implementation increases health insurance coverage by nearly tens of millions of persons. However, at least one study found that immigrants pay more into the health care system than they take out (Simon 1989). Others are concerned that illegal immigrants bring with them higher incidences of certain diseases and they link them to the resurgence of diseases like tuberculosis and the spreading of HIV/AIDS, or even that bioterrorists will enter with the illegal flow to launch a biological attack (LeMay 2013: 68).

Illegal immigrants affect public education by increasing demands placed on the public education system at the local levels, in terms of both their increased numbers and their need for bilingual education (Hayes 2012; Merino 2012; Miller 2014; Kivisto and Faist 2010).

Finally, two issues related to young illegal immigrants occupied public concern after 2001, and particularly after 2008, and its subsequent surge in deportations using expedited removal. Progressive forces in Congress have been introducing a bill annually since 2001 to enact what has become known as the Dream Act (Development, Relief, and Education of Alien Minors). Sen. Harry Reid, for example, then Senate majority leader, introduced a bill in May 2011. In past years the measure had a degree of bipartisan support, but is currently adamantly opposed by Congressional Republicans as an amnesty measure and what they term "backdoor citizenship" (Heritage Foundation 2014).

In all of their various versions over a decade, the Dream Act proposals provide for conditional permanent residency to illegal alien students of good moral character who graduated from U.S. schools, having lived in the United States for at least five years, completed two years of military service, or were enrolled in a two- to four-year institution of higher education. The Congressional Budget Office, in its markup of Senator Reid's bill, estimated that it would reduce deficits by $1.4 billion over the period 2011–2020, and would increase government revenues by a projected $2.3 billion over 10 years (Pew Hispanic Center 2013).

Conservative critics on the right of U.S. politics argue that one solution, or at least one approach, to deal with the issue is to end the birthright citizenship of persons born in the United States of illegal immigrants. They charge undocumented and unauthorized immigrant mothers come to the United States while pregnant in order to have their child be a native-born citizen. Several scholars argue Congress should abolish or modify birthright citizenship (in Erler and Stock 2012). Others argue there is no legal basis to do so without an outright amendment of the Constitution, citing legal precedents such as the Fourteenth Amendment, enacted on July 9, 1968, the Naturalization Act of 1790 (1 Stat.103), and U.S. Federal Law (8 USC 1401). The birthright citizenship debate was heated up again in 2013 when Sen. David Vitter (R-LA) and Rep. Steve King (R-IA) introduced bills to end birthright citizenship for children of unauthorized immigrants (Pew Hispanic Center 2010.)

Frustrated with Congressional inaction and entrenched opposition by the Republicans in both houses of Congress, President Obama used his executive authority to implement most of the provisions contained in the Dream Act. In 2012, there were 4 million unauthorized immigrant adults living with their U.S.-born children. Among those, 3.7 million, approximately 1 million, people have temporary relief from deportation by two separate administration programs. Roughly 575,000 unauthorized immigrants aged 16 to 30 who were brought into the country by their parents are shielded under President Obama's Deferred Action for Childhood Arrivals (DACA) (DHS 2014; U.S. Citizenship and Immigration Services 2014).

Similarly, a degree of protection was afforded to 5,000 children, mainly from Central America, who came unaccompanied by adults, and have been granted "Temporary Protected Status" based on conditions in their home countries (El Salvador, Guatemala, and Honduras) that make it difficult and dangerous for them to return (DHS 2014; U.S. Citizenship and Immigration Services 2014).

President Obama followed that executive action with one called: "Deferred Action for Parents of Americans and Lawful Permanent Residents" (DAPA) on November 20, 2014. However, both orders have been put on legal hold from implementation by an order of Federal District Judge (Texas), Andrew Hanen, a 2002 Bush appointee. Prior to Judge Hanen's restraining order, pending further judicial review by a full panel of the Circuit Court, 26 states had filed a suit opposing the DACA and DAPA actions as unconstitutional exercises of executive power. Twelve liberal states supported President Obama's DACA and DAPA orders, as did the Major Cities Chiefs (of Police) Association (National Immigration Law Center 2015).

Solutions

As has hopefully been made clear by this chapter, illegal immigration is a problem for which there is simply no easy solution, at least not in terms of congressional enactments of domestic legislation. The problem is what may be called a public policy conundrum. What makes for good (i.e., popular) politics makes for bad (i.e., ineffective or inefficient) policy and vice versa. The politics of illegal immigration reform has become all the more complicated and perhaps intractable by the spread of the illegal immigrant population across the nation, now to about 30 states. The shift in the composition of the post-1970 immigration from European nations to those from Asia and Latin America exacerbate the conundrum nature of the issue.

Congressional enactments, especially since the 9/11 attacks, presidential executive orders or proclamations, and judicial rulings have shaped the illegal immigration policy debate since 1986. Illegal immigration reform measures are likely, as do virtually all major policy decisions, to have significant intended and unintended consequences. Perhaps a greater measure of success regarding the illegal immigration reform problem will be involved in congressional enactment of Comprehensive Immigration Reform, such as S.744, a bill passed on June 27, 2013, by the U.S. Senate by a bipartisan vote of 68 to 32, with 52 Democrats and 14 Republicans voting for the measure. However, to date, comprehensive immigration reform has been stymied in the House of Representatives by the refusal of Speaker John Boehner (R-OH) to even bring the House measure to a floor vote (Lee 2013).

References

Aleinikoff, T. Alexander. 2000. "Reorganizing the U.S. Immigration Function." In Lydio Tomasi, ed., *In Defense of the Alien, XXII*. New York: Center for Migration Studies: 22–32.

Aleinikoff, T. Alexander. 2001. "Policing Boundaries: Migration, Citizenship, and the State." In Gary Gerstle and John H. Mollinkopf, eds. *E Pluribus Unum? Contemporary and Historical Perspectives on Immigrant Political Incorporation*. New York: Russell Sage.

Americans for Immigration Control. www.Immigration Control.com.

Bach, Robert L. 2000. "Looking Forward: New Approaches to Immigration Law Enforcement." In Lydio Tomasi, ed. *In Defense of the Alien, XXII.* New York: Center for Migration Studies, 239–251.

Bean, Frank D., and Gillian Stevens. 2003. *America's Newcomers: Immigrant Incorporation and the Dynamics of Diversity.* New York: Russell Sage.

Birkland, Thomas A. 2004. "The World Changed Today: Agenda-Setting and Policy Change in the Wake of 9/11 Terrorist Attacks." *Review of Policy Research* 21, no. 2 (March): 179–201.

Bodnar, John. 1985. *The Transplanted: A History of Immigrants in Urban America.* Bloomington, IN: Indiana University Press.

Border Action Network. http:www.borderaction.org/. Accessed on February 20, 2015.

"Border Felony Case Questions Migrant Aid." *Denver Post,* January 6, 2006: A-15.

Borjas, George J. 1994. "The Economics of Immigration." *Journal of Economic Literature* XXXII (December):1667–1717.

Borjas, George. 1997. The New Americans: Economic, Demographic and Fiscal Effects of Immigration. Washington, DC: National Academy of Sciences Press.

Borjas, George J., ed. 2000. *Issues in the Economics of Immigration.* Washington, DC: National Bureau of Economic Research.

Broder, David. 2002. "Security in the Homeland." *Washington Post Weekly Edition.* September 2–8: 4.

Camarota, Steve A. 1999. *Immigrants in the United States—1998: A Snapshot of America's Foreign-Born Population.* Washington, DC: Center for Immigration Studies.

Camarota, Steve A. 2005. *Economy Slowed, but Immigration Didn't: The Foreign-Born Population, 2000–2004.* Washington, DC: Center for Immigration Studies.

Camarota, Steve A. 2006. "Immigration's Impact on American Workers." Testimony prepared for the House Judiciary Committee, August 29, 2006. Online at http://cis.org/articles/2006/sactestimony082906.html.

Camarota, Steve A. 2012a. Amnesty and the Employment Picture for the Less Educated. http://www.cis.org/amnesty-and-the-employment-picture-for-less-educated. December 2012. Accessed on February 20, 2015.

Camarota, Steve A. 2012b. "Socio-Demographic Variables of U.S.-Born Hispanics That May Matter Politically." http://www.cis.org/blog/17. Accessed on February 15, 2015.

Cato Institute. 2009a. "CATO Institute Finds $180 Billion Benefit to Legalizing Illegal Immigrants." htpp://www.washingtonindependent.com. Accessed on February 15, 2015.

Cato Institute. 2009b. http://www.cato.org/measuring-the-economic-benefits-of-illegal-Immigrants. Accessed on February 15, 2015.

Center for Immigration Studies. 2004. "The High Cost of Cheap Labor." http://www.cis.org/the-high-cost-of-cheap-labor. Accessed on February 15, 2015.

Center for Immigration Studies. 2006. http://www.cis.org/article/2006/sactestimony/082906.html.

Center for Immigration Studies. 2012. http://www.cis.org/amnesty-and-the-employment-Picture-for-the-less-educated. Report of December 2012. Accessed on February 15, 2015.

Center for Immigration Studies. 2014. http://cis.org/vaughn/contrary-to-administration-claims-only-tiny-fraction-of-'surge'border-jumpers-deported. Accessed on February 15, 2015.

Center for Immigration Studies. 2015. http://www.cis.org/node/5883. Accessed on February 15, 2015.

Chiswick, Barry R., ed. 1982. *U.S. Immigration Issues and Policies*. Washington, DC: American Enterprise Institute.

Chiswick, Barry R. 2005. *The Economics of Immigration: Selected Papers of Barry R.Chiswick*. Cheltenham, UK: Edward Edgar Publishing.

Congressional Budget Office. 2007. http://www.cbo.gov/sites/default/files/12-6-immigration.pdf. Accessed on February 15, 2015.

Congressional Budget Office. 2014. http://www.cbo.gov/sites/default/files/documents/USBP%20stats%20FY2014%20sector%20profile.dpt. Accessed on February 20,2015.

Crotty, William. 2003. "Presidential Policymaking in Crisis Situations: 9/11 and Its Aftermath." *Policy Studies Journal* 31, no. 3 (August): 451–465.

Crummy, Karen E. 2005. "The Reluctant Enforcer." *Denver Post*, May 31: A-12.

Department for Professional Employees. 2013. "Guest Worker Programs and the STEM Workforce. Fact Sheet 2013." AFL-CIO. http://dpeaflcio.org/guest-worker-programs-and-the-science-technology-engineering-and-mathematics-stem-workforce.

Department of Homeland Security. 2011. "Persons Obtaining Permanent Resident Status, Fiscal Years 1820–2010." *Yearbook of Immigration Statistics, 2010*. Washington, DC: Department of Homeland Security.

Department of Homeland Security. 2013a. *Characteristics of H-1B Specialty Occupation Workers, Fiscal Year 2012, Annual Report*. Washington, DC: U.S. Department of Homeland Security.

Department of Homeland Security. 2013b. http://www.dhs.gov/sites/default/OIS-enforcements_ar_2013.pdf. Accessed on February 15, 2015.

Department of Homeland Security. 2014. http://www.dhs. gov/sites/default/. . ./14_1120_memo_deferred_action.pdf.

Erler, Edward, and Margaret Stock. 2012. *The Cost to Americans and America of Ending Birthright Citizenship.* National Foundation for American Policy.

Ewing, Walter A. 2005. "The Economics of Necessity." *Immigration Policy in Focus, Report of the American Law Foundation* 4, no. 3 (May).

Fawcett, James T., and Benjamin V. Carino. 1987. *Pacific Bridges: The New Immigration from Asia and the Pacific Islands.* New York: Center for Migration Studies.

Feere, Jon. 2010. "Birthright Citizenship in the United States: A Global Comparison." Center for Immigration Studies, August. http://www.cis.org/birthright-citizenship. Accessed on February 20, 2015.

Fix, Michael, and Jeffrey Passel. 2002. *Lessons of Welfare Reform: Immigrant Integration."* The Urban Institute, Presentation, March 5, 2002.

Foner, Nancy, and George M. Frederickson. 2004. *Not Just Black and White: Historical And Contemporary Perspectives on Immigration, Race, and Ethnicity in the United States.* New York: Russell Sage.

Francis, Samuel T. 2001. *America Extinguished: Mass Immigration and the Disintegration of American Culture.* Monterey, VA: Americans for Immigration Control.

Gallup. 2014. http://www.gallup.com/poll/1660/ immigration.aspx. Accessed on February 15, 2015.

Gardner, Robert. 2000. "Restructuring the INS: Draft Design Proposal." In Lydio Tomasi, ed., *In Defense of the Alien, XXII.* New York: Center for Migration Studies.

General Accounting Office. 1995. *Illegal Aliens: National Net Cost Estimates Vary Widely.* Washington, DC: U.S. Government Printing Office.

General Accounting Office. 2000a. *H1-B Foreign Workers: Better Controls Needed to Help Employers and Protect Workers*. Washington, DC: U.S. Government Printing Office.

General Accounting Office. 2000b. *Illegal Aliens: Opportunities Exist to Improve Expedited Removal Process*. Washington, DC: U.S. Government Printing Office.

General Accounting Office. 2004. *Overstay Tracking: A Key Component of Homeland Security and a Layered Defense*. GAO-04–82. Washington, DC: U.S. Government Printing Office.

Gerstle, Gary, and John Mollenkopf, eds. 2001. *E Pluribus Unum? Contemporary and Historical Perspectives on Immigrant Political Incorporation*. New York: Russell Sage.

Gorman, Siobhan. 2004. "The Endless Flood." *National Journal* 6 (February 7): 378–384.

Gotcham, Benjamin, and Rutilio Martinez. 2005. "Mexicans in the U.S. Send Billions Home—And It All Comes Back." *Denver Post*, February 19: C-13.

Halperin, Morton H. 2003. "Safe at Home." *American Prospect* 14, no. 10 (November): 36–40.

Hayes, Patrick, ed. 2012. *The Making of Modern Immigration: An Encyclopedia of People and Ideas*. Santa Barbara, CA: ABC-CLIO.

Haynes, Wendy. 2004. "Seeing Around Corners: Crafting the New Department of Homeland Security." *Review of Policy Research* 21, no. 3 (May): 369–396.

Heritage Foundation. 2014. "The Dream Act in the NDAA: Wrong for National and Homeland Security." http://www.heritage.org/research/reports/2014/the-dream-Act-in-the-NDAA. Accessed on February 20, 2015.

"House of Cards? Point-Counterpoint Commentary." *Denver Post*, February 19, 2005: C-12.

Huddle, Donald. 1993. *The Costs of Immigration*. Washington, DC: Carrying Capacity Network.

Hyong, Y. 2003. "Building a Department of Homeland Security: The Management Theory." *Public Manager* 32, no. 11 (Spring): 55–57.

Information Plus. 2006. *Immigration and Illegal Aliens: Burden or Blessing?* Farmington Hills, MI: Thomson/Gale.

Jacobsen, Gary C. 2003. "Terror, Terrain and Turnout: Exploring the 2002 Midterm Elections." *Political Science Quarterly* 118, no. 1 (Spring): 1–23.

Jasso, G. et al. 2000. "The New Immigrant Pilot Survey (NIS-P): Overview and New Findings about U.S. Legal Immigrants at Admission." *Demography* 37: 127–138.

"Jobs, Impact Ample in Shadow Economy." *Denver Post*, December 4, 2005: A-12.

Kamau, Pius. 2005. "Illegal Immigrants Jam Our Emergency Rooms." *Denver Post*, December 22, 2005: B-7.

Kemp, Roger. 2003. "Homeland Security: Trends in America." *National Civic Review* 92, no. 4 (winter): 45–53.

Kivisto, Peter, and Thomas Faist. 2010. *Beyond a Border: The Causes and Consequences of Contemporary Immigration*. Thousand Oaks, CA: Sage Publication.

Krauss, Elisha. 2003. "Building a Bigger Bureaucracy: What the Department of Homeland Security Won't Do." *Public Manager* 32, no. 1 (Spring): 57–59.

Krauss, Erich, and Alex Pacheco. 2004. *On the Line: Inside the U.S. Border Patrol*. New York: Citadel Press.

Lamm, R. D., and G. Imhoff. 1985. *The Immigration Time Bomb*. New York: Truman Tally.

Lee, Esther Yu-Hsi. 2013. "Breaking: Senate passes historic immigration reform." ThinkProgress. http://www.thinkprogress.org/immigration/2013/27/comprehensive-immigration-reform.Accessed on February 21, 2015.

Lee, Margaret. 2006. *U.S. Citizenship of Persons Born in the United States of Alien Parents.* Congressional Research Service Report, ilw.com. Accessed on May 30, 2010.

Lehrer, Eli. 2004. "The Homeland Security Bureaucracy." *Public Interest* 1156 (Summer): 71–86.

Leinwand, Donna. 2005. "Illegals Going Back by the Planeload." USA Today, February 16, 2005. http://usatoday30 .usatoday.com/news/nation/2005–02–16-illegals-deportation_x.htm.

LeMay, Michael. 1994. *Anatomy of a Public Policy: The Reform of Contemporary American Immigration Law.* Westport, CT: Praeger.

LeMay, Michael. 2001. "Assessing Assimilation: Cultural and Political Integration of Immigrants and Their Descendants." In Lydio Tomasi, ed., *In Defense of the Alien, XXIII.* New York: Center for Migration Studies, 163–176.

LeMay, Michael. 2004. *U.S. Immigration: A Reference Handbook.* Santa Barbara, CA: ABC-CLIO.

LeMay, Michael. 2006. *Guarding the Gates: Immigration and National Security.* Westport, CT: Praeger Security International.

LeMay, Michael. 2007. *Illegal Immigration: A Reference Handbook.* Santa Barbara, CA: ABC-CLIO.

LeMay, Michael., ed. 2013. *Transforming America: Perspectives on Immigration, Vol. 3: Immigration and Superpower Status: 1945 to the Present.* Santa Barbara, CA: ABC-CLIO.

Light, Paul C. 2002a. *Homeland Security Will Be Hard to Manage.* Washington, DC: Brookings Institution Center for Public Service.

Light, Paul C. 2002b. "Homeland Security Debate on Hold." Washington, DC: Brookings Institution Center for Public Service, Interpreter Releases, August 25.

Los Angeles Times. http://www.latimes.com/la-ed-birthright_ citizenship_in_the_United_States. Accessed on February 20, 2015.

Manning, Bayless. 1977. "The Congress, the Executive and Intermestic Affairs: Three Proposals." *Foreign Affairs* (January), Online, http://www.foreignaffairs.com/articles/27035/bayless-manning.

Marshall, Ray. 2009. *Immigration for Shared Prosperity—A Framework for Comprehensive Reform.* Washington, DC: Economic Policy Institute.

Martin, David. 2000. "Expedited Removal, Detention, and Due Process." In Lydio Tomasi, ed. *In Defense of the Alien, XXII.* New York: Center for Migration Studies: 161–180.

Martin, Philip. 2001. "Temporary Workers at the Top and Bottom of the Labor Market." In Lydio Tomasi, ed. *In Defense of the Alien, XXIII.* New York: Center for Migration Studies, 44–55.

McCarthy, Kevin F., and George Vernez, 1997. *Immigration in a Changing Economy: California's Experience.* Santa Monica, CA: Rand Corporation.

Meissner, Doris. 2000. "Management Challenge and Program Risks." In Lydio Tomasi, Ed., *In Defense of the Alien, XXII.* New York: Center for Migration Studies, 1–5.

Meissner, Doris. 2003. "Senate Testimony of Doris Meissner." http://www.hsgac.senate.gov/download/?id-00030998-d4df-4aa-aaa69. Accessed on February 15, 2005.

Merino, Noel. 2012. *Illegal Immigration.* Boston, MA: Cengage/Greenhaven Press.

Miller, Debra. 2014. *Immigration.* Boston, MA: Cengage/Greenhaven Press.

Minuteman HQ. http://www.minutemanhq.com/CO. Colorado. Accessed on February 20, 2015.

Minuteman Project. http://www.minutemanproject.com. Accessed on February 20, 2015.

Moffett, Dan. 2015. "What Is a Guest Worker Program?" http://immigration.about.com/od/Browse-Topic/f/What-Is-A-Guest-Worker-Program.htm.

Moore, Stephen. 1998. *A Fiscal Portrait of the Newest Americans*. Washington, DC: National Immigration Forum and the CATO Institute.

Mosisa, Abraham. 2002. "The Role of the Foreign-Born Workers in the U.S. Economy." *Monthly Labor Review*, May 2002 (3): 1–14.

National Association of State Budget Officers. 2005. http://www.nasbo.org/. Accessed on February 15, 2015.

National Conference of State Legislatures. 2005. "Immigrant Policy: News from the States, 2005." http://www.ncsl.org/programs/immig/immigstatelegis080105html. Accessed on July 20, 2006.

National Immigration Forum. 1998. *Fiscal Impact of the Newest Americans*. Washington, DC: National Immigration Forum and the Cato Institute.

National Immigration Law Center. 2014. "Deferred Action for Parents of Americans and Lawful Permanent Residents." Online at http://www.nilc.org/dapa&daca.html. Accessed on February 22, 2015.

National Research Council. 2001. *Building a Workforce for the Information Economy*. Washington, DC: National Academy.

Nevins, Joseph. 2001. *Operation Gatekeeper: The Rise of the "Illegal Alien" and the Making of the U.S.-Mexico Boundary*. New York: Routledge.

New York Times. http://www.nyt/com/2995/08/19/national/19ranch.html.

O'Beirne, Kated. 2002. "Bureaucratic Nightmare on the Way." *National Review*, Public opinion page, *Press Enterprise*. Riverside, CA: August 25: D-1.

O'Hanlon, Michael E. 2005. *Defense Strategy for the Post-Saddam Era*. Washington, DC: Brookings Institution.

Obsatz, Sharyn. 2002a. "Between Two Worlds." *Press Enterprise*. Riverside, CA: August 27, 2002: B-5.

Obsatz, Sharyn. 2002b. "Vandals Turn Desert Deadly," *Press Enterprise*. Riverside, CA: September 14: A-1, 10.

Papademetriou, Demetrios, Alexander Aleinkopf, and D. W. Meyers. 1999. *Reorganizing the U.S. Immigration Function: Toward a New Framework for Accountability*. Washington, DC: Carnegie Endowment for International Peace.

Passel, Jeffrey S., and Rebbecca L. Clark. 1994. *How Much Do Immigrants Really Cost?* Washington, DC: Urban Institute.

Perez, Miguel. 2006. "Hire Education: Immigrants Aren't Taking Jobs from Americans." *Chicago Sun Times* (August 22).

Pew Hispanic Center. 2005. Report of May, 2005. "More Jobs for New Immigrants but at Lower Wages." Washington, DC: Pew Hispanic Center: 1–22.

Pew Hispanic Center. 2010. "Unauthorized Immigrants and Their U.S.-Born Children." Pew Hispanic Center.

Pew Hispanic Center. 2012. "A Portrait of Unauthorized Immigrants in the U.S." http://phc.org/portrait-of-unauthorized-immigrants-in-u.s. December 6, 2012. Accessed on February 20, 2015.

Pew Hispanic Center. 2013. http://www.pewhispanic.org/2013/12/18/3-views-about-unauthorized-immigrants-and-deportation-worries. Accessed on February 20, 2015.

Pew Hispanic Center. 2014a. http://www.pewhispanic.org/2014/09/03/as-growth-stalls-unauthorized-population-becomes-more-stable. Accessed on January 26, 2015.

Pew Hispanic Center. 2014b. http://www.pewresearch.org/fact-tank/2014/12/30/u-s-Apprehensions-of-Mexicans-fall-to-historic-lows. Accessed on February 15, 2015.

Pollack, Andrew. 2005. "2 Illegal Immigrants Win Arizona Ranch in Court," *New York Times*, August 19, 2005. http://www.nytimes.com/2005/08/19/national/19ranch.html.

Portes, Alejandro, and Ruben G. Rumbaut, eds. 2001. *Ethnicities: Children of Immigrants in America.* New York: Russell Sage.

Ries, Lora. 2001. "An Update from Capitol Hill." In Lydio Tomasi, ed. *In Defense of the Alien, XXIII.* New York: Center for Migration Studies.

Rumbaut, Ruben G. 2000. "Transformation: The Post-Immigrant Generation in an Age of Diversity." In Lydio Tomasi, ed. *In Defense of the Alien, XXIII.* New York: Center for Migration Studies.

Salzman, H. et al. 2013. *Guestworkers in the High-Skill U.S. Labor Market: An Analysis of Supply, Employment, and Wage Trends.* Washington, DC: Economic Policy Institute.

Schuck, Peter H. 2009. "Taking Immigration Federalism Seriously." *The Forum* 7, no. 3: 4–14.

Schultz, Jeffrey D. 2000. *Encyclopedia of Minorities in American Politics: African Americans and Asians Americans.* Westport, CT: Greenwood Press.

Simcox, David. 1997. *Measuring the Fallout: The Cost of the IRCA Amnesty after 10 Years.* Washington, DC: Center for Immigration Studies.

Simon, Julian L. 1989. *The Economic Consequences of Immigration.* Boston: Basil Blackwell.

Singer, Audrey. 2004. "Welfare Reform and Immigrants: A Policy Review." In Philip Kresedemas and Anna Aparicio, eds. *Immigrants, Welfare, Reform, and the Poverty of Policy.* Westport, CT: Praeger Press.

Smith, James P., and Barry Edmonston, eds. 1998. *The New Americans: Studies of the Economic, Demographic, and Fiscal Effects of Immigration.* Washington, DC: National Research Council, National Academy of Sciences Press.

"Smuggling Deaths Net Convictions." *Denver Post*, March 25, 2005: A-1, 16.

Social Security Trust Fund. 1998. *Board of Trustees Report.* Washington, DC: SSTF, U.S. Government Printing Office.

Southern Poverty Law Center. 2013. "Close to Slavery: Guestworker Programs in the United States." http://www .splcenter.org/get-informed/publications/close-to-slavery-guestworker-programs-in-the-united-states. Accessed on February 15, 2015.

Spencer, Jim. 2005. "Immigration Economics vs. Emotion." *Denver Post*, December 14, 2005: B-1.

Stevens, Gillian. 2001. "U.S. Immigration Policy and Language Characteristics of Immigrants." In Lydio Tomasi, ed. *In Defense of the Alien, XXIII.* New York: Center for Migration Studies.

"Study on Day Laborers Tallies Woes of 117,600." *Denver Post*, January 13, 2006: A-12.

Suarez-Orozco, Marcelo M., ed. 1998. *Crossings: Mexican Immigration in Inter-Disciplinary Perspectives.* Cambridge, MA: David Rockefeller Center for Latin American Studies, Harvard University Press.

Suro, Roberto. 2015 "California Dreaming: The New Dynamism in Immigration Federalism and Opportunities for Inclusion on a Variegated Landscape." *Journal Migration and Human Security* 3, no. 1 (2015): 1–25.

Time, Inc. 2010. "Arizona's Next Immigration Target: Children of Illegals." Time.com/. June 11, 2010.

United States Bureau of the Census. 2010. American Community Survey. Washington, DC: U.S. Government Printing Office.

United States Department of Labor, Bureau of Labor Statistics. "Occupational Employment and Wages." Washington, DC: Bureau of Labor Statistics, May 2004–May 2012.

U.S. Citizenship and Immigration Services. 2014. "Consideration of Deferred Action for Childhood Arrivals by Fiscal Year, Quarter, Intake, Biometrics, and Case

Status: 2012–2014. FY2014, 3rd Quarter. http://www.
uscis.gov/sites/default/files/USCIS/Resources/Reports%20
and%20Studies/Immigration%20Forms%20Data/All%20
Form%20Types/DACA/DACA_fy2014_qtr3.pdf.

Vernez, George, Robert Schoeni and Kevin McCarthy. 1996.
The Mixed Economic Progress of Immigrants. Santa Monica,
CA: The Rand Corporation.

Wolbrecht, Christina, and Rodney E. Hero. 2005. *The Politics
of Democratic Inclusion.* Philadelphia: Temple University
Press.

Wolchok, Carole Leslie. 2000. "Where Do We Go from
Here? The Future of the Expedited Removal Process." In
Lydio Tomasi, ed. *In Defense of the Alien, XXII.* New York:
Center for Migration Studies.

Zuniga, Victor, and Ruben Hernandez-Leon, eds. 2005. *New
Destinations: Mexican Immigration to the United States.* New
York: Russell Sage.

Introduction

This chapter presents eight original essays on the topic of illegal immigration from a variety of viewpoints from all sides of the issue. It gives voice to activists, both pro and con on the issue and on illegal immigration reform measures, and from various disciplinary perspectives, allowing the reader to hear viewpoints beyond and different from the expertise of the author. They are presented here in point/counterpoint arrangement.

On Hospitality to the Stranger: Some Moral Implications of Immigration Reform
The Rev. Canon Pablo Ramos

This is the truth of stewardship: the service to others, especially the service to our neighbors in the same form that it was thought of in the Old Testament, and as Jesus thought of it in the parable of the Good Samaritan, takes us to the practice of stewardship itself, especially in the exercise of the charity to others, in particularly to the immigrants who come to this

---

A U.S. Customs and Border Protection Air and Marine agent looks for signs of illegal activity along a trail while on patrol near the Texas-Mexico border, September 5, 2014. Since illegal immigration spiked in the Rio Grande Valley in the summer of 2014, the Border Patrol dispatched more agents, the Texas Department of Public Safety sent more troopers, and Governor Rick Perry deployed as many as 1,000 guardsmen to the area. (AP Photo/Eric Gay)

country after a long journey of suffering in search of better perspectives of life. These people are not statistics or objects of political agreements or new laws that do not help them in any way. There are our brothers and sisters.

I remember hearing someone say, "Hospitality opens the door of a community into something out of the ordinary." It is not coincidence that hospitality and hospital come from the same word in Latin—both lead to the same result: healing, health. When you open the door to anyone you are sending this message, "You are important to God and to me." You may be thinking that what you are saying is this, "come to visit us." But what the stranger hears is, "I am worthy."

Today men and women live on a constant pilgrimage (especially the immigrants coming to this country) as lone travelers in search of a moment of peace, fresh water, and a sign of encouragement that allow us to keep walking in search of the ultimate freedom (the collect for peace says to serve God is perfect freedom). For this reason the stewardship of hospitality invites us to get rid of the fear and turn our communities into places where our hospitality reigns. Hospitality is a virtue that allows us to break the narrowness of our fears and to open our home to the stranger with the intuition that salvation comes in the form of a weary traveler.

We are people easily dominated by the negative power of fear—fear pervades most recondite corners of our being to the point of controlling our choices and decisions. Fear is a cruel being that has taken hold of us and our communities. Fear makes us pull away, become fearful and distant to the stranger. Fear prompts us to try to close or fortify our borders. Fear takes away our ability to host in simplicity.

Our society seems to be wrapped in an alarming rate of growing violence and aggression—leading us to live defensively. Communities that live attached to their property are inclined to be suspicious of the one that approaches us. But our vocation in the midst of this world is to receive what we see as a hostile being as a brother, the enemy as a friend. We are called to create a place of no fear or worries; a place where we can give the grace of the common union.

Historically, churches have been concerned with the construction of temples: places for song, conferences, and exhortations. Places where some believers can take their sacrifice and offerings. Places where believers hope to find prosperity, psychological orientation and fight against the demons that overwhelm them. Places where some are proud of what they built and where they get motivated to build more. It is in the temple of today, just as it was in the Old Testament, where some believe God lives and forgiveness can be found.

The forgiveness that Jesus offers serves as an alternative to include anyone of any ethnicity, any age, any gender, any sexual orientation. For example, when Jesus presented his authority to forgive sins he did it in conflict with the authority of the time, in the temple, and against Jewish law. Jesus did not proclaim another temple, but an alternative. Jesus offers his forgiveness in homes, at the table, in friendship with the sinners.

God provides for the life of his children. Through the blessing of the Lord, we know that to host those who come to us pleases the Lord. I want to emphasize that hospitality is fundamental to and an integral tool of stewardship, and that we need to focus on two characteristics of hospitality. First, hosting a stranger is to host the Lord. Second, the hospitality that we offer must be born from the richness of our heart and not only from our checkbook. The Letter to the Hebrews gives us a great stimulus that could be something of value for the stewardship of hospitality: "Do not neglect to show hospitality to strangers, for by doing that some have entertained angels without knowing it" (Hebrews 13:2).

In the New Testament numerous accounts value hospitality to the stranger as hospitality to the Lord. Today, in the church at the Eucharistic Table, when strangers and foreigners are welcomed and recognized, they become members of the community. Jesus's encounter with the Samaritan woman at the well suggests the notion of hospitality and how to host the Lord in your life. Like the Samaritan woman who comes to recognize who Jesus is, we as well, can hear this good news and recognize a God that comes to us through our encounters with the stranger. This story encourages us to be aware of our own willingness or neglect to offer hospitality to the "other." Through the other God opens us to his presence.

The stewardship of hospitality invites us to recognize that in receiving the stranger we receive the Lord and the One that is loved by the Lord. The hospitality that we are invited to give is simple: it comes fundamentally from affirming the value of a person, even though in this action the Lord is not recognized. A story illustrates a piece of this truth.

> *An old rabbi asked his students one day when they could say the night was over and the day begun. "Is it," a student responded, "when you can see an animal at a distance and tell whether it is a sheep or a dog?" "No," replied the rabbi. Another asked, "Is it when you can see a tree in the distance and tell whether it is a fig tree or a palm tree?" "No," replied the rabbi. The students were puzzled and no other responses were proposed. "So, what is it?" they asked. "It is when looking at the face of the stranger, you see him as a friend. Because if you don't see a friend, it is still dark."*

The symbolic meaning of the kiss on the cheek as a personal sign of welcome is that our hospitality should be personal—born from the heart. It is not enough simply to indicate a location and provide a brochure or bulletin. We must pay special attention to the person.

Conclusion

In this essay I am not saying that hospitality is always a pleasant experience. The exercise of hosting or receiving is not always easy. Patience and good will can often be tested in the practice of hospitality. Instead, I want to re-emphasize the importance of the service of hospitality. In this essay I have suggested two related and important ideas in relationship to hospitality that have biblical foundations. First, in hosting the stranger we receive angels, which means the presence of the Lord among us. This must be done with faith and respect. Second, our hospitality should be personal, sincere and cheerful. What makes Christian hospitality amazing is the fact that it is offered without any pretentions. Christian hospitality is spontaneous. Our hospitality does not seek recognition in doing a good deed or for fulfilling an obligation—it is simply a pleasure. We live to be able to express this type of hospitality. This is the essence of our spiritual life. Who knows what the Lord wants to do in the lives of His people in this place and among us? As Jesus, with the help of the Holy Spirit, let's be hospitable disciples.

Many politicians today describe the United States as a Christian nation. If that is so, then we must be a nation that welcomes the stranger. As we grapple with proposals to amend our immigration laws, we must remember that there are, indeed, moral as well as legal implications to immigration reform.

The Rev. Canon Pablo Ramos has worked in the Diocese of Utah since 1998, and currently serves as Canon for the Latino Ministry, Vicar of San Esteban, El Buen Pastor and San Francisco; he is also cochair of the antiracism committee.

Examining the Adequacy and Enforcement of U.S. Immigration Laws
Jessica Vaughan

Current immigration law enforcement is in a state of collapse. The vast majority of illegal aliens face no threat of deportation regardless of when or how they arrived. New illegal arrivals continue from land, air, and sea; and the size of the illegal population stopped declining several years ago. The Obama administration's deliberate dismantling of enforcement has imposed enormous costs on American communities in the form of lost job opportunities and stagnant wages for native workers, higher tax bills to cover increasing outlays for social services and benefits, compromised national security, and needless public safety threats. One of the most urgent tasks now before Congress is to restore integrity to our immigration laws by ending the massive catch and release scheme put into place by the Obama administration, implementing more effective deterrents to illegal settlement, and providing the tools for more efficient enforcement.

Statistics published by the Department of Homeland Security (DHS) show clearly that over the last several years, even as illegal border crossings have grown and the number of overstaying visitors is large, the number of deportations has plummeted and the number of illegal aliens allowed to stay and work in the United States has increased. The drop in enforcement activity has become particularly acute since the president's executive action went into effect in late November 2014.

Since 2011, the number of illegal crossers apprehended by the Border Patrol has increased by 43 percent, from 340,000 to 487,000 (Simanski 2014). It is generally believed that border apprehensions are an indicator of the number of attempted illegal border crossings, and that approximately half of those who attempt illegal entry are successful. U.S. Customs and Border Protection (CBP) states that "The uptick is largely due to the increase in unaccompanied children and family units who turned themselves in to Border Patrol agents in South Texas this summer." These cases totaled 137,000 in 2014 alone.

Although the apprehension statistics are concerning enough, they do not tell the whole story. CBP has yet to disclose how these cases were disposed of—that is, how many of those apprehended were removed or returned, and how many were released into the United States? Of those released, how many have concluded their immigration proceedings or absconded from those proceedings? For example, separate government statistics indicate that only a few hundred of the surge arrivals have been deported (Vaughan 2014).

It is generally accepted that 40 percent of the illegally residing population is comprised of aliens who overstayed beyond the time or purpose authorized by their status. According to an unpublished report prepared by DHS based on arrival and departure records, in 2012 approximately 263,000 aliens who were admitted on B-1 or B-2 visitor status or under the Visa Waiver Program were identified as having stayed in the country beyond their authorized duration of stay (DHS 2012). Overstayers are not a high priority for deportation. In 2013, only 3 percent (11,596 out of 368,485) of the aliens deported by U.S. Immigration and Customs Enforcement (ICE) were overstays (ICE 2013).

Total deportations of all three DHS immigration enforcement agencies (Border Patrol, ICE, and CBP-OFO) have declined 37 percent since 2009, from 978,000 to 616,000. This has occurred despite an increasing number of apprehensions and continuing overstay arrivals (DHS Office of Statistics Annual Reports).

The number of ICE deportations from the interior has dropped 58 percent since the peak in 2008, from 236,000 to 102,000 in 2014 (Vaughan October 2014).

The number of criminal aliens deported from the interior has declined by 43 percent since 2012, from 153,000 to 87,000, despite increases in the number of criminal aliens encountered and screened by officers. In 2014, ICE deported 69,000 fewer criminals from U.S. communities than it did in 2012. This has occurred despite the fact that ICE has the ability to identify more criminal aliens than ever before, thanks to the nationwide implementation of the Secure Communities program, which links the DHS databases to the national fingerprint matching system.

In 2013, ICE released 36,007 convicted criminal aliens from its custody (Vaughan May 2014). Of these, 193 had homicide convictions, 426 had sexual assault convictions, and 303 had kidnapping convictions. As of September 2014, 5,700 of them (16 percent) had been arrested again for subsequent offenses, and 1,000 have been convicted again. ICE has taken only 1,600 back into custody (DHS Records 2015). There were 174,283 convicted criminals with pending deportation proceedings who were at large, released by ICE (DHS Secretary Johnson 2014).

Moreover, many convicted criminal aliens are allowed to walk out of ICE custody without being enrolled in a program of supervision. ICE officers report that fewer aliens are being enrolled in the Intensive Supervision Appearance Program (ISAP), in which criminal aliens wear an electronic monitoring bracelet and check in frequently with monitors. While once this program was used for lower level offenders, now it is rarely used.

The number of aliens who have received final orders of removal but who are still in the United States has risen to nearly 900,000 as of September 2014 (Ibid). This number has risen by 40,000 in just two years. They were never a priority for enforcement under this administration, but now the president's recent executive action specifically nullified all removal orders and enforcement actions involving "non-criminals" taken before January 1, 2014.

References

Department of Homeland Security. 2012. "Nonimmigrant Overstays, Fiscal Year 2012, Unpublished report reviewed by author.

Department of Homeland Security. 2015. DHS Records provided to Sen. Churck Grassley on January 30, 2015.

Department of Homeland Security, Annual Reports, Office of Immigration Statistics Yearbooks and Annual Reports.

ICE. 2014. Weekly Departures and Detention Report, September 22, 2014.

ICE Removals 2013, obtained by FOIA request by author, includes those labeled non-Immigrants, Border Crossing

Card Holders, temporary workers, students, and Other categories of admission.

Johnson, Jeh. 2014. Testimony of the DHS Secretary before the House Homeland Security Committee on December 2, 2014.

Simanski, John. 2014. "Immigration Enforcement Actions, 2013." Department of Homeland Security, CBP Border Security Report, Fiscal Year 2014.

Vaughan, Jessica. M. 2014. Testimony before the House Immigration Subcommittee, December 10, 2014.

Vaughan, Jessica. May 2014. "ICE Documents Detail 36,700 Criminal Alien Releases in 2013." Center for Immigration Studies.

Vaughan, Jessica. October 2014. "ICE Enforcement Collapses Further in 2014." Center for Immigration Studies.

Jessica M. Vaughan serves as Director of Policy Studies for the Center for Immigration Studies, a Washington, D.C.–based research institute that examines the impact of immigration on American society and educates policy makers and opinion leaders on immigration issues. She has been with the center since 1992, and her area of expertise is immigration policy and operations, covering topics such as visa programs, immigration benefits, and immigration law enforcement.

Should the United States Enact Tougher Laws to Stem Illegal Immigration?
Karen K. Clark

The United States does not need to enact tougher laws to stem illegal immigration. Myths and politically infused ideas about illegal immigration create an emotionally charged environment that promotes segregation, racism, and divided communities while undermining deliberate discussion about productivity, economic development, and the exploitation of labor groups.

Much of the immigration controversy reflects the relationship between the United States and Mexico. While there are significant numbers of illegal European and Canadian immigrants who work "off-the-books" without paying taxes or processing appropriate paperwork for long term stay (roughly 40 percent of unauthorized immigrants), many view the issue of illegal immigration as simply a problem of allowing Mexicans to cross the southern border illegally.

Modern efforts to limit immigration reflect misunderstandings or ignorance of historical patterns. Those who advocate stricter limits ignore the fact that their European heritage reflects its own pattern of illegal immigration. Between the 16th and 20th centuries, millions of Europeans arrived claiming lands that belonged to the indigenous population. Violence, repeated violations of treaties and laws, and even genocidal efforts were used consistently against native peoples. European immigrants felt entitled to enter occupied nations and take control of their lands and resources. Many U.S. national parks were established after the forced relocation of the indigenous people. This removal was not an unfortunate aberration. Rather, it was one of countless acts leading to the development of modern America. Manifest Destiny was more than a political declaration; it was a deeply held belief those of Northern European ancestry held that did not limit their migration, while those of Mexican, Chinese, and Native American ancestry were expected to abide by a myriad of laws and government efforts to limit their migration and settlement.

Throughout American history immigration policies favored those of European descent, although there had been immigration waves of nonwhites when their labor fulfilled a need, such as the construction of railroads. Unfortunately, the history of immigration policy has exhibited a racial bias that continues to shape current debate.

Both Mexican and Chinese immigrants were used to construct railroads throughout the United States. Chinese laborers were paid less than half the wages of white laborers during the construction of the Pacific and Transcontinental Railroads. Mexican immigrants were brought in to work as railroad maintenance workers in the Bracero Program during World War II. Once the troops returned, labor shortages dissipated and the workers who had been here legally became, if they stayed, illegal immigrants. The United States developed a closed border policy in the 1920s. Prior to then, the U.S.-Mexican border was open and people from both sides moved freely into and out of each other's respective countries.

Since the closed border policies developed, immigration strategies have reflected economic conditions, but the problem isn't as simple as greater opportunities for economic prosperity luring migrants to the United States. Acknowledging that corporations and large-scale business alliances create migration is paramount to understanding resettlement trends.

Such business practices are not colonial rules. They reflect a political reality that irrevocably stimulates human displacement. Migration results inevitably. Contemporary pronouncements against immigration fail to take into account the fact that the United States creates migration patterns while laying blame on those whose environments are altered. America is the world's largest consumer culture yet it fails to recognize the implications of this fact. Consequences of mass consumption require alterations to lifestyles elsewhere and create demand for cheap labor and production within U.S. borders. The idea that trade can be facilitated cheaply and quickly across borders through policy like the North American Free Trade Agreement (NAFTA) while pretending that labor and human migration patterns will not follow suit is illogical and impractical.

Reducing immigration without causing labor shortages in agriculture and the hospitality sectors has proven problematic. There are an estimated 1.6 million illegal farm workers in the United States. This number does not include those who work in meat or egg processing plants. Those working in the agricultural sector are roughly 15 percent of the estimated 12 million undocumented immigrants in the United States. Several congressmen from states now dependent on such labor have made attempts to legalize them. Recognizing the needs of large-scale farming operations, Senators John McCain (R-AZ) and Edward Kennedy (D-MA) proposed legislation in 2006 and 2007 that would have allowed farm workers a gradual path towards citizenship working under recognized labor contracts. Both efforts were defeated by members of the Republican Party. Some Democrats voted against the proposals fearing a 'yes' vote would create reputations for supporting amnesty—then politically unpopular. To be clear, the programs are not the same as amnesty, but to voters whose emotions are manipulated by commercial media outlets, the differences among various immigration policies and related terms can easily be lost.

Unfortunately, this political environment leads to productivity loss on American farms. For example, New Mexico, the world's largest producer of chili peppers, has had multiple years of partially harvested crops. Restrictions and a decrease in visas issued to Mexican citizens resulted in many crops not being picked, packaged, or sold—leading to increased costs, diminished supplies, and substantial losses to farmers and their communities. American citizens have not been willing to fulfill those labor roles while simultaneously resisting the idea of paying higher produce costs, particularly during a hardship economy, and thus, unfortunately, denying the fact that this kind of labor is essential to United States agriculture.

Paradoxes in immigration policy are a recurrent theme. Under President Ronald Reagan, the Immigration Reform and Control Act (IRCA) was passed in 1986. It represented the first widespread effort to enhance both border security and restrict immigration. It reduced the allocation of visas for legal migration by Mexican citizens and increased penalties for visa overstayers.

Ironically, these restrictions were passed in the same time frame as NAFTA. The dichotomous concept that one can facilitate greater movement of goods across borders while restricting movement of people created an increase in the black market for illegal labor. Illegal labor increases tend to decrease wages and working conditions, exacerbating the declining work environment and the degradation of a community forced into economic shadows. Another irony is that IRCA, meant to be tough on illegal immigration, granted amnesty to undocumented immigrants who had entered before 1982, and amnesty programs are anathema to those wanting the toughest immigration laws and policies.

Regrettably, scapegoating immigrants has been endemic in American history. In contemporary politics, this translates to enhanced security on the Mexican border. Anti-immigrant sentiment is largely based on fear of crime. While Mexico has experienced spikes of violent crime associated with narcotics trade, little of this crime has crossed the border. Cuidad Juarez experiences an unusually high rate of homicide as a result of Mexican cartel activity. However, El Paso, Juarez's neighbor to the north, is consistently rated as one of the safest cities in America.

Within the Unites States, communities with higher percentages of immigrants tend to have lower rates of crime than communities without significant numbers of foreign-born. The notion that immigrants and crime are related is a political artifact not borne by data or scientific evidence. Anecdotal insinuations of Al Qaeda or terrorist networks using the Mexican border to cross into the United States are not based in fact. There are no reports by any local, state, or federal agencies that indicate this scenario has been used. It appears to be sensationalistic fears of one group imposed on another.

Meanwhile, militarization of the border has done little to affect crime rates in Mexico or the United States. Illegal immigration, while absorbing much of the media's attention, has been declining over recent years. Between October 2010 and September 2011, the rate of apprehensions by the U.S. Border Patrol's Tucson, Arizona, sector has declined by 42 percent. Arrests throughout all border patrol stations along the southern border were the lowest since 1972. While some are quick to suggest this is due to security enhancements, there was little done then to distinguish it from other periods after 2003. The better explanation is that the weak economy is not drawing labor. Most illegal immigrants work in the hospitality and construction industries. Lowered demand in these industries following the bust of the housing bubble predictably reduced the number of undocumented immigrants.

The most effective method to contain illegal immigration would be to enhance investigation and penalties against corporations and employers using undocumented labor. Increasing restrictions on visas and work programs or expanding security measures will do little to impact exploitive labor patterns that require illegal immigrants. Recognizing the impact of trade policies and consumption patterns on migration will likely produce a more cohesive and effective set of immigration policies.

References

Andreas, Peter. 2009. *Border Games: Policing the U.S.-Mexico Divide*. Ithaca, NY: Cornell University Press.

Booth, William. 2011. "National Guard Deployment on Mexico Border Has Mixed Results." *Washington Post*, December 5. http://www.washingtonpost.com/world/national-security/national-guard-deployment-on-us-mexico-border-has-mixed-results/2011/11/21/gIQAly 6qXO_story.html?hpid=zl (Accessed December 5, 2011).

Elliot, Debbie. 2011. "Tough Alabama Law Changes Way of Life." Morning Edition/NPR, October 6, 2011. http://www.npr.org/2011/10/06/141103839/tough-ala-immigration-law-changes-way-of-life?ps=rs (Accessed December 5, 2011).

Greenblatt, Alan. 2008. "Immigration Debate: Can Politicians Find a Way to Curb Illegal Immigration?" *Congressional Quarterly*, 18, 5 (February 2008): 97–120.

Massey, Douglas S., Jorge Durand and Nolan J. Malone. 2002. *Beyond Smoke and Mirrors: Mexican Immigration in an Era of Economic Integration*. New York: Russell Sage.

NPR Staff. 2001. "The Economic Reality of Tough Immigration Laws." All Things Considered/NPR, October 8, 2011. http://www.npr.org/2011/10/08/141183030/can-the-us-economy-really-function-without-undocumented-workers (Accessed December 5, 2011).

Preston, Julia. 2011. "US to Review Cases Seeking Deportations." *New York Times.* November 17, 2011. http://www.nytimes.com/2011/11/17/us/deportation-cases-of-illegal-immigratns-to-be-reviewed.html?_r=1&scp=2&sq=illegal%20immigration&st-cse (Accessed December 5, 2011).

Rau, Alia Beard. 2010. "Arizona Immigration Law Three Months Later: No Arrests." *The Arizona Republic/USA Today*, October 10, 2010. http://www.usatoday.com/news/nation/2010-10-29-immigration-law-three-months-laterN.htm (Accessed March 2011).

Rotella, Sebastian. 1998. *Twilight on the Line: Underworlds and Politics at the U.S.-Mexico Border.* New York: W.W. Norton and Company.

Karen K. Clark received her doctorate from the University of California in Irvine. She specializes in international criminality covering topics such as war crimes, immigration, and smuggling. She has published in various textbooks and academic journals and conducts book reviews for the Digest of Middle East Studies. *Dr. Clark is affiliated with research projects with the Homeland Security Department at San Diego State University.*

In Opposition to Birthright Citizenship
Judith Ann Warner

Opponents of birthright citizenship refer to children born to undocumented immigrants as anchor babies. These children increase U.S. population growth and are eligible at maturity to anchor or pull extended family members within the legal immigration quotas. It is purported that thousands of pregnant women from Mexico and other countries come to give birth in the United States. They can enter as temporary visitors or without authorization. After birth, they receive a U.S. birth certificate and passport for the child and gain a permanent link to this country (Simmons 2005; Warner 2008).

Birthright citizenship is considered unfair because it allows noncitizens and their American children to bypass the naturalization process of legal immigrants. Spouses and children who have applied for entrance to the United States face quotas that often result in a long wait for legal entrance. It is unfair for unauthorized women to use a loophole to gain entrance for their child, and through that child, legal residency for themselves (Lee 2006). Proposals to end birthright citizenship have been introduced by Republican members in the U.S. House of Representatives in 2005, 2007, 2009, 2011, and 2013.

Those opposed to birthright citizenship believe that unauthorized immigrants try to have children quickly after their arrival because it complicates their removal. Legal action taken to prevent deportation of undocumented parents with birthright-citizen children rarely succeeds. Under a legal change 10 years ago, parents were required to prove that their deportation would cause "exceptional and extremely unusual hardship" to the children (Warner 2010).

Birthright citizenship becomes an issue at the outset because of hospital costs. The medical cost of labor and delivery are estimated at from $1,500 to $1,800 per child. Legally, the government has to cover these costs. The baby receives the right to a public school education, federal welfare benefits, and the right to vote in adulthood (Kamau 2005).

Birthright citizenship carries many taxpayer costs in the high-immigration states of California, Texas, and Florida, and it disproportionately impacts U.S.-Mexico border communities. Along the U.S.-Mexico border, Mexican women may cross to give birth in U.S. hospitals in order for their children to be U.S. citizens. Later, these children may attend school in U.S. border cities in neighborhoods in which the family maintains an address. In effect, the child leads a bi-national life, spending the preschool years in a Mexican border city and then crossing the border to attend a U.S. public school, which is considered to be better (Beilenson 1996; Warner 2008).

Certain issues connected to birthright citizenship concern how the medical and other costs of these children born to noncitizens are to be covered. At present, states have to pay for natal hospitalization, education, and other social services to which these children are entitled. One result is a conflict between the states, whose taxpaying citizens may be reluctant to fund this, and the federal government, which regulates immigration and is viewed as rightfully owing the cost for permitting the situation. States are suing the federal government and pressuring for reimbursement for these additional costs since the federal government regulates immigration and states are not given that right.

Critics of birthright citizenship point out that few nations confer automatic citizenship by birth, *jus soli* citizenship. For example, a child born in France to a noncitizen can apply for citizenship at age 18, but only if they resided in France continuously for five years. Indeed, birthright citizenship is a feature of some North, Central, and South American nations, the new world, but not nations of other continents, the old world, unless there has been upheaval or an effort to recruit external population. The countries that grant birthright citizenship include Argentina, Brazil, Cameroon, Canada, India, Jamaica, Mexico, New Zealand, Pakistan, Spain, United States, and Venezuela (Feere 2010).

Almost all industrialized countries and all European nations require at least one parent to be a citizen or legal resident before conferring citizenship at birth. European countries have used *jus sanguinis* legal principles, requiring parents to be citizens before conferring citizenship. In Europe, immigrant parents and their children have been excluded from citizenship. Children of immigrants must apply for citizenship after fulfilling residency and age requirements. Over time, as the immigrant population in Europe has increased in size, some countries are liberalizing citizenship requirements. In 1999, Germany changed from a *jus sanguinis* policy to a more liberal *jus soli* policy. Great Britain and Ireland, which had maintained liberal *jus soli* policies, have reversed and passed more exclusive *jus sanguinis* laws (Warner 2010).

A 2011 Rasmussen poll indicated that a majority (61%) do not believe that children of illegal immigrants should be granted birthright citizenship while 28% do. Multiple bills and resolutions to end birthright citizenship have been introduced in Congress but not passed. Margaret Lee, author of a House Congressional Research Service Report, indicates that there are many legal issues related to the wording of the various congressional amendments, including which parents are included or excluded and the constitutionality of a congressional vote to end birthright citizenship. It is uncertain if the Supreme Court will allow a legal end to birthright citizenship (Lee 2006).

The Fourteenth Amendment grants citizenship to those born in the United States under the "complete and exclusive jurisdiction" of the United States. After an 1898 Supreme Court ruling in *United States v. Kim Ark,* it was argued that being born on U.S. soil was made more important than whether the parents were under the jurisdiction of the U.S. or had allegiance. It was thought that subordinating birthplace to jurisdiction would end the practice of coming to the United States to establish birthright children as an anchor (Warner 2010).

Terminating birthright citizenship might yield a small advantage in the war on terror. The U.S. birthright citizenship of Yasser Hamdi was an issue taken to the U.S. Supreme Court because he was classified an enemy combatant fighting for the Taliban in Afghanistan. Yasser Hamdi, born to Saudi parents in Louisiana, had birthright citizenship but spent little of his lifetime in the United States, living instead in Saudi Arabia. As a citizen, he received rights and benefits a noncitizen combatant did not receive. Ending birthright citizenship would remove constitutional protections in the case of enemy fighters such as Hamdi.

Those opposed to birthright citizenship make three points: (1) individuals who enter without documents should not be allowed to use children born on U.S. soil as an anchor to move ahead of legal applicants for immigration; (2) individuals who do not have primary or full allegiance to the United States should not be allowed to have children born to them in the United States gain instant citizenship, and (3) individuals who were born in the United States but develop enemy allegiance should not be able to use the fact of birth on U.S. soil to gain constitutional citizenship legal protections (Barton 2013; Erler 2012; Erler and Stock 2012; Porttens 2012; Schuck 2009; Lee 2006; Warner 2008; Reasoner 2011).

References

Barton, Paul C. 2013. "Birthright Citizenship Contested on Capitol Hill." *USA Today*, March 20.

Beilenson, Anthony. 1996. "Case for Correction by Constitutional Amendment." *The Social Contract*, 7, no. 1 (Fall).

Erler, Edward et al. 2012. *The Founders on Citizenship and Immigration: Principles and Challenges in America.* Arlington, VA: National Foundation for American Policy.

Erler, Edward, and Margaret Stock. 2012. "The Costs to Americans and America of Ending Birthright Citizenship," www.infop/com.

Feere, Jon. 2010. "Birthright Citizenship in the United States: A Global Comparison." http://www.cis.org/birthright-citizenship. August.

Fourteenth Amendment, July 9, 1868.

"GOP Mulls Ending Birthright Citizenship." *Washington Times*, November 3, 2005.

Kamau, Pius. 2005. "Illegal Immigrants Jam Our Emergency Rooms," *The Denver Post*, December 22, 2005: B-7.

Lee, Margaret. 2006. U.S. Citizenship of Persons Born in the United States of Alien Parents. Congressional Research Service Report, http://www.ilw.com. Accessed May 30, 2010.

Porttens, Kevin. 2012. "Immigration and the American Founding." *Free Market Forum*. www.hillsdale.edu/outreach/free-market-forum.

Reasoner, W. D. 2011. "Birthright Citizenship for Visitors." http://www.cis.org/birthright-citizenship-for-visitors. March 2011.

Schuck, Peter M. 2009. "Taking Immigration Federalism Seriously." *The Forum* 7(3): 4–14.

Simmons, Kathryn. 2005. "Anchor Babies Tie Illegal Immigrants to U.S." *NBC News*, November 25.

U.S. Federal law (8 U.S.C. 1401).

Warner, Judith A. 2008. *Battleground Immigration*. Westport, CT: Greenwood Press, 2v.

Warner, Judith A. 2010. *U.S. Border Security: A Reference Handbook*. Santa Barbara, CA: ABC-CLIO.

Wong Kim Ark vs. United States, 1898. United States Supreme Court.

Judith Ann Warner is a professor of sociology and criminal justice at Texas A&M International University (TAMIU). In 2008, she received the Distance Educator of the Year award, and in 1991, she received the Scholar of the Year award from TAMIU. She is coeditor of the Journal of Social and Ecological Boundaries *and has published in the areas of immigration, homeland security, and domestic violence. Her research interests include immigration, homeland security, and the intersection of race, class, and gender. She is the editor of* Battleground: Immigration *(Greenwood, 2008) and the author of* U.S. Border Security: A Reference Handbook *(ABC-CLIO, 2010).*

In Support of Maintaining Birthright Citizenship
Judith Ann Warner

Advocates of maintaining the birthright citizenship privilege contend that the unauthorized population is composed primarily of moral, hard-working individuals who should be supported in attaining legalization and naturalization. The U.S. Catholic Bishops' Committee on Migration and Refugee Services has stressed that citizenship is important to showing humans respect and giving immigrants dignity. The United States is the world's most open nation for immigrants; their successful adaptation and assimilation is dependent on offering them a stake in the nation through citizenship for themselves, through naturalization, or birthright citizenship for their children. Ending this form of citizenship would marginalize these immigrants and make the United States less successful as an immigrant-receiving nation. Children who are adapting and growing up accustomed to American culture could be yanked away from their homeland if this form of citizenship were ended (Warner 2008).

The stereotype of a woman with a birthright citizen child is that of a border crosser who has a motive to use an American hospital to have her baby. Yet a majority of undocumented parents born in Mexico or Central America have been living and working in the United States over a period of time. A politically strategic constituency that is opposed to ending birthright citizenship is Latinos. They are the group with the highest birthrate in the United States, and both the stereotype of the pregnant Latino woman and the idea of taking away citizenship from babies is offensive to them. Politicians are wary of politically alienating this important group (Warner 2010).

Undocumented immigrants maintain that they came to the United States to find a livelihood, not to have children. They believe that the attack on birthright citizenship is unfair and that all children should be born equal. Parents in families separated by immigration status have a hard time explaining to children why their father or mother is not present. The Pew Hispanic Center estimated that as the first decade of the 21st century drew to a close 14.6 million people were part of a mixed-status family in which at least one parent is undocumented. Sixty-four percent of the mixed-status-family children, 3.1 million, were birthright citizens (PHC 2010).

Birthright citizenship is not a way of avoiding the immigration bureaucracy indefinitely, and unauthorized immigrants pay a price in fear and waiting. Although the United States has a principle of family reunification in its legal immigration policy, it can take years or decades before the quota on admittance ends family separation. Visa petitions are processed slowly and some immigrants wind up as visa overstayers or try to enter unauthorized in order to be with their families. U.S. immigration law literally creates partially fugitive families that mix legal and unauthorized members. Undocumented individuals need to make serious decisions about where their families will live and work to try to avoid detection and family separation. Families of mixed nationality are deeply impacted by the debate on immigration. Parents are worried that they will not be able to stay with their citizen children or that their family will have to return to Mexico (Bosniak 2012; Goode 2015; PHC 2010; PHC 2011; Warner 2010; Manger 2015).

It is undeniable that birthright-child citizens are the ones who are harmed when parents are deported. The older birthright children of undocumented parents have a history of having lived in and adapted to the American culture. Benjamin Cabreras, from Mexico, and Londy Cabreras, from Guatemala, brought a lawsuit asking that they be able to stay with their two teenage daughters. In 2002, a Los Angeles immigration judge made a rare decision in ruling that the parents could maintain residency. The basis of the legal decision was that one daughter was academically gifted and that parental deportation would "savagely" and permanently interrupt her schooling. This case is now under appeal (LA Times 2011).

At present, in the Department of Homeland Security, the Immigration and Customs Enforcement branch can deport the undocumented parents of children who are citizens by birth. In practice, immigration judges can rule in favor of the parents and grant them legal status. Many immigration processors simply choose not to undertake deportation of parents with birthright children and they remain as unauthorized residents.

Nevertheless, cases are coming to immigration court and the parents do not always win. In Los Angeles, parents with a child who has hemophilia won the right to stay while the undocumented parents of a child with a mild learning disability were deported (Warner 2010).

When parents are deported, some leave their children with relatives, others depart with the child, and yet others seek to remain illegally by disappearing underground. Family fragmentation is a common result of deporting parents of birthright citizen children. Breaking up families is a dubious venture. Removing parents of birthright children could result in a massive number of children needing foster care at a tremendous cost to the states. At present, although birthright children receive a public education at taxpayer cost, those with an undocumented parent(s) often are less likely to receive health and other benefits (PHC 2010).

Despite being U.S. citizens, children born to undocumented immigrants are more likely to live in poverty and crowded housing and are less likely to have health coverage than children born to citizens, experts say. Citizen children in mixed-status families are eligible for public assistance, but their parents often fear that seeking government help could lead to deportation or hurt their chances for future legalization. Michael Fix, vice president of the Migration Policy Institute, a think tank, indicated that undocumented parents do not want to apply for benefits because they fear discovery and deportation as a public charge. Although immigrants are stereotyped as coming to the United States to receive public benefits, many believe in independence for themselves and their children (Fix and Van Hook 2010; Hanson 2009; Warner 2008, 2010).

Supporters of birthright citizenship feel that eliminating it creates another social barrier between those who are socially included and those who are socially excluded. Social divisions that exclude a part of the population from full participation in this country are a violation of democratic principles. Ending birthright citizenship would result in the first generation of native-born noncitizens in this society. These individuals would become part of a stateless class and subject to prejudice, discrimination, and the resultant feelings of alienation. In France, a nation which practices heritage or *jus sanguinis* citizenship, extensive rioting occurred among the second generation of immigrants because they were treated as a lesser class. If the United States disenfranchises children born in the United States to non-native parents, it could create an alienated group that will engage in destructive forms of social struggle, as occurred in France (Warner 2008).

Peter Nyers contends that 9/11 greatly impacted immigrants because of the idea that some individuals become so-called citizens by accident. Yaser Esam Hamdi, designated an enemy combatant during the war in Afghanistan, received U.S. Constitutional protections because he was born to Saudi parents on a three-year temporary work permit. He only resided in the United States as a toddler. Despite a debate over whether Hamdi was an essential citizen or an accidental citizen, it becomes evident that territorial birthright is a transparent and reliable way to establish citizenship. It is a legal concept that permits an international system of citizenship rights, as well as inequalities and exclusions based on place of birth (Nyers 2005).

Ending the use of birthright citizenship as a legal concept would have severe administrative repercussions for children born to undocumented parents. Stateless children would have a compromised citizenship status because of their parents' unauthorized entrance or illegal stay. Citizenship might be established by the parents' country of origin, but some parents come from different countries of origin. Many children might be required to petition to another country to establish legal status. In addition, not having birthright citizenship would create massive bureaucratic problems as the citizenship of each baby's parents would need to be verified. The present rule makes it easy to administer the system of birth certificate processing. If all parents had to provide papers to prove their children's citizenship, it would overburden immigration enforcement.

References

Bosniak, Linda S. 2012. "Birthright Citizenship, Undocumented Immigrants and the Slavery Analogy." *Social Science Research Network*, December 12, http://ssrn.com/abstract=2194874. Accessed February 20, 2015.

Fix, Michael, and Jennifer Van Hook. 2010. *The Demographic Impacts of Repealing Birthright*. Washington, DC: Migration Policy Institute.

Goode, Victor. "Race, Immigration and the Birthright Controversy." Legal Services of California Race Equity Project. http://www.equity.lsuc.net/race-immigratio n-and-the-birthright-controversy. February 20, 2015.

Hanson, Gordon. 2009. *The Economics and Policy of Illegal Immigration in the United States*. Washington, DC: Migration Policy Institute.

LA Times 2011. "Tampering with Citizenship." htpp://www .latimes.com/news/opinion/editorials/la-ed-citizen-20110113.0.5847728. Accessed February 20, 2105.

Manger, Chief J. Thomas. 2015. "Law Enforcement Immigration Task Force on Safe Act." http:// immigrationforum.org/blog/law-enforcemen t-immigration-task-force-on-safe-act. February 11, 2015 Letter, Major Cities Chiefs Police Association.

Neyers, Peter. 2005. *Rethinking Refugees Beyond States of Emergency*. New York: Routledge.

Pew Hispanic Center. 2010. "Unauthorized Immigrants and Their U.S.-Born Children." PHC, August 11, 2010. http:// www.perhispanic.org.

Pew Hispanic Center. 2011. "Statistical Portrait of the Foreign-Born Population of the United States, 2009." http://www.pewhispanic.org/factsheet/factsheet. php?FactsheetID=69.

United States Conference of Catholic Bishops. 2012. "Birthright Citizenship: The Real Story." Issue Briefing

Series, Issue #2. Migration and Refugee Services, Office of Migration Policy and Public Affairs.

Warner, Judith A. 2008. *Battleground Immigration*. Westport, CT: Greenwood Press. 2v.

Warner, Judith A. 2010. *U.S. Border Security: A Reference Handbook*. Santa Barbara, CA: ABC-CLIO.

Judith Ann Warner is a professor of sociology and criminal justice at Texas A&M International University (TAMIU). In 2008, she received the Distance Educator of the Year award, and in 1991, she received the Scholar of the Year award from TAMIU. She is coeditor of the Journal of Social and Ecological Boundaries *and has published in the areas of immigration, homeland security, and domestic violence. Her research interests include immigration, homeland security, and the intersection of race, class, and gender. She is the editor of* Battleground: Immigration *(Greenwood, 2008) and the author of* U.S. Border Security: A Reference Handbook *(ABC-CLIO, 2010).*

Mitigating Federal Immigration Law: Inclusion at the Local Level
Roberto Suro

Interactions among local, state and federal governments as regards immigration policies have undergone dramatic changes since the passage of Proposition 187 in California in 1994, and after the U.S. Supreme Court's 2012 decision in *Arizona v. United States* (132 S.Ct. 2492) (Suro 2015). States have been portrayed as uniquely capable intermediaries between national policies and immigration's highly local impacts (Su 2014).

In one of the most extensive post-*Arizona* analyses, Hiroshi Motomura argues in his 2014 book, *Immigration Outside the Law*, for distinguishing "direct" involvement in immigration law which refers to governmental decisions whether or not to admit or exclude aliens, an undisputed federal domain, as characterized by Ming Chen as "at the border" policies (Chen

2014). By contrast, Motomura describes a realm of "indirect" involvement where state and local governments can play a role in several different ways. They can become involved in enforcement through cooperative agreements with federal authorities or undertake their own efforts to make life difficult for unauthorized immigrants. Still other forms of indirect involvement, in Motomura's view, are state and local policies that "neutralize" federal enforcement policies, effectively shielding the unauthorized from federal regulation and thus permitting them to integrate into local communities regardless of immigration status (Motomura 2014). The latter kind of state and local policies have the potential to change life for the unauthorized and may eventually help change federal policy. They are mitigating federal laws and policies that determine immigration status in the sense that they are reducing the penalty to be paid for violating those policies.

Indeed, the cumulative effect of such mitigating state and local policies can be to create the potential for *inclusion* of immigrants regardless of status. Maria Lorena Cook usefully defines the term: "By inclusion I mean an individual or group's engagement with processes or organizations that *recognize* the individual or group by conferring membership or by providing resources such as entitlements or protections. . . . Inclusion provides a sense of security, stability, and predictability, understood primarily as an ability to plan for the future (Cook 2013).

State and local jurisdictions have varied greatly in their willingness to cooperate with federal immigration enforcement since some policing powers were devolved in 1996. The Secure Communities program was launched in 2008 and identified unauthorized immigrants for removal by checking the fingerprints of persons arrested or booked in custody by local authorities. President Obama ended it as one of the executive actions announced in November 2014, saying federal agents should focus on deporting "felons, not families" (Linthicum 2014). During its 2008 to 2014 lifespan, Secure Communities provoked a variety of state and local governments to take actions that neutralize federal regulations, to borrow Motomura's expression. For example, in October 2014 the Catholic Legal Immigration Network, Inc. had counted three states, 26 cities, 233 counties and the District of Columbia as having restricted cooperation (CLINIC 2014). However, some state and local governments are doing more than that. They are taking proactive steps to welcome immigrants regardless of their status under federal law. These *mitigate* the condition of illegality.

On November 19, 2005, Illinois Governor Rod Blagojevich signed the "New Americans Executive Order," which launched a package of efforts to coordinate policies and programs promoting integration or other services to immigrants and to help the state assert its voice on federal immigration policies. This initiative was the result of a public-private partnership that involved foundation founding, think-tank advice and an explicitly influential advisory role for local and national advocacy groups and civil society organizations from the immigrant communities (Illinois.gov 2005). That model of creating a coordinating office for immigrant services has been adopted in Michigan, New York, Massachusetts as well as a number of cities including Los Angeles, Philadelphia and Baltimore. In many of these cases the explicit intent has been to entice the settlement of immigrants as part of an economic development strategy (Turner 2012). Such rustbelt cities as Columbus, Cleveland and Lansing that were facing population losses have recruited immigrants with packages of incentives and services, and in some of the most successful cases, like Dayton, which has attracted more than 3,000 Turkish newcomers, local citizens and business groups have jointed municipal officials in developing detailed action plans for immigrant settlement (Altman 2014; Preston 2013).

While such welcoming programs were spurred by local concerns and local policy entrepreneurs, other inclusionary policies have echoed federal initiatives, for example, President Clinton's executive order in 2000 that requires any state or local agency receiving federal funds to bridge language barriers with beneficiaries who have limited proficiency in English. However, the federal government has not dictated how this requirement is to be met nor has it undertaken a significant accountability effort. As a result, a remarkable variety of approaches have emerged from state and local agencies of all sorts, from schools to courtrooms to city halls, utilizing everything from the deliberate employment of bilingual staff, to the translation of printed materials, and the use of interpretation technologies (MPI 2014).

All these local initiatives have two other characteristics in common. To varying degrees they all create points of interaction between immigrants and government offices, local business, civil society organizations and ordinary citizens. The welcoming initiatives in particular have also often stimulated the creation of civil society organizations within immigrant communities to mediate interactions with the host community. The second common characteristic is that these sub-federal initiatives erase, or at least blur, the many levels of immigration that are at the heart of federal policies, adopting a sort of "don't ask, don't tell" approach to immigration status (Montalvo et al. 2014).

For an unauthorized immigrant, such sub-federal policies *mitigate* the status of illegality, lessening the severity of a negative condition, or reducing the penalty for an offense. These policies actively encourage interactions between unauthorized immigrants, public officials, and community institutions that might not happen otherwise. As a matter of public policy, they create safe spaces where some of the harshest negative consequences of federal illegality are alleviated if not erased.

References

Altman, Alex. 2014. "Put Out the Welcome Mat." *Time*, June 5, 16.

Chen, Ming Hsu. 2014. "Immigration and Cooperative Federalism: Toward a Doctrinal Framework." *University of Colorado Law Review* 85(4): 1087.

CLINIC (Catholic Legal Immigration Network, Inc.). 2014. "State and Localities that Limit Compliance with ICE Detainer Requests." In *State and Local Immigration Project*. Washington, DC: Catholic Legal Immigration Network, Inc.

Cook, Maria Lorena. 2013. "Is Incorporation of Unauthorized Immigrants Possible? Inclusion and Contingency for Nonstatus Migrants and Legal Immigrants." In *Outsiders No More? Models of Immigrant Political Incorporation*, edited by Jennifer Hochschild, Jacqueline Chattopadhyay, Claudine Gay, and Michael Jones-Correa. Oxford: Oxford University Press. http://dx.doi.org/10.1093/acprof:oso/97801992113.003.0003.

Illinois.gov. 2005. "Gov. Blagojevich Announces Landmark Immigration Policy." Springfield, IL: State of Illinois, Office of the Governor.

Linthicum, Kate. 2014. "Obama Acts on Immigration: An Unpopular Tool for Deportation Is Gone; Obama Ends Secure Communities Program, Saying U.S. Should Expel 'Felons, Not Families'." *Los Angeles Times*, November 21, AA.1.

Montalvo, Jorge and Karen Phillippis, Marcony Almeida-Barros, Teresa Reyes. 2014 "Immigration and the States: Advancing State Policy Priorities." Presented at the National Immigrant Integration Conference, Los Angeles, CA, December 14–16.

Motomura, Hiroshi. 2014. *Immigration Outside the Law*. Oxford: Oxford University Press.

MPI (Michigan Policy Institute). 2014. "Language Access: Translation and Interpretation Policies and Practices." Michigan Policy Institute. http://migrationpolicy.org/

programs/language-access-translation-and-interpretati on-policies-and-practices.

Preston, Julia. 2013. "Ailing Cities Extend Hand to Immigrants: National Desk." *New York Times*, October 7, A.18.

Su, Rick. 2014. "The Role of the States in the National Conversation on Immigration." In *Strange Neighbors: The Role of States in Immigration Policy*, edited by Carissa Byrne Hessick and Gabriel J. Chin. New York: New York University Press.

Suro, Roberto. 2015. "California Dreaming: The New Dynamism in Immigration Federalism and Opportunities for Inclusion on a Variegrated Landscape." *Journal on Migration and Human Security* 3 (1): 1–25.

Turner, Kim. 2012. *United States: Good Ideas from Successful Cities*. Toronto, Canada: Maytree Foundation. http://citiesofmigration.ca/wp-content/ uploads/2012/03Municipal_Report_Main_Report2.pdf.

Roberto Suro holds a joint appointment as a professor in the Annenberg School for Communication & Journalism and the Sol Price School of Public Policy at the University of Southern California. He is also director of the Tomás Rivera Policy Institute, an interdisicplinary university research center exploring the challenges and opportunities of demographic diversity in the 21st-century global city. Suro's latest book is Writing Immigration: Scholars and Journalists in Dialogue *(U of CA Press, 2011) coedited with Marcelo Suarez-Orozco and Vivian Louie. Prior to joining the USC faculty in August 2007, he was director of the Pew Hispanic Center, a research organization in Washington, DC, which he founded in 2001. Suro worked as foreign and domestic bureau chief for* The New York Times *and at* The Washington Post *as deputy national editor and as a staff writer on the national desk. He is the author of several books and several dozen book chapters, research reports, and other publications related to Latinos and immigration.*

Obama's "Executive Action" on Immigration and Judicial Review
Alemayehu G. Mariam

On November 20, 2014, President Barack Obama announced a series of executive actions purportedly aimed at 1) enforcing tougher controls to prevent illegal immigration into the U.S.; 2) prioritizing deportation of felons and 3) requiring certain undocumented immigrants to pass a criminal background check and pay taxes in order to temporarily stay in the U.S. without fear of deportation (White House, 2014). In taking "executive action," President Obama robustly asserted, "I have the legal authority to take as president—the same kinds of actions taken by Democratic and Republican presidents before me—that will help make our immigration system be more fair and more just."

House Speaker John Boehner lamented the President's actions. "The American people want both parties to focus on solving problems together; they don't support unilateral action from a president who is more interested in partisan politics than working with the people's elected representatives." House Judiciary Committee Chairman Bob Goodlatte chafed. "The president's decision to recklessly forge ahead with a plan to unilaterally change our immigration laws ignores the will of the American people and flouts the Constitution." Sen. Mitch McConnell groused. "The plan [Obama is] presenting is more than just, as the president himself has acknowledged, an overreach—it's also unfair."

In a Memorandum dated November 20, 2014, Jeh Charles Johnson, Secretary of Department of Homeland Security (DHS) set up a Deferred Action for Parental Accountability (DAPA) program which directed his agency to exercise "prosecutorial discretion" in "issuing, serving, filing, or canceling a Notice to Appear" as well as in implementation of "a broad range of other discretionary enforcement decisions, including deciding: whom to stop, question, and arrest; whom to detain or release; whether to settle, dismiss, appeal, or join in a motion on a case; and whether to grant deferred action, parole, or a stay of removal instead of pursuing removal in a case" (Department of Homeland Security, 2014). The new policy rescinded 6 major policy memoranda dating back to 2009.

In December 2014, federal judge Arthur Schwab in Pittsburgh ruled, "This[Obama's] executive action 'cross[es] the line,' constitutes 'legislation,' and effectively changes the United States' immigration policy. The president may only 'take care that the laws be faithfully executed . . .'; he may not take any executive action that creates laws" (U.S. v. Elionardo Juarez-Escobar, 2014). In February 2015, a federal judge in Texas issued a preliminary injunction in Texas v. U.S. blocking DAPA (State of Texas v. United States, 2015). In a 123-page Memorandum Opinion and Order the court ruled the Obama Administration had failed to comply with the Administrative Procedures Act. The court reasoned DAPA "represents a substantive change in immigration policy . . . a massive change in immigration practice. It does more than supplement the [Immigration and Nationality Act] . . . it contradicts it (State of Texas v. United States, 2015, p. 111).

Does the president have the constitutional or statutory authority to grant "administrative relief" to undocumented aliens on a large scale? There are those who argue the President does not have the authority to issue DAPA. Derrick Morgan, vice president of The Heritage Foundation, argues Obama "gave quasi-legal status and work permits to millions of illegal immigrants" by his pen (Morgan, 2014). He surmised, "Obama's executive action could usher in an era of government by executive fiat. A future president may decide to use 'prosecutorial discretion' to ignore environmental or tax laws."

Marshall Fitz, director of immigration policy at the Center for American Progress, argues that the President is merely acting in faithful execution of the laws. Fitz asserts that DAPA is "completely legal and grounded in ample historical precedent—similar policies have been adopted 39 times by 11 presidents over 60 years— . . . [and] . . . is no different than when President Ronald Reagan allowed children of unauthorized immigrants to stay in the country in 1986 . . . [or] President George H.W. Bush's Family Fairness policy of 1990 . . ." (Fitz, 2014).

Alex Nowrasteh takes the middle of the road and places blame on the president and Congress for the immigration mess. "The first is for the president to issue an executive order on dubious constitutional grounds to provide temporary relief for problems caused by a fundamentally broken system. The second resolution is for Congress to change those terrible laws and make them work so they don't attract executive orders like honey attracts flies" (Nowrasteh, 2014).

It is unclear why the President chose to implement DAPA as an "executive action" instead of by "executive order," which could have strengthened his hand as his predecessors had done. Executive actions do not have precise legal definition; but they have been used by presidents to take action or refrain from taking action such as actions issued by President Obama in January 2014 to increase federal back ground checks for fire arm purchases (White House, 2013). Such actions need not comply with the APA. Executive orders and proclamations are directives or actions by the President. When exercised, they must have a demonstrable basis in the Constitution, statutes or the President's inherent authority to ensure the laws are "faithfully executed."

The ultimate resolution in the DAPA challenge is likely to revolve around four questions: 1) whether the President abused his broad discretion in implementing DAPA, 2) whether DAPA represents "a substantive change in immigration policy and practice" as the District Court ruled in order granting the above-referenced injunction, 3) whether re-issuance of DAPA in compliance with the APA could resolve the question of its implementation, and 4) whether DAPA represents substantive lawmaking on the part of the President in violation of separation of powers principles under Art. I, § 7, cl. 3 (presentment clause) of the United States Constitution.

I believe DAPA is within the guided but broad discretion of the President in implementing the INA. DHS is in charge of enforcing the immigration laws of the United States. The U.S. Supreme Court has recognized the existence of deferred action and DHS's authority to grant it (Reno v. American-Arab Anti-Defamation League, 1999).

DHS makes discretionary decisions about prosecutions, deportations and other sanctions tens of thousands of times every year. DAPA appears to systematize the detection, apprehension and prosecution of alleged immigration law violators by enforcing tougher controls, focusing resources on felons and requiring criminal background checks on undocumented immigrants to *temporarily* stay in the U.S. without fear of deportation. DHS takes such actions on a case-by-case basis every day. DAPA aims to facilitate "batch processing" of such decisions.

There is ample presidential precedent to support DAPA. In 1980, President Jimmy Carter exercised parole authority and allowed some 123,000 "Mariel Cubans" into the U.S. In 1987, President Reagan barred deportation of children of newly-legalized immigrants under the Immigration Reform Act of 1986. President George H.W. Bush in 1990 and 1992 issued executive orders that granted Deferred Enforced Departure (DED) to certain nationals of the People's Republic of China and El Salvador. In 1997, President Bill Clinton issued an executive order granting DED to certain Haitians who had arrived in the U.S. before Dec. 31, 1995. In 2009–2010, the Obama administration began a policy of granting parole to the spouses, parents, and children of military members and DED to Liberians.

References

Department of Homeland Security. 2014. Policies for the Apprehension, Detention, and Removal of Undocumented Immigrants. November 20, 2014. Online at http://www.dhs.gov/sites/default/files/publications/14_1120_memo_prosecutorial_discretion.pdf.

Fitz, Marshall. 2014. "Obama Is Just Doing His Job." U.S. News and World Report, November 21, 2014. Online at http://www.usnews.com/debate-club/is-obamas-immigration-executive-order-legal/obama-is-just-doing-his-job.

Morgan, Derrick. 2014. "Government by Executive Fiat." U.S. News and World Report, November 21, 2014. Online at http://www.usnews.com/debate-club/is-obamas-immigration-executive-order-legal/government-by-executive-fiat.

Nowrasteh, Alex. 2014. "Bad Laws Lead to Bad Executive Orders." U.S. News and World Report, November 21, 2014. Online at http://www.usnews.com/debate-club/is-obamas-immigration-executive-order-legal/bad-laws-lead-to-bad-executive-orders.

Reno v. American-Arab Anti-Discrimination Committee. 1999. (97–1252) 525 U.S. 471 (1999) 119 F.3d 1367. Online at https://www.law.cornell.edu/supct/pdf/97–1252P.ZS.

State of Texas v. United States. 2015. Case # 1:14-cv-00254. Online at http://documents.latimes.com/obama-defer-deportation/.

U.S. v. Elionardo Juarez-Escobar. 2014. Case # 2:14-cr-00180-AJS. Online at http://online.wsj.com/public/resources/documents/2014_1216_immigrationruling.pdf.

White House. 2013. "Now is the Time: The President's Plan to Protect Our Children and Our Communities by Reducing Gun Violence." Online at https://www.whitehouse.gov/sites/default/files/docs/wh_now_is_the_time_full.pdf.

White House. 2014. Fixing the System: President Obama Is Taking Action on Immigration. Online at https://www.whitehouse.gov/issues/immigration/immigration-action.

Professor Alemayehu G. Mariam, PhD and JD, teaches political science at California State University, San Bernardino. He is also a defense lawyer practicing in the areas of criminal and constitutional law. He is one of the foremost advocates of human rights in Africa. His weekly human rights blogs are disseminated widely.

Resolving the Issue of Illegal Immigration—
A Question of Balance
David E. Krahl

The pervasive question of what to do about illegal immigration is being bantered about in the mainstream media and on 24-hour cable news channels, by political candidates of every political stripe and persuasion, by liberals and conservatives, in the blogosphere, on discussion boards, by political action committees, in state legislatures, in Congress, by humanitarian and religious organizations, by voters—and by college professors and their students.

This essay will argue that the United States should adopt tougher strategies to control illegal immigration and that the U.S. government has both the moral obligation and the constitutional authority to do exactly that.

Illegal Immigration as a Contemporary Social Issue

Illegal immigration as a contemporary social issue has been linked to a host of social ills: organized crime, violence, drug trafficking, and terrorism. It has economic implications in that it results in an increase in unskilled labor into an already faltering economy. Another argument is that since "illegals" are, by definition, "undocumented," they do not contribute to the viability of the national tax base, and are a drain on existing social programs, resources, benefits, and services. They are considered to be "free riders" in an already overburdened system.

Although illegal immigration had been a much discussed issue prior to the 9/11 terrorist attacks—mostly as a reflection of nativist sentiments and xenophobic beliefs—it was the 9/11 attacks that catapulted illegal immigration into the front of the political discourse.

The control of illegal immigration rests with the Department of Homeland Security, tasked with enforcing federal laws. Unfortunately, these laws are neither inclusive nor expansive enough to provide tactical remedies to a problem that is clearly front-and-center in the collective consciousness of the American public.

In attempts to deal with the problem at the state level, several states have enacted statutes to control the ebb-and-flow of "illegals" across their borders. The success of these statutes, however, has been limited. Several federal courts have held that the statutes represent unconstitutional usurpations of the power of the federal government to regulate immigration. Thus, we must rely upon the federal government implementing a comprehensive workable set of strategies to mitigate the problem of illegal immigration.

Geographic and Demographic Considerations

The debate on illegal immigration most often focuses on the border between Mexico and the United States. Four states are directly affected: California, Arizona, New Mexico, and Texas. No other states are directly affected by this specific pattern of illegal immigration. Illegal immigration from Canada into the U.S. has been largely ignored.

From a simple geographic point of view, there are just 14 states where illegal immigration is *not* actually or potentially problematic to some degree based on the fact that they do *not* have a border that is directly contiguous to another nation (Mexico or Canada), or a border that is contiguous to a body of water that could be used as an entry point into that state by illegal immigrants. The remaining 36 states fulfill either, or both, of those criteria. These states account for 86 percent of the total U.S. population, and comprise about three-fourths of the nation's land area. Given this vast area, it makes sense for the federal government to take the lead in addressing the issue in a comprehensive fashion.

Just as striking are the linear miles of land-based borders and coastlines that are adjacent to the United States. The land-based U.S.-Mexico border stretches for 1,933 miles, while the U.S.-Canada border extends for 5,525 miles. Additionally, the U.S. coastline totals to 12,429 miles along the Atlantic and Pacific seaboards and the Gulf of Mexico. The Great Lakes shoreline which, in essence, serves as a functional boundary between the United States and Canada, adds another 4,960 miles. Given the sheer length of these borders, and the large number of states adjacent to them, how does this not make the federal government preeminently responsible for securing them?

Constitutional Considerations

Currently, much of the federal law on immigration is subsumed under Title 8 of the Code of Federal Regulations, the Immigration and Nationality Act of 1952, as amended; Title VIII of the United States Code, as amended; the Immigration Reform and Control Act of 1986; the Immigration Marriage Fraud Amendments of 1986; the Immigration Act of 1990; the Illegal Immigration Reform and Immigrant Responsibility Act of 1996; various administrative decisions issued by the United States Citizenship and Immigration Services' Administrative Appeals Office; and various court cases pertaining to the vast body of federal immigration law.

The constitutional basis for all of these lies in Article I, Section 8, which stipulates that congressional authority includes the power to ". . . *establish a uniform rule of naturalization*" along with the power to coin money, to borrow money on the credit of the United States, to declare war, to raise and support armies and maintain a navy, to regulate commerce with foreign nations, and a whole host of other congressional authorizations. The implications of this provision for the control of modern illegal immigration are profound.

Ironically, in attempting to expand the authority of the states to deal with illegal immigration, it was actually Congress who took the lead: When revising immigration laws, it indicated that the states could cooperate with the federal government in the identification, apprehension, detention, and removal of aliens not lawfully present in the United States. However, states have limitations on their legislative authority to control immigration (28 U.S.C. Section 1251).

These limitations have been further articulated in recent court decisions regarding the constitutionality of state immigration statutes. Following Congress's lead, immigration laws were enacted by state legislatures in South Carolina, Arizona, Utah, Georgia, Indiana, and Alabama. However, federal district courts have found that there has been a substantial amount of overreach on the part of the states, affirming that regulating immigration is the sole province of the federal government.

For example, in June 2011, U.S. District Court Judge Sarah Evans Barker put on hold a portion of an Indiana statute that authorized the arrest of anyone who had been ordered deported by an immigration court. A few days later after Judge Barker's ruling, U.S. District Court Judge Richard M. Gergel, in a test of the South Carolina immigration statutes, held that only the federal government, and not the states, can regulate immigration. In December 2011, Judge Gergel also prevented the state of South Carolina from giving the police the authority to arrest and hold suspected illegal immigrants while their immigration status was being checked. Similar kinds of decisions were rendered in federal district court ruling on state statutes in Georgia, Alabama, and Arizona. These lower court decisions are under appeal, and the United States Supreme Court may ultimately decide that the states have not overstepped their authority.

Enhanced Federal Strategies for Control of Illegal Immigration

Contrary to the views of many in the public, the federal government is currently doing much to combat illegal immigration.

Most prominently, there is extensive electronic monitoring, fencing, and boots-on-the ground patrolling along most of the U.S.-Mexican border. Moreover, several additional efforts are in the planning stages, including making E-Verify mandatory, refining a database that matches the entry of foreign nationals to their actual departure, and multiple amnesty proposals. E-Verify is an Internet-based system that allows businesses to determine the eligibility of their employees to work in the United States. It was established in 1997 for implementation at the state level, but has been of limited success because there is no *mandatory* requirement for its use. As of August 2011, only ten states had imposed mandatory E-Verify requirements on its employers (Alabama, Florida, Georgia, Indiana, Louisiana, North Carolina, South Carolina, Tennessee, Utah, and Virginia).

In May 2011, the Supreme Court issued the *United States Chamber of Commerce v. Whiting* decision (558 F. 3d.856) that strengthened state authority to make participation in E-Verify mandatory for all employers. In the *Whiting* decision, the Court upheld an Arizona law that required employers within the state to use E-Verify to confirm employment eligibility of all new hires. Furthermore, the decision allowed the state to suspend or revoke an employer's business license if the employer has knowingly hired unauthorized workers.

Although its net effect may indeed be to reduce the number of illegal immigrants, the *Whiting* decision is also likely to complicate the body of employment verification laws for employers from one state to the next. Proposals are before the federal government to establish a single, mandatory, reliable, and secure employment verification system that is consistent from one state to the next, from border to border, and from coast to coast.

Foreign Nationals Database. A second federal strategy under proposal is the implementation of a nationwide, comprehensive database that links data on foreign nationals who enter the country with data on those who leave. In essence, we know when foreign nationals enter the United States. However, there is no comprehensive database that indicates when they actually depart. As a result, even though they may have entered the country legally, their legal status may change after they arrive. Because we don't know when they leave, or even if they leave, we have no realistic estimation on who is actually here *illegally*, how long they have been here, or how many people have stayed longer than they have permission to. The development and implementation of a database that integrates these two types of data would go a considerable distance in estimating the scope and magnitude of the illegal immigration problem, as well as tracking down those who have overstayed their legal status.

Amnesty. A third strategy to ease the problem associated with illegal immigrants is to implement one of several proposals that would grant amnesty. To some, amnesty sends the wrong message: even though an individual is here illegally, he or she is receiving a "get-out-of-jail-for-free" card. However, amnesty proposals do not necessarily involve blanket amnesty. Rather, they employ a strategy of "conditional" amnesty. Conditional amnesty is based on the idea that if you're here illegally, you can receive amnesty under certain conditions—having been here for a lengthy period of time, not having committed any criminal acts, and being willing to become a naturalized citizen by going through the lengthy process that naturalization presently entails. And the use of conditional amnesty would go a long way in also ensuring that the provisions of the DREAM Act could be continued.

Summary

Despite a vast body of federal immigration law, some states have enacted legislation that is more directly responsive to their unique, individual needs. The perception on the part of these states is that federal law does not go far enough to address the problem of illegal immigration. However, to date, federal courts have stuck down a number of provisions of these state statutes. The prevailing sentiment expressed by the federal courts is that these state statutes have overreached their actual authority to control illegal immigration.

Any real solutions must involve the federal government and the states working together. Obviously, the federal government has the constitutional authority on its side; at the same time, the federal government cannot implement strategies like E-Verify, a national database, and a conditional amnesty program without considerable buy-in and assistance from the states.

References

Adrian, James. 2005. "Criminal Networks, Illegal Immigration and the Threat to Border Security." *International Journal of Police Science & Management* 7, no. 4: 219–229.

Buckler, Kevin. 2008. "Public Opinion on Illegal Immigration: A Test of Seven Core Hypotheses." *Journal of Crime & Justice* 3, no. 1: 113–147.

Cornelius, Wayne. 2005. "Controlling 'Unwanted' Immigration: Lessons from the United States, 1993–2004." *Journal of Ethnic & Migration Studies* 31, no. 4: 775–794.

Coutin, Susan Bibler. 2005. "Contesting Criminality: Illegal Immigration and the Spatialization of Legality." *Theoretical Criminology* 9, no. 1: 5–33.

Leerkes, Arjen, Mark Leach, and James Bachmeier. 2012. "Borders behind the Border: An Exploration of State-Level Differences in Migration Control and Their Effects on U.S. Migration Patterns." *Journal of Ethnic & Migration Studies*, 38, no. 1: 111–129.

Tichenor, Daniel. 2002. *Dividing Lines: The Politics of Immigration Control in America*. Princeton, NJ: Princeton University Press.

Todaro, Michael P. and Lydia Maruszko. 1987. "Illegal Migration and US Immigration Reform: A Conceptual Framework." *Population and Development Review* 13, no. 1: 101–114.

Varsanyi, Monica. 2011. "Neoliberalism and Nativism: Local Anti-Immigrant Policy Activism and an Emerging Politics of Scale." *International Journal of Urban and Regional Research* 35, no. 2: 295–311.

Vaughns, Katherine L. 2005. "Restoring the Rule of Law: Reflections on Fixing the Immigration System and Exploring Failed Policy Choices." *University of Maryland Law Journal of Race, Religion, Gender & Class* 5, no. 2: 151–186.

Woodland, Alan D. and Chisato Yoshida. 2006. "Risk Preference, Immigration Policy and Illegal Immigration." *Journal of Development Economics* 81, no. 2: 500–513.

Dr. David E. Krahl is an Assistant Professor of Criminology and Criminal Justice at the University of Tampa. In his professional career, Krahl has extensive and diverse management and administrative experience in the different areas of the criminal justice system including the police, courts, and corrections. Krahl also has treatment, intervention, and prevention experience in the field of substance abuse and chemical dependency at both the adult and juvenile levels.

Introduction

This chapter profiles people and organizations involved in the issue of illegal immigration.

The biographical section is an extensive but partial list of the individuals who are key players in the arena of illegal immigration reform. The chapter covers executive branch officials, including several U.S. presidents; several state governors who have taken prominent action on the problem or are chief executives of high-immigrant population states; legislative branch officials—key senators and members of the House of Representatives; a federal judge; and nongovernmental actors, including important advocates for and against illegal immigration reform legislation, as well as scholars, or "think tank" actors, who have had a particular impact on the debates over illegal immigration policy reform. They are presented here in alphabetical order by last name.

The biographical section is followed by profiles of important organizations. It discusses national domestic government agencies first.

The domestic government section is followed by a list of some of the more important international organizations active in the

---

Undocumented student Alma Castrejon, originally from Mexico, who has two college degrees but is unable to work, joins other undocumented students and community members protesting outside the Unites States Immigration Customs Enforcement (ICE) offices on August 24, 2011. The protestors called for the termination of the "Secure Communities Program" in front of the Federal Building in Los Angeles. (AP Photo/Damian Dovarganes) *global scene, with particular emphasis on those involved in refugee issues and concerns.*

In addition to governmental agencies and organizations, there are numerous important nongovernmental organizations involved (often known as NGOs or nonprofits). This chapter discusses those most active in advocacy for or against immigration and illegal immigration matters. For each organization, it discusses their positions on immigration reform. The chapter lists and discusses scholarly organizations involved in the policy arena of immigration reform. These are presented as examples of so-called immigration-related "think tanks" or centers for the study of immigration and immigration policy.

Biographies

Roy Beck (b. 1948)

Beck took his degree in journalism from the University of Missouri. In the late 1970s he wrote on business news at the *Cincinnati Enquirer*, then covered religion and politics, including covering Congress as chief Washington correspondent for the Booth chain of daily newspapers. He has written two books on immigration, one on its impact on the environment and the other on its impact on the U.S. labor market and on local communities. He has published on the topic in the *Atlantic Monthly, New York Times, National Review, Washington Post*, and *Christian Science Monitor*. He has studied immigration policy as an area of special concern while covering Congress. He is a frequent speaker on immigration matters before a wide variety of groups and organizations. His career in print media coverage of immigration policy making finally led him to develop the **Numbers USA Web site.**

Michael Bennet (b. 1964)

Senator Bennet (D-CO) is the senior senator from Colorado and a member of the Senate's "Gang of Eight" who sponsored and crafted S.744, the comprehensive immigration reform bill that passed the Senate in 2013. He was first appointed to the U.S. Senate in 2009, and elected in 2010. Before being elected to the Senate he was in private business and public service—Superintendent of Denver Public Schools. He took his BA degree from Wesleyan University and his JD from Yale Law School, where he was editor-in-chief of the *Yale Law Journal*. He is a member of the Senate Education Committee, the Agriculture, Nutrition, and Forestry, Committee on Finance, and Health, Education, Labor, and Pensions.

Sandford D. Bishop (b. 1947)

Rep. Sandford D. Bishop (D-GA) graduated with his B.A. from Morehouse College in 1968. He took his J.D. from Emory University in 1971. He served in the U.S. Army from 1971 to 1972. He was a practicing attorney from 1971 to 1992. His political career began with his election to and service in the Georgia House of Representatives, 1976–1990, and then the Georgia senate, 1990–1992. He was elected to the U.S. House of Representatives in 1992. He serves on the Agriculture Committee and on the Permanent Select Committee on Intelligence. He is the ranking minority member on the Technical and Tactical Intelligence subcommittee. He serves on the House Appropriations Committee. His most notable effort on the immigration issue has been his sponsoring in the House of the 1998 Guest Worker Program bill. He is a member of the Law Enforcement Caucus and the Congressional Black Caucus.

Diane Black (b. 1951)

Rep. Diane Black (R-TN) is a leading sponsor among the 24 Republicans who have led the effort to enact the Birthright Citizenship Act of 2013, which would strip citizenship of native-born persons whose parents are in the United States in unauthorized immigrant status. She has a BA in nursing, 1991; and an AA degree in nursing, 1971. First elected to the House in 2010, she serves on the House Ways and Means Committee and the House Budget Committee. Black is a member of the Tea Party Caucus and the Congressional Coast Guard Caucus.

John Boehner (b. 1949)

Rep. John Boehner (R-OH) is Speaker of the House. He effectively killed any chance of enactment of comprehensive immigration reform by refusing to bring the House version of S.744 to a House floor vote. Speaker Boehner took a business degree from Xavier University in 1977. He was elected to the House in 1990. In 1994 he was a prominent supporter of the Contract with America. He was a member of the House Agricultural Committee, and the "Gang of Seven" in 1992. He served as the House majority leader in 2006, and was elected Speaker of the House in 2010, and again in November, 2014 as the 53rd Speaker of the House. As Speaker he controls the flow of legislative proposals in the House and has consistently resisted taking up comprehensive immigration reform, but rather, supports piecemeal consideration of bills focused on border control and restriction and opposed "amnesty" proposals.

Janet Brewer (b. 1945)

Janet Brewer was the Republican governor of Arizona until she chose not to run for reelection in 2014. She is and was a frequently outspoken critic of the Obama administration and its immigration policy. During her five years in office as governor, she advocated and secured passage in 2010 of the state's harsh immigration law (the harshest law passed by any state), which was subsequently overturned as unconstitutional by the U.S. Supreme Court in *Arizona v. United States* (132 S.Ct. 2492, 2010).

Jerry Brown (b. 1938)

Jerry Brown is the governor of California, the state with the nation's largest Hispanic population and the most unauthorized/undocumented immigrants. He attended a Jesuit seminary in 1956, but left the Jesuit order in 1960 and enrolled in the University of California, Berkeley, from which he took his BA in classics. He graduated Yale Law School with his JD degree in 1964. In 1970 he was elected California Secretary of

State. He was first elected governor of California in 1974, and reelected in 1978. After his governorship, he lectured widely, led delegations to China and the Soviet Union, studied Spanish in Mexico, spent six months in Japan studying Japanese culture and Buddhist practice, worked with Mother Teresa in India, and was a CARE ambassador to Bangladesh during the devastating floods of 1987. He married Anne Gust, in a ceremony officiated by Sen. Dianne Feinstein and at a Catholic ceremony in the San Francisco church where he was baptized. In 1998 he served as mayor of Oakland and was reelected in 2002. In 2006 he was elected California's 31st attorney general. Governor Brown was elected for his third gubernatorial term in 2010 and reelected in 2014. He officially supports President Obama's executive actions for DACA and DAPA.

George Walker Bush (b. 1946)

Former president George W. Bush was enrolled at Phillips Academy in Andover, Massachusetts, in 1961. He worked on his father's Senate bid in 1964. He graduated Yale University in 1968, and then enlisted in the Texas Air National Guard. In 1973 he entered the Harvard Business School, taking his MBA in 1975. He founded an oil and gas exploration company that year. In 1978 he lost a bid to the U.S. House. In 1978 he worked on his father's campaign for the presidency. He joined a group of investors buying the Texas Rangers baseball team in 1989. He was elected governor of Texas in 1994 and reelected in 1998. In 2000 he won the presidency after losing the popular vote but being certified as winner in Florida: he won the Electoral College vote and a U.S. Supreme Court case that prevented recounts of disputed votes in Florida. He was inaugurated in 2001. He won reelection in 2004 and served until 2008. On September 11, 2001, terrorists struck the Pentagon and the World Trade Twin Towers in New York City. President Bush launched a "war on terrorism," and his administration authored and Congress passed the USA Patriot Act, granting the executive branch sweeping powers to deal with terrorism that have had significant impact on illegal immigration control efforts. Congress also passed the administration-backed law to create a Department of Homeland Security that dissolved the INS and moved its activities to the new department. The administration is noted for its crackdown on illegal immigrants and efforts to enforce expedited removal. He appointed the first director of National Intelligence, a position that has the potential to impact on efforts to control international terrorism (which will in turn affect illegal immigration). He is currently promoting enactment of a guest-worker program and favors a comprehensive approach to immigration reform.

Thomas Carper (b. 1947)

Senator Carper (D-DE) is the ranking member of the Homeland Security Committee, which oversees the DHS. He favors earned legalization and a guest-worker program. He received his BA in economics in 1968, went on to become a navy flight officer, than earned his MBA from the University of Delaware. He served two terms of governor of Delaware, after his election in 1992. He served five terms in the House of Representatives before being elected to the U.S. Senate in 2001.

James Earl Carter Jr. (b. 1924)

Jimmy Carter was born in Hope, Georgia. In 1941 he entered the Georgia Institute of Technology. In 1943 he entered the Annapolis Naval Academy, where he graduated in 1946. In 1962 he was elected to the Georgia state senate. In 1970 he was elected governor of Georgia. Carter was elected president in 1976 and served until 1980. In 1978 he deregulated the oil industry, pushed the Panama Canal treaty through the Senate, and signed the Camp David Accords. His most significant contribution to immigration policy was the establishment of the Select Commission on Immigration and Refugee Policy (SCIRP), whose recommendations led to the Immigration Reform and Control Act of 1986 (IRCA). The commission's work has formed the basis for much of the debate over illegal immigration reform since then. In 1980, the hostage crisis in Iran and the failure of the Immigration and Naturalization Service (INS) to track Iranian students in the United States contributed to his failed reelection bid. Carter's humanitarian work has led to his involvement in negotiations regarding the Haitian crisis, and he has worked with the United Nations on refugee problems and as an external election observer in several countries around the world. He was awarded the Nobel Peace Prize in 2002.

Linda Chavez (b. 1947)

Linda Chavez is founder and chairperson of the Center for Equal Opportunity, a policy research and advocacy organization headquartered in Virginia. She also writes a weekly syndicated column and is a political analyst for Fox News, hosts a daily radio show in Washington, D.C., and has written three books: *Towards a New Politics of Hispanic Assimilation* (1991), *An Unlikely Conservative* (2002), and *Betrayal* (2004). She served as chairperson of the National Commission on Migrant Education (1988–1992), as White House director of public liaison in 1985, as staff director of the U.S. Commission on Civil Rights (1983–1985), and as a member of the Administrative Conference of the United States (1984–1986). She was a Republican nominee for the U.S. Senate from Maryland in 1986. In 1992 she was elected to the UN Human Rights Commission, where she served a four-year term. She chairs the Latino Alliance of the Republican Party. In 2000, she was honored by the Library of Congress as a "Living Legend" for her contributions to America's cultural and historical legacies. In January 2001, President Bush nominated her to be the secretary of labor, but after considerable controversy she withdrew her name from consideration. She was born in Albuquerque, New Mexico, and received her BA from the University of Colorado in 1970. Chavez served as editor of the quarterly journal *American Educator* (1977–1983). She also served the American Federation of Teachers as assistant to its president (1982–1983) and as assistant director of legislation

(1975–1977). She is a strong advocate of legal-immigration reform and control of illegal immigration, and she opposes amnesty for illegal immigrants.

William Jefferson Clinton (b. 1946)

Former president William Clinton entered Georgetown University in 1964 and clerked for Arkansas senator J. William Fulbright in 1966. He graduated from Georgetown in 1968 and went on to Oxford University as a Rhodes Scholar. In 1970 he entered Yale Law School and received his law degree there in 1973. He began teaching at the University of Arkansas Law School in 1973 and lost an election for the U.S. House of Representatives in 1974. He was elected Arkansas attorney general in 1976. He lost his first bid for governor of the state in 1980 but was elected to that office in 1982 and reelected in 1984. In 1986 he chaired the National Governors Association, and in 1988 he was reelected governor. Clinton was elected president in 1992, and reelected in 1996. His most significant illegal immigration policy role was shepherding the Personal Responsibility and Work Opportunity Reconciliation Act of 1996 through Congress and signing it into law. This welfare reform act had numerous and important immigration-related provisions, and it was soon followed by the Illegal Immigration Reform and Immigrant Responsibility Act of 1996. A 1998 sexual affair scandal led to his impeachment in 1998. He was acquitted by the U.S. Senate in 1999 and served out his term as president. After his term ended, Clinton served with distinction in disaster relief efforts for the United Nations, most notably efforts to alleviate the devastation created by the Asian tsunami of 2004 and to aid refugees. He founded the Clinton Initiative, and is an outspoken advocate for comprehensive immigration reform.

J. Richard Cohen (b. 1941)

J. Richard Cohen is president of the Southern Poverty Law Center, the civil rights advocacy organization headquartered in Montgomery, Alabama, founded in 1971 by Joe Levin, Julian Bond, and Morris Dees. It is a leading advocacy group on immigration reform, antifascism, and antipoverty issues. Cohen is a graduate of Columbia University and the University of Virginia Law School. He joined the SPLC in 1986, after which it won a series of landmark lawsuits against some of the nation's most violent white supremacist organization. In 1997, the national legal magazine, *The American Lawyer*, selected him as 1 of 45 public sector lawyers "whose vision and commitment are changing lives." He recently won a case in which the Christian Knights of the Ku Klux Klan were handed a record $37.8 million judgment against the Klan group for the burning of a South Carolina church. He has led the SPLC into cooperative work with a host of proimmigrant rights groups advocating on behalf of legal and illegal immigrants.

John Conyers Jr. (b. 1929)

Conyers (D-MI) is the ranking member on the House Judiciary Committee, which considers all legislative bills dealing with immigration matters. He is author of several books on civil rights matters. He was educated at Wayne State University. He was first elected to the Congress in 1965 and is the oldest, longest-serving member of Congress. He serves on the House Judiciary Committee and the Constitution Committee, and on the Intellectual Property, Competition, and Internet. He is founding member of the Congressional Black Caucus, and has strongly supported comprehensive immigration reform. He served in the National Guard and the U.S. Army Corps of Engineers in the Korean War. He earned his BA degree in 1957 and his JD in 1958 at Wayne State University.

John Cornyn (b. 1952)

John Cornyn is the junior senator from Texas. He was born in Houston, Texas, and received his BA from Trinity University in 1973, his JD from St. Mary's Law School in 1977, and an LLM degree from the University of Virginia in 1995. He served as the San Antonio District Court judge from 1984 to 1990, on the Texas Supreme Court from 1990 to 1997, and as Texas attorney general from 1998 to 2002. As attorney general, he argued that federal law bars public hospitals from giving illegal immigrants anything but emergency treatment, immunizations, and communicable disease treatment. He was elected to the U.S. Senate in 2002. He serves on the Armed Services Committee; on Budget, Environment and Public Works; on the Judiciary Committee and its subcommittees of Administrative Oversight and Courts, Constitution, Civil Rights, and Property Rights, of which he is chair; on Crime, Corrections and Victims' Rights; and on Immigration, Border Security, and Citizenship. He was the Senate cosponsor of the Comprehensive Enforcement and Immigration Control Act of 2005, a bill to reform illegal immigration policy that was a more conservative approach than the Kennedy-McCain bill. In the Senate today, he sponsors and supports the Secure Our Borders First Act of 2015. In 2015, he became assistant majority leader. He has sponsored the Cross-Border Trade Enhancement Act of 2015. He serves on the Senate Homeland Security and Government Affairs Committee and has opposed any proposal he deems is an amnesty provision.

Andrew Cuomo (b. 1957)

Andrew Cuomo is the 56th governor of New York, one of the biggest immigrant-receiving states in the nation. He was elected governor in 2011. He previously served as New York's attorney general from 2007 to 2010. He has been outspoken on the need for comprehensive immigration reform. He also served as U.S. Secretary of the Department of Housing and Urban Development from 1997 to 2001. He graduated from Fordham University in 1979, and took his law degree from Albany Law School in 1982. In 2014, he published his book: *All Things Possible: Setback and Success in Public Life.*

Thomas J. Donohue (b. 1938)

Thomas Donohue is president and CEO of the U.S. Chamber of Commerce, which is a leading advocate for expansion of the various guest-worker programs to deal with immigration matters and the illegal immigration problem. He has been with the chamber since 1997 and established its Institute for Legal Reform. He was born in New York City and has his BA degree from St. John's University and an MA degree in business administration from Adelphi University. Although the chamber is officially nonpartisan, it more commonly supports Republicans; yet in 2015 Donohue said: "If the Republicans don't change their immigration policy position, they shouldn't even bother to run a candidate [for president] in 2016."

Richard Durbin (b. 1944)

Dick Durbin (D-IL) is one of the Senate's "Gang of Eight," who helped craft S.744, the bipartisan comprehensive immigration reform measure that passed the Senate in 2013. He is the 47th senator from Illinois, and has served in the Senate since 1996, having been reelected in 2002, 2005, and 2014. He is a member of the Senate Judiciary Committee and of the Appropriations Committee, and is ranking member on the Subcommittee on Constitution, Civil Rights, and Human Rights. He is the assistant Democratic leader in the Senate, commonly known as minority whip. As such, he is a leader of the Democrats in the Senate and their chief vote counter.

Dianne Feinstein (b. 1933)

Feinstein is California's senior senator. She was elected in 1992 and reelected in 2000. She received a BA from Stanford University in 1955. Prior to serving in the Senate, she served on California's Women's Parole Board, 1960–1966; on the San Francisco Board of Supervisors, 1970–1978; and as mayor of San Francisco, 1978–1988. Senator Feinstein serves on several committees important to immigration: the Appropriations Committee; Agriculture and Rural Development; Interior; Labor, Health and Human Services, Education, and Related Agencies; Judiciary; Immigration; and Technology, Terrorism and Government Information. A tough critic of the Immigration and Naturalization Service (INS) and now Immigration and Customs Enforcement (ICE), she has been notably involved in bills to strengthen the Border Patrol (1993), sponsored increased fees to fund the "fencing-in" pilot program in the San Diego area, and was instrumental in the legislative battles leading to the Department of Homeland Security. Feinstein is a sharp critic of some of the alleged abuses of civil liberties in the administration of the USA Patriot Act. Her most recent legislative proposal of note to illegal immigration is a bill to make it a federal crime to tunnel under a U.S. border. She has been and continues to be a sharp critic of the Department of Homeland Security.

Jeff Flake (b. 1962)

Senator Flake (R-AZ) is a member of the Senate's "Gang of Eight" and sponsor of S.744, the bipartisan comprehensive immigration reform bill that passed the Senate in 2013. He was a cattle rancher before entering electoral politics. He is a graduate of Brigham Young University and served on a Mormon mission. He has a B.A. in international relations and a M.A. in political science. He served in the House of Representatives from 2001 to 2013. He is an influential member of the Senate Judiciary Committee.

William Gheen (no birth date available)

William Gheen is president and spokesman of the Americans for Legal Immigration PAC (ALIPAC) and manages all operations and activities. He has led its fight against illegal immigration and any form of amnesty since 2004. He is a veteran campaign consultant and North Carolina native with over 15 years' experience in Internet and grassroots organizing, marketing, research, campaign management, and event coordination. He has a B.A. degree in political science from East

Carolina University and has experience with over 40 campaigns for public office. He has created new voter outreach methods for campaigns and issue advocacy. He served as the NC senate sergeant-at-arms, 1997–2003, and as legislative assistant in the NC General Assembly, and as a registered lobbyist, and has helped pass several laws addressing illegal immigration while maintaining the national operations of ALIPAC.

Jim Gilchrist (b. 1949)

Jim Gilchrist is an American political activist and the cofounder and president of the Minuteman Project, an activist group whose aim is to prevent illegal immigration across the southern border of the United States. He served in the U.S. Marine Corps, and is active with the Constitution Party. He organizes individuals and groups of volunteers to patrol the U.S.-Mexican border to intercept undocumented immigrant border-crossers.

Robert Goldsborough (no birth date available)

Goldsborough founded the Americans for Immigration Control in 1982. He is a columnist for *Middle America News* and is a harsh critic of U.S. immigration policy, calling for drastically reduced legal immigration and stricter control over illegal immigration. He is especially critical of any legalization program and any guest-worker program. He is prominent in the English-only movement.

Bob Goodlatte (b. 1952)

Rep. Bob Goodlatte took his B.A. in 1974 from Bates College, and his JD from Washington and Lee Law School in 1977. He began his political career working for Congressman Caldwell Butler in 1977. He practiced law from 1970 until 1992, when he was first elected to the House. He serves on the Agriculture Committee, and as the new Chairman of the House Judiciary Committee and its Crime, Terrorism and Homeland Security Subcommittee, and on the Select Committee on Homeland Security and its Subcommittee on Infrastructure and Border Security. He has sponsored a law imposing tougher penalties on commercial counterfeiters. He has compiled a conservative voting record. He sponsored a bill to end the visa lottery. He is chair of the House Judiciary Committee and has sponsored the Secure Our Borders First bill.

Trey Gowdy (b. 1964)

Gowdy (R-SC) is a member of the House Judiciary Committee and serves as chair of its Subcommittee on Immigration and Border Security, and as chairman of the House Select Committee on the Events Surrounding the 2012 Terrorist Attack in Benghazi. He continues to serve on the House Committee on Ethics, Oversight and Government Reform, and Judiciary. He has been a leading spokesman against any comprehensive immigration reform measure in the House, sponsoring its "Secure Our Borders First Act" currently in the House committee. He is sponsor of HR1148: To amend the Immigration and Nationality Act. Gowdy graduated from Baylor University in 1986 with a degree in history, and the University of South Carolina School of Law in 1989, where he was a member of the scholastic honor society: "Order of the Wig and Robe." He served six years as a federal prosecutor prior to his election to the House of Representatives.

Lindsey Graham (b. 1955)

Senator Graham (R-SC) is one of the Senate's "Gang of Eight," which sponsored and helped pass, in 2013, S.744, the bipartisan comprehensive immigration reform bill. He was a member of the Senate Judiciary Committee; and is on the Senate Armed Services Committee, 2008–2014. He graduated with a BA degree from the University of South Carolina in 1977, and took his JD from the South Carolina School of Law in 1981. He served in the U.S. Air Force from 1982 to 1988, and is an Air Force Reserves officer. He served in the House of Representatives from 1995 to 2002, and was elected to the Senate in 2002, 2008, and 2014. He is a declared candidate for the Republican Party nomination for president in 2016.

Charles "Chuck" Grassley (b. 1933)

Senator Grassley (R-IA) is chairman of the Senate Judiciary Committee, which oversees all legislative matters concerning immigration, and its Subcommittee on Immigration, Refugees and Border Security. He served in the House of Representatives from 1975 to 1981, and was first elected to the U.S. Senate and 1981 and reelected in 1987, 1993, 1997, 2003, and 2010.

Luis Guitierrez (b. 1953)

Guitierrez (D-IL) is a key member of the House of Representatives' "Gang of Eight" who sponsored the House version of S.744. He is emerging as a key progressive congressman on immigration matters. He is in his 12th term, having served since 1992. He is a Northwestern Illinois University graduate. He is a leading member of the Congressional Hispanic Caucus, serving as chairman of its Immigration Task Force, and has played an instrumental role in President Obama's decision to use executive action regarding DACA and DAPA. He is a leading Latino and immigrant spokesperson. He serves on the House Judiciary Committee and on its Subcommittee on Immigration and Border Security.

Andrew Hanen (b. 1953)

Andrew Hanen is an article III federal judge for the United States District Court for the Southern District of Texas. He was appointed to the federal bench by President George Bush in 2002. Judge Hanen took his undergraduate degree from Denison University in 1975, and his JD from the Baylor University School of Law in 1978. He was confirmed by the U.S. Senate in May 2002, on an unopposed vote of 97–0. His February 16, 2015, decision in a case brought by the attorneys general of 25 Republican-dominated states put an injunction (a judicial hold) to halt implementation of key elements of the immigration initiative by the Obama administration's DOJ regarding the president's executive actions known as DAPA. He ruled that President Obama lacked the authority to implement the new immigration program regarding granting a deferred status to illegal immigrants who are the parents of U.S. citizens or legal residents. The Obama administration has filed a suit challenging his ruling with the Federal Circuit Court.

Orrin Hatch (b. 1934)

Senator Hatch (R-UT) is a key member and chair of the Senate Judiciary Committee, and the most senior Republican in the Senate, having been elected in 1977. Senator Hatch is noted for his sponsorship of the Americans with Disabilities Act. He failed in his bid for the Republican Party's nomination for president in 2000. He attended Brigham Young University and the University of Pittsburgh and has his JD from the University of Pittsburgh Law School. He is chair of the Senate Committee on Finance, and is in his seventh term in the Senate and is president pro tempore of the Senate.

Ruben Hinojosa (b. 1940)

Hinojosa (D-TX) is chairman of the Congressional Hispanic Caucus. He is in his 9th term in the Congress, having first been elected to the House of Representatives in 1996. He has a BA degree in business and an MA in business administration from the University of Texas-Austin. He is ranking member of the House Financial Services Committee. In 2014 he received the Hispanic Heritage Award for his advocacy of Latino/Hispanic issues.

Donald Huddle (no birth date available)

Donald Huddle is a leading economist and scholar of ways to measure the cost-benefit ratio of immigration generally and illegal immigration specifically. He is professor emeritus of Rice University, in Economics. His 1993 study for the carrying capacity set off the debate over the "burden or benefit" controversy regarding illegal immigration. Since 1993, he has authored numerous and influential articles on the subject of the cost and benefits of immigration and is generally viewed as a leading authority on the subject. His groundbreaking journal article, based on the 1993 study, is: Huddle, Donald and David Simcox. "The Impact of Immigration on the Social Security System," *Population and Environment* 16, no. 1 (September 1994).

Cristina Jimenez (no birth date available)

Cristina Jimenez is the cofounder and managing director of the United We Dream advocacy organization based in Washington, D.C. It is a leading advocacy organization for the "Dreamers," and lobbies congress and the Obama administration for pro-Dreamer policy. United We Dream was important in pushing President Obama to issue his executive actions on DACA and DAPA. Ms. Jimenez was born in Ecuador and came to the United States at age 13, attending both high school and college as an unauthorized immigrant. For the last decade she has organized immigrant youth and workers to advocate for proimmigration policies at the local and national levels. Jimenez was recognized among Forbes "30 and under 30 in Law and Policy," and the *Chronicle of Philanthropy* named her one of its five nonprofit leaders who will influence public policy. She cofounded the New York State Youth Leadership Council and the Dream Membership Program at Queens College, and served as an immigration policy analyst for the Drum Major Institute for Public Policy. She is an immigrant rights organizer at Make the Road New York. She took her master's degree in public administration and public policy from the School of Public Affairs at Baruch College, CUNY, and graduated cum laude with a BA in political science and business at Queens College, CUNY.

Jeh Johnson (b. 1957)

Jeh Johnson is the secretary of the Department of Homeland Security, appointed by President Obama in 2013, and thus

oversees the implementation of all laws, policies, and procedures pertaining to illegal immigration and legal immigration.
He is an American civil and criminal trial lawyer. He is a graduate of Morehouse College and took his JD from Columbia Law
School. He served s the Air Force General Counsel and, then in
2009, as the general counsel in the Department of Defense. He
was also an United States Assistant States Attorney in the South
District of New York.

Ron Johnson (b. 1955)

Sen. Ron Johnson (R-WI), who as of 2015, is the new chair of
the Homeland Security and Government Affairs Committee.
He is a sponsor of the Secure Our Borders First Act of 2014.
He is a University of Minnesota graduate. He was elected to
the U.S. Senate in 2011 and serves also as a member of the
Committee on Foreign Relations.

Don M. Kerwin Jr. (no birth date available)

Don Kerwin is executive director of the Center for Migration
Studies in New York, the leading progressive "think tank,"
which is a proimmigration organization studying and advocating for comprehensive immigration reform. He became
director in 2011, succeeding Lydio Tomasi as such. He is the
author of *Migrant Children, Uninvited Guests, and Welcoming
the Stranger*, 2014. Prior to his coming to the CMS, he worked
for the Catholic Legal Immigration Network, Inc. (CLINIC)
between 1992 and 2008, serving as its executive director for
15 years. He coordinated CLINIC's political asylum project
for Haitians. CLINIC, a subsidiary of the United States Conference of Catholic Bishops (USCCB), is a public interest legal
corporation supporting a national network of charitable legal
programs for immigrants. Between 2008 and 2011, Kerwin
served as vice president for Programs at the Migration Policy
Institute, where he frequently wrote on immigration, labor standards, and refugee policy issues. He also served as an associate

fellow at the Woodstock Theological Center coordinating its Theology of Migration Project, and as a member of the American Bar Association's Commission on Immigration, a member of the Council on Foreign Relations' Immigration Task Force, a board member for the Jesuit Refugee Services-USA, a board member for the Capital Area Immigrant Rights Coalition, and as adviser to the USCCB Committee on Migration. He currently serves on the board of directors for the Border Network for Human Rights in El Paso, Texas.

Peter King (b. 1944)

King was born in Manhattan; his parents were Irish immigrants and Democrats; his father was an NYPD detective. He received a BA degree from St. Francis College in 1965 and took his JD degree from the University of Notre Dame in 1968. He served in the Army National Guard from 1968 to 1973. He practiced law from 1968 to 1972, worked as deputy attorney for Nassau County from 1972 to 1974, and was later both the executive assistant to the county executive and general counsel. He was elected to the Hempstead Town Council from 1977 to 1981 and served as Nassau County comptroller in 1977. Now in his 12th term, he was first elected to the House in 1992. He has a moderately conservative voting record. King serves on the Financial Services Committee, on the International Relations Committee and its subcommittee on International Terrorism, and on the Select Committee on Homeland Security and its subcommittees on Emergency Preparedness and Response, and Intelligence and Counterterrorism. He has sponsored English-only legislation and generally opposes aid to illegal immigrants.

Amy Klobuchar (b. 1960)

Senator Klobuchar (D-MN) is a leading minority member of the Senate Judiciary Committee and on its subcommittee on Immigration. She is the senior senator from Minnesota, first elected to the U.S. Senate in 2007. She graduated from Yale University in 1982, and the University of Chicago Law School in 1985. Prior to her service in the Senate, Amy Klobuchar was the county attorney for Hennepin County, Minnesota, from 1999 to 2007. She has strongly supported President Obama's use of executive actions in DACA and DAPA, and advocates comprehensive immigration reform, having voted for S.744.

Mark Krikorian (b. 1961)

Mark Krikorian has a BA degree from Georgetown University and took a master's degree from the Fletcher School of Law and Diplomacy at Tufts University. He also studied for two years at Yerevian State University in the then-Soviet nation of Armenia. He has held various editorial and writing positions, and in 1995, he joined the Center for Immigration Studies in Washington, D.C., and serves as its executive director. He frequently testifies before Congress and has published numerous articles in such periodicals as the *Washington Post*, the *New York Times, Commentary*, and the *National Review*. He has appeared on *60 Minutes, Nightline*, the *News Hour* with Jim Lehrer, CNN, National Public Radio, and similar television and radio programs.

Jon Kyl (b. 1942)

Sen. Jon Kyl was born in Oakland, Nebraska. He was the junior senator from Arizona; he was elected to that office in 1994 and reelected in 2000, and retired from the Senate in 2013. He moved to Arizona and went to college and law school there, practiced law in Phoenix, and headed its chamber of commerce. He won the heavily Republican 4th District in 1986. In the House he became a leading Republican on missile defense and the balanced-budget amendment. He had a solidly conservative record and in the Senate became a major force on defense policy and a champion of the missile-defense system. Senator Kyl served on the Judiciary Committee and cosponsored, with Sen. Dianne Feinstein, a constitutional amendment on victims' rights. Before 9/11 Kyl and Feinstein also cosponsored a bill to prepare for attacks by terrorists with chemical and biological weapons. In 2001, the two introduced a bill to establish a comprehensive lookout database that would combine data from the CIA, FBI, and the State Department to make it available to the Border Patrol and consular officials. Senator Kyl worked to beef up the Border Patrol and to track legal immigrants who overstayed their visas; he supported cuts in legal immigration and new rules for family-based immigration. He worked for more federal reimbursement of states and localities for the costs of hospitalizing and incarcerating illegal aliens. He cosponsored a limited guest-worker bill that competed with the more comprehensive Kennedy-McCain proposal. Of importance to illegal immigration matters, Senator Kyl served as chair of the Republican Policy Committee and on the Judiciary Committee and its subcommittees on Constitution, Civil Rights and Property Rights, and on Immigration, Border Security and Citizenship; and at the time of his retirement, chaired the Subcommittee on Terrorism, Technology, and Homeland Security. He cosponsored the Cornyn/Kyle bill, the Comprehensive Enforcement and Immigration Control Act of 2005.

Patrick Leahy (b. 1940)

Senator Leahy (D-VT) is the ranking member of the Senate Judiciary Committee, which considers all proposals dealing with immigration matters, and served as its chair from 2007 to 2015. He is president Pro Tempore Emeritus, 2012–2015, of the Senate. He has served in the U.S. Senate since 1975. He is a graduate of St. Michael's College and took his JD from Georgetown University Law School. Senator Leahy is a member of the Appropriations Committee and the ranking member of the Senate Judiciary's subcommittee on Immigration.

Joseph I. Lieberman (b. 1942)

Former senator Lieberman took his BA from Yale University in 1964 and received an LLB from Yale in 1967. He was a practicing attorney from 1964 to 1980. In his political career, he served in the Connecticut state senate from 1970 to 1980, including serving as its majority leader from 1974 to 1980. He was attorney general of Connecticut from 1983 to 1988, at which time he was elected to the U.S. Senate, where he served until 2014. In 2000, Lieberman ran (with Al Gore) as the Democratic nominee for vice president and also for reelection to the U.S. Senate. He lost the former election but won the latter. In terms of illegal immigration policy reforms, he was the leading spokesman for and the Senate sponsor of the bill for the establishment of the Department of Homeland Security with its broad implications for restructuring the INS.

Zoe Lofgren (b. 1947)

Rep. Zoe Lofgren (D-CA) is a member of the House Judiciary Committee, the House Science, Space and Technology Committee, and the Committee on House Administration. She was first elected to the House in 1995, representing the Silicon Valley area. She graduated Stanford University with a BA degree in political science in 1970. She took her law degree, cum laude, from Santa Clara University School of Law in 1975. She practiced and taught immigration law. She is the ranking member and former chair of the Subcommittee on Immigration and Border Security, a lifetime immigration attorney and law professor, and is recognized as a champion of comprehensive immigration reform and a national leader on immigration policy. She played a key role in negotiating a comprehensive reform bill in the House in 2013 (one of the House of Representatives' "Gang of Eight"). Lofgren was a key sponsor of the Dream Act, and then Speaker Nancy Pelosi presented her with the gavel used to preside over the passage of the bill in the House of Representatives. She is chair of the California Democratic Congressional Delegation of 38 Democratic members from California, the most diverse and largest delegation in the House of Representatives.

John McCain (b. 1936)

John McCain, the senior senator from Arizona, was born in the Panama Canal Zone. A career naval officer from 1958 to 1980, he is the son and grandson of navy admirals and is a decorated navy pilot who was shot down in Vietnam and spent five years as a prisoner of war. In March 1973 McCain returned to the United States, where he served his final term in the navy as a Senate liaison. In 1980 he retired and moved to Arizona, ran in 1982 for a House seat, and won in both 1982 and 1984. In 1986 he ran and won a U.S. Senate seat. He strongly supported President Bush in the war on terrorism after 9/11. His independent and bipartisan stands, and particularly his crusades for campaign finance regulation and against pork-barrel spending, have often made him unpopular among his colleagues. He brings to his work a strong sense of righteousness and conviction. His most notable legislative achievement was enactment of the McCain-Feingold campaign-finance law in 2001. He ran for president in 2000 but failed to get his party's nomination. After his failed presidential bid, he became more active in the Senate—increasingly allying with Democrats and opposing most Republican positions on campaign finance and on tobacco-related matters. He took a significant role in the post-9/11 legislative battles and called for government-run airport security. Senator McCain was the Republican presidential nominee in 2008, losing to President Obama. He cosponsored with Senator Kennedy of Massachusetts the comprehensive bill to reform illegal immigration policy, and is today a member of the "Senate Gang of Eight," which advocated and helped pass S.744, the current most comprehensive immigration reform bill, and has advocated for an extensive guest-worker/earned legalization program.

Claire McCaskill (b. 1953)

Senator McCaskill (D-MO) is the ranking minority member of the Homeland Security Committee and a leading supporter and often outspoken critic of the Department of Homeland Security. She took her JD from the University of Missouri Law School, Columbia. From 1978 to 1982 she was the Kansas City prosecutor. In 1999 she was elected the Missouri State auditor, and in 2004, governor of Missouri. She was elected to the U.S. Senate in 2006 and reelected in 2012. She chaired the Commerce Committee and the Armed Services Committee.

Michael McCaul (b. 1962)

Rep. Michael McCaul (R-TX) is the newly selected chairman of the House of Representatives Committee on Homeland Security. First elected to the House in 2002, he is in his sixth term. He is also chairman of the U.S.-Mexico International Parliamentary Group and serves on the Committee on Foreign Affairs. His conservative voting record earned him recognition by the American Conservative Union's coveted ACU Ratings Award. Prior to his election to the House, he served as Chief of Counterterrorism and National Security in the U.S. Attorney's office, Western District of Texas, and led the Joint Task Force charged with detecting, deterring, and preventing terrorist activity. He served as Texas Deputy Attorney General and as a federal prosecutor in the Department of Justice's Public Integrity Section, Washington, D.C. He has a BA degree in history from Trinity University, and took his JD from St. Mary's University School of Law. He is also a graduate of the Senior Executive Fellows Program of the School of Government, Harvard University.

Mitch McConnell (b. 1942)

Senator McConnell (R-KY) became Senate majority leader after the 2014 Senate elections, only the second senator from Kentucky to serve as majority leader. As such, he plays the key role in all Senate legislative proceedings and, in particular, a leading role in forming the Senate Republicans' position on immigration reform. He previously served as Senate minority leader in the 110th–113th Congresses, and as majority whip in the 108th and 109th Congresses. He served as chairman of the National Republican Senatorial Committee, 1998–2000. He was first elected to the Senate in 1984. He graduated cum laude from the University of Louisville College of Arts and Sciences, and took his JD from the University of Kentucky College of Law where he served as president of the Student Bar Association. Prior to his elective office in the Senate, he served as deputy assistant attorney general to President Gerald Ford, and as judge-executive of Jefferson County, Kentucky, from 1978 to 1985. He serves as a senior member of the Appropriations, Agriculture and Rules Committees in the Senate.

Robert Menendez (b. 1954)

Senator Menendez (D-NJ) is one of the Senate's "Gang of Eight," who sponsored and wrote the bipartisan S.744 bill to enact comprehensive immigration reform that passed the Senate in 2013. He served as chair of the Senate Foreign Relations Committee, 2013–2015, and is now its ranking member. He served in the House of Representatives from 1993 to 2006. He is a member of the Banking subcommittee and is on the Housing, Transportation and Community Development Committee. He took his BA from St. Peter's College, Jersey City, and his JD from Rutgers University School of Law. While in the House, he chaired the House Democratic Caucus from 2003 to 2006. He is a strong advocate of comprehensive immigration reform.

Candice Miller (b. 1954)

Miller was born in Detroit. She attended Macomb County Community College and Northwood University and served as secretary-treasurer of a marina. In elected offices, she served as trustee of the Harrison Township Board, as a Harrison Township supervisor, then as Macomb City treasurer before being elected Michigan's secretary of state, a position she held from 1994 to 2002. She was first elected to the House in 2002 and now serves on the Armed Services and Governmental Reform committees and is vice chair of the Intergovernmental Relations and Census subcommittee. She has a solidly conservative voting record and describes herself as a "Bush Republican"; she was very active in passage of North American Free Trade Agreement (NAFTA). She recently sponsored a constitutional amendment that would stipulate that only citizens be counted for the purpose of census data to determine representation to Congress and has sponsored the Birthright Citizenship Act and the Secure Our Borders First Act of 2015.

Janet Murguia (b. 1960)

Janet Murguia was elected, in 2014, president of the National Council of La Raza, the largest national Hispanic civil rights and advocacy organization in the United States, and is a leading political activist for Hispanic interests and the Latino community, including education, health care, immigration reform, civil rights, and the economy. In her role as spokesperson for La Raza, she is frequently interviewed by news outlets and has appeared on many news programs. Murguia serves as a board member of the Independent Sector, a coalition of nonprofits, foundations, and corporations, and is an executive committee member of the Leadership Conference on Civil Rights, and she sits on the board of the Hispanic Association on Corporate Responsibility and the National Hispanic Leadership Agenda. She serves on the advisory board of the National Hispanic University. In 2001 she joined the University of Kansas as its vice chancellor for University Relations and managed its strategic planning and marketing efforts on four campuses. She has a BS degree in journalism, 1982; a BA degree in Spanish, 1982; and a JD degree from Kansas University, 1985.

Demetrios Papademetriou (b. 1946)

Demetrios Papademetriou has published in the United States and abroad on immigration and refugee policies, with an emphasis on the labor market and developmental repercussions. He has taught at American University, the University of Maryland, and Duke University, and is on the graduate faculty of the New School for Social Research. He has served as director of emigration policy and research at the U.S. Department of Labor and chaired the secretary of labor's Immigration Policy Task Force. He also served as U.S. representative to the Migration Committee of the Organization for Economic Cooperation and Development (OECD). Before his governmental service, he was executive editor of the *International Migration Review* and directed the research activities of the Center for Migration Studies in New York. Papademetriou now directs the Carnegie Endowment's International Migration Policy Program and also serves as chair of the OECD Migration Committee. He concentrates on U.S. immigration policies and practices, the migration politics and practices of advanced industrial societies, and the role of multilateral institutions in developing and coordinating collective responses to voluntary and involuntary international population movements. He is a leading authority/scholar of immigration policy matters.

Jeffrey S. Passel (no birth date available)

Jeffrey Passel is a senior demographer at the Pew Research Center, and a nationally known expert on immigration to the United States, and on the demography of racial and ethnic groups. He served as the principal research associate at the Urban Institute's Labor, Human Services and Population Center. He has authored numerous studies on immigrant populations in America, and focused on undocumented immigration, the economic and fiscal impact of the foreign-born, and the impact of welfare reform on immigrant populations. *American Demographics* magazine named him, in 2004, a "Demographic Diamond." He served as senior statistician in the U.S. Bureau of the Census, 1974–1989, and is a fellow of the American Statistical Association, the American Association for the Advancement of Science, and a former member of the Population Association of America. He took his PhD in statistics from Johns Hopkins University, an MA from the University of Texas at Austin, and a BS from the Massachusetts Institute of Technology.

Nancy Pelosi (b. 1940)

Nancy Pelosi was first elected to the House in 1987. She was born in Baltimore, Maryland, and now resides in San Francisco. She took her BA from Trinity College in 1962. She also studied at the Institute of Notre Dame, and at Washington University. She was a PR executive from 1986 to 1987 and served as California Democratic Party northern chairman from 1977 to 1981; she was state chair from 1981 to 1983, and served as the Democratic Senatorial Campaign Committee finance chair from 1985 to 1987. She once again serves as the minority leader in the House of Representatives, after a distinguished term as Speaker of the House, 2001–2014. She has an almost perfect liberal voting record. She has been elected and reelected by huge margins. Currently, as minority leader she has taken very vocal stances on immigration and guest-worker programs. She joined with Senator Feinstein on sponsoring bills to increase border security along the California-Mexico border, and voted for the House comprehensive immigration reform bill in 2013.

Rick Perry (b. 1950)

Rick Perry was the 47th governor of Texas, 2000–2015, campaigned for the Republican Party presidential nomination in 2010, and is a declared candidate for the Republican Party presidential nomination again in 2016. He was elected lieutenant governor of Texas in 1998, and assumed the governorship when George W. Bush resigned the office to become president in 2000. Governor Perry was the longest-serving governor in Texas history. He was elected to a full term in 2002, and reelected in 2006 and 2010. He is an outspoken critic of President Obama's immigration policy and use of executive action regarding DACA and DAPA.

Harry Reid (b. 1939)

Sen. Harry Reid (D-NM) is now the Senate minority leader, after serving as Senate majority leader from 2007 to 2014. As minority leader he continues to play a key role in all legislative proceedings concerning immigration matters and is the Democratic Party leader in the Senate. He was first elected to the Senate in 1986, and reelected in 1992, 1998, 2004, and 2010. He is Nevada's senior senator. He graduated from Utah State in 1961 and took his JD from George Washington University. He was elected to the House of Representatives in 1982, and to the Senate in 1986. He has strongly supported comprehensive immigration reform and helped manage successfully the bipartisan passage in the Senate of S.744, the comprehensive reform bill.

Marco Rubio (b. 1971)

Senator Rubio (R-FL) is one of the Senate's "Gang of Eight" who sponsored S.744, the bipartisan comprehensive immigration reform bill that passed the Senate in 2013. He is a declared candidate for the Republican Party nomination for president in 2016. He was elected to the U.S. Senate in 2010. Senator Rubio serves on the Foreign Relations Committee, Commerce, Science and Transportation, Small Business and Entrepreneurship. He has a BA degree for the University of Florida, and took his JD from the University of Miami Law School. He served in the Florida House from 2000 to 2009, and as its Speaker in 2007–2009, before being elected to the U.S. Senate.

Charles E. Schumer (b. 1950)

Now the senior senator from New York, Charles Schumer took his BA from Harvard in 1971 and his JD from there in 1974. He served in the New York Assembly from 1974 to 1980 and then in the U.S. House from 1980 to 1998. He was elected to the Senate in 1998. He was critically important in crafting compromises making possible the passage of the Immigration

Reform and Control Act of 1986 and has continued to play a critical role in all immigration-related bills since then, essentially taking the lead among progressive senators in the role played by the late senator Ted Kennedy. He is a leading member of the Senate's "Gang of Eight" and sponsor of S.744, the bipartisan comprehensive immigration reform bill that passed the Senate in 2013. In the Senate he serves on several committees including Banking, Housing and Urban Affairs; International Trade and Finance; Judiciary and its subcommittees of Administrative Oversight and the Courts; Criminal Justice Oversight; Immigration (where he is the ranking minority member); and Rules and Administration.

James Sensenbrenner (b. 1943)

Sensenbrenner was first elected to the House in 1978. He was born in Chicago. He received an AB degree from Stanford University in 1965 and his JD degree from the University of Wisconsin in 1968. He practiced law from 1968 to 1969 and was elected to the Wisconsin assembly (1968–1974) and the Wisconsin senate (1974–1978). He was staff assistant to Congressman Arthur Younger in 1965. He serves as the chair of the powerful Judiciary Committee in the House and on the Select Committee on Homeland Security. He staunchly supported the use of force in Iraq and creation of the Department of Homeland Security but was critical of Attorney General Ashcroft's possible violations of civil liberties and calls for additional investigative powers for law enforcement. Sensenbrenner insisted on sunset provisions (which would expire after four years) for the USA Patriot Act and the Patriot Act II. He sponsored a bill to split the INS into two separate agencies, and when these agencies were moved to the new Department of Homeland Security, he expressed strong concerns that internal problems would remain unresolved. He has long opposed racial quotas and preferences and was vocal in his support of Milwaukee's school-choice program. He has won election and reelection by wide margins and has often been unopposed in the general election. His most notable recent legislation concerning illegal immigration is his sponsorship of the REAL ID Act.

Jeff Sessions (b. 1946)

Senator Sessions (R-AL) is chair of the Senate Judiciary's Subcommittee on Immigration and National Interest. He was first elected to the Senate in 1997 and reelected for his third term in 2008. In 2011 he was the ranking minority member of the Budget Committee, and the subcommittee on Banking. He is sponsor of a bill to block any funding for amnesty. He serves on the Senate Armed Forces Committee, the Environment and Public Utility Committee. He took his BA degree from Huntingdon College in 1969, and his JD from the University of Alabama School of Law in 1973. Prior to his election to the U.S. Senate, he served as a President Reagan appointee to the U.S. attorney, Alabama Southern District. Senator Sessions is an outspoken opponent of comprehensive immigration reform and any sort of amnesty provision.

Frank Sharry (no birth date available)

Frank Sharry directs one of the nation's leading immigration policy organizations and is an advocate of upholding America's tradition as a nation of immigrants. He is a leading spokesperson for proimmigration policies and frequently appears in print and on television. Prior to joining the National Immigration Forum (NIF), he was executive director of the Centro Presente, which helps Central American refugees. He helped found the Massachusetts Immigration and Refugee Advocacy Coalition and led efforts to resettle refugees from Vietnam and Cuba; he also led the campaign against passage of California's Proposition 187. He is currently starting up a new organization called America's Voice to advocate for broad immigration reform rooted in the American values of earned citizenship, the rule of law, and the promise of the American Dream. For the past 25 years he has been involved in every major legislative and policy debate related to immigration. He was also executive director of Centro Presente, a local organization working with Central Americans in the greater Boston area.

Christopher H. Smith (b. 1953)

Rep. Christopher Smith (R-NJ) received a B.S. from Trenton State College in 1975. He was a sales executive in a family-owned sporting goods business from 1975 to 1980. He served as executive director of New Jersey Right to Life from 1976 to 1978. He was elected to the U.S. House of Representatives in 1980. He serves on the International Relations Committee and chairs its subcommittee on International Operations and Human Rights, Western Hemisphere. He also holds vice chair positions on the Veterans Affairs Committee and on the Health Committee. His most notable immigration reform measure was sponsoring the Trafficking Victims Protection Act in 2003. He is a member of the Caucus on Human Trafficking, the Pro-Life Caucus, and the Congressional Poland Caucus. He was officially a Democrat prior to 1978, and switched to the Republican Party since then. He took his BA from the College of New Jersey.

Lamar S. Smith (b. 1947)

Smith was born in San Antonio. He took a BA from Yale in 1969 and his JD from Southern Methodist University in 1975. He worked for the U.S. Small Business Administration from 1969 to 1970 and was a business writer for the *Christian Science Monitor* from 1970 to 1972. He practiced law from 1975 to 1976. He was elected to the Texas House of Representatives from 1981 to 1982. He served on the Bexar County Committee from 1982 to 1985 and was elected to the U.S. House of Representatives in 1986. Smith serves on the Judiciary Committee, where he is chair of its Immigration and Claims Subcommittee; on the Science Committee; and on the Standards of Official Conduct Committee, which he also chairs. Since his arrival in the House, he has been an outspoken critic of immigration policy and is one of the House's strongest advocates for restricted immigration, illegal immigration reform, strengthening of the Border Patrol, and opposition to amnesty proposals. He chaired the House Ethics Committee, 1999–2001, and previously chaired the House Judiciary Committee.

Roberto Suro (no birth date available)

Roberto Suro is the founding director of the Pew Hispanic Center, a Washington-based research and policy-analysis organization that he founded in 2001. He was born in Washington, D.C., to Puerto Rican and Ecuadorian parents, and has chronicled Hispanic and related issues as a journalist for some 30 years. He began a career in journalism in Chicago in 1974. During his career as a journalist, he researched and wrote about Latinos for the *Washington Post*. He has also worked as a foreign correspondent for *Time* magazine and the *New York Times* in Latin America, Europe, and the Middle East. He was bureau chief for the *New York Times* in Rome, Italy. He is author of *Strangers among Us: Latino Lives in a Changing America* (1999), and he is author of two Twentieth Century Fund papers on immigration matters: "Remembering the American Dream" and "National Policy and Watching America's Door: The Immigration Backlash and the New Policy Debate." He is a graduate of Yale University, where he took his BA in 1973, and Columbia University, where he received an MS degree in 1974. He is currently professor at the University of Southern California. He is an affiliate of the Brookings Institution as a nonresident senior fellow in metropolitan policy (since 2005), the Migration Policy Institute as a nonresident fellow (2007–2010), on the advisory board, since 2008, of E Pluribus Unum Prizes, awards for initiatives to promote immigrant integration. He is a member of the Network for Multicultural Research in Health and Healthcare; is a senior investigator (since 2007) in the School of Medicine, UCLA; and serves on the Pacific Council on International Policy's Mexican Council of Foreign Relations and Bi-national Task Force on the U.S.-Mexico Border (since 2009).

John H. Tanton (no birth date available)

John Tanton is a widely recognized leader in the anti-immigration and "official English" movements in the United States. Tanton cofounded the Federation for American Immigration Reform and NumbersUSA in 1996, founded Pro-English in 1993, founded the Center for Immigration Studies in 1985, and cofounded and became chair of U.S. English in 1982. Tanton played a central role in mobilizing neoconservatives, the New Right, and the Christian Right against center-left politics in the United States, and he mobilized backlash sentiment against immigrants. He co-organized E Pluribus Unum in 1992, the Emergency Committee on Puerto Rican Statehood in 1990, and he became founder and chairman of US Inc. in 1982. He has worked with the Sierra Club, the National Audubon Society, and Zero Population Growth, and he is founder and publisher of Social Contract Press, which publishes books that shape a nationalist ideology and focus on the perceived threat of immigration to the white, English-speaking population. He is a retired eye surgeon, and a graduate of Michigan State University and the University of Michigan Medical School, 1960; and has an MS from the University of Michigan, 1964, in Ophthalmology and is Diplomate, American Board of Ophthalmology, 1956. He is coauthor, with Wayne Lutton, of *The Immigration Invasion*.

Bennie Thompson (b. 1948)

Rep. Bennie Thompson (D-MS) is the ranking minority member of the House of Representatives Committee on Homeland Security. He served as an alderman from 1968 to 1972 and then as mayor, 1973–1980, of Bolton, Mississippi. He was founding member and president of the Mississippi Association of Black Mayors. He was first elected to the House of Representatives in 1993 and is currently the longest-serving African American elected official in the state of Mississippi. He authored, in 2000, legislation creating the National Center for Minority Health and Health Care Disparities. In 2006 he was elected the first Democratic chairman of the House Homeland Security Committee. He has served on the Agriculture, Budget and Small Business committees. Thompson has a BS degree from Tougaloo College and an MS degree from Jackson State University.

Lydio F. Tomasi (no birth date available)

Father Lydio F. Tomasi, CS, PhD, is executive director emeritus of the Center for Migration Studies in New York. He is its founding member and directed the agency from 1968 to 2001. He was the founding editor of *Migration World Magazine*, a bimonthly review of current issues in migration policy. He was also editor of the annual volume, *In Defense of the Alien*, the proceedings of an annual conference held on immigrants' rights and immigration policy. His younger brother, and CMS cofounder, is Archbishop Silvano Tomasi, who serves as the Permanent Observer to the Holy See at the United Nations and Specialized Organizations in Geneva, Switzerland. Father Tomasi was born in Vincenza, Italy, attended the Pontifical Gregorian University in Rome where he earned his philosophy and theology licenses, and was ordained in 1962. In 1984, he received his PhD in sociology from New York University.

Georges Vernez (b. 1939)

Dr. Vernez took his PhD in urban and regional development from the University of California, Berkeley. He has directed and conducted studies on a broad range of immigration issues, including most notably a comprehensive assessment of the implementation of the Immigration Reform and Control Act of 1986, with particular focus on its effects on undocumented immigration, the supply of labor, and relations between the United States and Mexico. He has analyzed issues related to the effects of immigration on the demand for state and local services and on labor markets, and issues related to the social and economic adjustments of immigrants in the United States. He has also made comparative studies of policies on immigration and refugee movements and their outcomes in Western nations, and he has recently completed a comprehensive assessment of the demographic, economic, institutional, and distributional effects of 30 years of immigration in California. He is currently conducting a study of the performance of immigrant women in the U.S. labor market and a study of the social benefits from increasing the educational attainments of Hispanics. In 1991 he became the founding director of the RAND Institute on Education and Training, which examines all forms of education and training.

David Vitter (b. 1961)

Sen. David Vitter (R-LA) has been a leading opponent of any comprehensive immigration reform measure in the Senate, an ardent opponent of any amnesty bill, and one of the key sponsors and authors of the Birthright Citizenship bill of 2013. He is the leader of a congressional coalition to secure the borders and to stop illegal immigration, and an outspoken critic for reforming the Army Corps of Engineers to ensure better hurricane and flood protection. He was first elected to the House of Representatives in 1999, and to the U.S. Senate in 2004, and reelected in 2010. He serves as chairman of the Committee on Small Business and Entrepreneurship; and on the Committee on Banking, Housing and Urban Affairs, the Committee on Environment and Public Works, and the Committee on the Judiciary. In 2015 he began service as the Republican Party's deputy whip in the Senate. He has an AB degree from Harvard University, a BA degree from University College, Oxford, and a JD from Tulane Law School.

Ron Wyden (b. 1949)

Sen. Ron Wyden took his BA from Stanford University in 1971, and his JD from the University of Oregon in 1974. He served as the codirector and cofounder of the Oregon Gray Panthers from 1974 to 1980 and then as director of Oregon's Legal Services for the Elderly, 1977 to 1979. He was also professor of gerontology at the University of Oregon, 1976, and at Portland State University of Oregon, 1980. He served in the U.S. House of Representatives from 1980 to 1996, when he was elected to the U.S. Senate. His Senate committees of note are Aging; Budget; Commerce, Science and Transportation; Energy and Natural Resources; and Environment and Public Works. His most notable action on the immigration issue was his cosponsorship, with Sen. Gordon Smith, of the 1998 guest-worker bill. As senator from a state near the Canadian border, immigration matters continue to be a major focus of his legislative agenda. He continues to be an important advocate of a guest-worker program and of the earned legalization provision accompanying it. He is a relentless critic of the national security community's abuse of secrecy, and forced the declassification of the CIA Inspector General's 9/11 Report, helped shut down the controversial Total Information Awareness program, and focused on both the Bush and Obama administrations' reliance on secret law, and he successfully fought to have controversial antileaks provisions removed from the latest intelligence authorization bill.

Directory of Organizations and Agencies

National Government Agencies and Organizations

There are many federal agencies involved in the administration and implementation of U.S. immigration policy. They are all involved in immigration policy reform affairs as well, and they have an impact on illegal immigration reform, either through attempts to control or mitigate illegal immigration or by indirectly providing service to illegal immigrants. Twenty principal federal agencies follow, with their contact information and a brief description of their involvement in the issue.

U.S. Census Bureau

The bureau collects and does analysis of statistical data on the population, including immigrants. Its data form the basis for the most accurate information available to project or analyze the level and distribution of illegal immigrants throughout the United States and to track trends in the illegal immigration flow over time. Its numerous statistical studies and reports make possible the tracking of all immigrants. Its reports provide demographic data as to the gradual incorporation of immigrants into the major institutions of American society.

U.S. Commission on Civil Rights

The commission is an independent, bipartisan, fact-finding agency of the executive branch established under the Civil Rights Act of 1957. It investigates complaints as to discrimination; appraises federal laws and policies with respect to discrimination because of race, color, religion, sex, age, disability, or national origin; studies and collects information relating to such discrimination; serves as a clearinghouse for such information; and submits reports, findings, and recommendations to the president and the Congress, many of which concern rights of immigrants and refugees, the problems generated by the illegal immigration flow, and civil rights guaranteed to all persons, including illegal immigrants, as basic human rights.

U.S. Commission on Immigration Reform

This was a bipartisan commission on immigration reform authorized by the Immigration Act of 1990 that was mandated to review and evaluate implementation and impact of U.S. immigration policy and to transmit reports of its findings and recommendations to the U.S. Congress. It issued its first interim report on September 30, 1994, its second interim report in 1995, and two final reports in 1997: "U.S. Refugee Policy: Taking Leadership" and "Becoming an American: Immigration and Immigration Policy." Like the SCIRP commission report of the 1980s, the recommendations contained in these two reports formed the basis for several legislative proposals aimed at better coping with the illegal immigration problem.

U.S. Department of Agriculture

The department's immigration role is largely supportive of other departments and agencies. Given the importance of illegal immigrants to the agricultural sector, particularly the flow of seasonal agricultural workers, the Department of Agriculture plays a crucial role in supplying information and data on the need for temporary agricultural workers. It assists immigrants through programs such as its Food and Nutrition Service. Although legally and technically it cannot provide such service to illegal aliens, given the poor quality of documentation control, the department undoubtedly does help, if inadvertently, to provide services to illegal as well as legal immigrants.

U.S. Department of Education

The department is the agency of the federal government that establishes policy for, administers, and coordinates most federal assistance to education. The immigration role of the department is to assist, supplement, and complement the efforts of states, the local school systems and other state agencies, the private sector, public and private educational institutions, public and private nonprofit educational research institutions, and community-based organizations to serve the educational needs of immigrants, particularly in the educational aspects of the naturalization process. By federal law and especially as the result of several critical court decisions, education must be provided to the children of illegal immigrants despite the status of the parents. Federal programs that assist local school districts, in providing health services or school lunch programs, for example, are therefore extended to the children of illegal immigrants as well as to those whose parents are in the United States as permanent legal residents.

U.S. Department of Health and Human Services

HHS impacts immigration policy through administration of programs such as the Administration for Children and Families; Health Care Financing Administration; Division of State Legalization Assistance; Financial Support Administration; U.S. Public Health Service Office of Refugee Health; and Office of Planning, Research and Evaluation. Its intergovernmental role is significant in coping with illegal immigration. It is an important actor involved with illegal immigration. Should an expanded guest-worker program with "earned legalization" be enacted, HHS would undoubtedly have a major role in its implementation.

U.S. Department of Homeland Security

Established in 2002 with the merging of the functions of many federal agencies into this newest cabinet-level department of the federal bureaucracy, the DHS is now the principal agency to administer immigration-related policy. Its immigration-related functions are implemented by two bureaus headed by an undersecretary: a Bureau of Border and Transportation Security and a Bureau of Citizenship and Immigration Services.

The department deals with all visa, passport, and citizenship matters; monitors all U.S. borders; ensures mass transit security; and provides airport and seaport security. It supervises the U.S. Border Patrol operations, the principal agency charged with controlling the illegal immigration flow and problem. Its antiterrorism responsibilities also involve monitoring the illegal immigration flow for suspected terrorist and terrorist cells. It has newly established policy related to bioterrorism, as well, that overlaps its illegal immigration control functions.

U.S. Department of Housing and Urban Development

HUD's mission is to promote a decent, safe, sanitary, and suitable home environment for every American. Its impact on immigration matters is primarily through programs designed to assist low-income persons; to create, rehabilitate, and maintain the nation's affordable housing; to enforce fair housing laws; to help the homeless; to spur economic growth in distressed neighborhoods; and to help local communities meet their development needs. Federal law specifically bans the provisions of HUD aid to illegal aliens, but the extensiveness of document fraud in the matter likely results in its providing some benefits to persons who are in fact in the United States illegally.

U.S. Department of Labor

The department oversees all labor-related policy and law, including matters related to temporary labor. Other agencies within the department with immigration-related policy roles are its Office of Federal Contract Compliance Program and its Wage and Hour Division. Its role related to the implementation of IRCA, to date the most directly related federal program attempting to control and decrease illegal immigration, was significant. Strict enforcement of U.S. labor laws may be one of the more effective ways to discourage employers from using the "cheap" labor source of undocumented workers. The department also plays a role in informing Congress or in certifying the need for temporary workers. It plays an important role in H-1A, H-1B, H-2A and H-2B guest-worker programs. Its data collection has helped certify the extent of discrimination against workers who are or were suspected of being undocumented workers.

U.S. Department of State

The Department of State is primarily involved in legal immigration, of course, but its consular affairs division, which issues visas, has a role in illegal immigration mostly related to visa overstayers. It has occasionally been embroiled in scandals in which "sting operations" have led to consular officials who have been caught selling visas and work certification cards (commonly referred to as green cards, although in fact they are now white cards) to illegal aliens, allowing them to enter the country with false documents or work authorizations.

U.S. Equal Employment Opportunity Commission

Housed in the Department of Health and Human Services, the EEOC administers three programs: affirmative employment, special emphasis/diversity, and discrimination complaint. It attempts to promote and ensure equal opportunity for all employees and fosters a culture and environment free from discrimination. It impacts illegal immigration primarily through its antidiscrimination program and monitoring the employer sanctions provisions of current policy.

U.S. Government Accountability Office

The Government Accountability Office is an agency that works for the U.S. Congress and the American people. Congress asks GAO to study the programs and expenditures of the federal government. The GAO is commonly called the investigative arm of Congress or the congressional watchdog. It is independent and nonpartisan. It studies how the federal government spends taxpayer dollars, and advises Congress and the heads of executive departments about ways to make government more effective and responsive. It evaluates federal programs, audits federal expenditures, and issues legal opinions, many of which over recent years have focused on the INS and the DOJ's efforts and programs and now the DHS's programs related to illegal immigration law and policy. Its reports are among the most reliable estimates of the size, nature, and impact of illegal immigration on the economy, on state and local government finances and services, and on society more generally. A number of its reports directly linked to the illegal immigration problem are listed in the print sources that follow.

U.S. House Committee on the Judiciary

This standing committee of the U.S. House of Representatives deals with all bills introduced to the Congress that concern immigration law and policy matters. Its members have become leading voices in efforts to reform policy to deal with illegal immigration and border control and security issues particularly or to stop or block such legislative efforts. Generally speaking, any bill introduced in Congress on immigration matters, pertaining to legal or illegal problems, will be sponsored by one or more members of the Judiciary Committee. Generally speaking, the House Committee has favored a "piecemeal" approach to immigration reform rather than a comprehensive reform measure. It notably favors restricting illegal immigration, the removal of illegal immigrants now in country, and a "tougher, crack down" stance on border control and management.

U.S. Senate Committee on the Judiciary

This standing committee of the U.S. Senate deals with all legislative matters concerning immigration policy and law. Like its counterpart in the House, its members and staff become principal actors in the illegal immigration reform effort. While both the House and the Senate committees are strongly supportive of efforts to beef up the Border Patrol and increase border security at airports and seaports, the Senate Judiciary Subcommittee has been notably more amenable to a guest-worker program than has its counterpart in the House. It has favored and has passed a comprehensive immigration reform bill (S.744) where the House has failed to even bring such a proposal to the floor for a vote.

U.S. Social Security Administration

The SSA's role in immigration policy matters is also supportive of other agencies. Its data bank is used to verify a person's identity and to guard against fraud, waste, abuse, and mismanagement in administration of the benefit programs based upon contributory financing of social insurance programs to ensure that protection was available as a matter of right as contrasted with a public assistance approach whereby only those persons in need would be eligible for benefits, whether natural-born citizens, naturalized citizens, or legal resident aliens who had worked in and contributed to the system. As a system, it collects benefit payments from all workers, including illegal aliens, who pay into the system. The large number of illegal workers who pay into the system yet who do not withdraw benefits from it results in a net benefit estimated to be in the billions of dollars annually. Given the increasing age of the citizen workforce, the illegal aliens, who generally are much younger and therefore work longer and pay into the system for longer periods of time, are significant in filling the gap or shortfall between income and payments of the system. In no small measure, these estimated billions of dollars in contributions from illegal workers help to keep the Social Security system solvent. Although they are only a stopgap factor in the financial strength of the Social Security system, their impact is nonetheless important. If policy designed to cut off that illegal alien flow were to be efficient, the Social Security system would suffer a noticeable decrease of considerable size.

International Organizations
Human Rights Watch
An organization dedicated to protecting human rights of people around the world, it stands with victims and activists to prevent discrimination, to uphold political freedom, and to protect people from inhumane conduct in wartime and bring offenders to justice. It investigates and exposes human rights violations and holds abusers accountable, challenging governments to respect international human rights laws. It is an independent, nongovernmental organization supported by private individuals and foundations worldwide. It plays a critical role in providing information on the exploitation of illegal

immigrant workers in many countries around the world. It has been critical in the past of procedures of the United States dealing with expedited removal and with the way in which claims of "fears of persecution" have been handled with respect to persons applying for refugee status; it strongly criticized the manner in which Haitian refugees were detained and processed.

International Committee of the Red Cross

Established in 1863, the ICRC is an impartial, neutral, independent organization whose humanitarian mission is to protect the lives and dignity of victims of war and internal violence and to provide them with assistance. It also directs and coordinates international relief activities of the Red Crescent Movement in situations of conflict. It endeavors to prevent suffering by promoting and strengthening humanitarian law and universal humanitarian principles. It plays an especially important role in dealing with refugees. In the post-tsunami and post-Katrina natural disasters, it provided relief to survivors without regard to their legal status as residents.

International Immigrants Foundation

Founded in 1973, the IIF has consultative status with the UN Economic and Social Affairs Council, and is associated with the Department of Public Information as a charitable, nongovernmental, nonpolitical, nonprofit, tax-exempt organization. Its stated mission is to help immigrant families and children to achieve their aspirations for a better life in the United States. It does so without regard to and without checking on the legal status of the immigrant. The organization addresses its mission by providing support to promote positive intercultural relations. It supports family reunification goals of legal immigration policy and supports legalization programs as a more effective way to bring illegal immigrants out of the shadow of illegality.

UN Department of Humanitarian Affairs

The UN Department of Humanitarian Affairs, established by the General Assembly, was created to "mobilize and coordinate the collective efforts of the international community, in particular those of the UN system, to meet in a coherent and timely manner the needs of those exposed to human suffering and material destruction in disasters and emergencies. This involves reducing vulnerability, promoting solutions to root causes and facilitating the smooth transition from relief to rehabilitation and development."

UN High Commissioner for Refugees

The UN agency responsible for all matters relating to refugees, it leads and coordinates international action for the worldwide protection of refugees and the resolution of refugee problems. Its primary purpose is to safeguard the rights and well-being of refugees, the right to asylum and safe refuge in another state, and the right to return home voluntarily. It was established by the 1951 UN Convention relating to the Status of Refugees and its 1967 protocol. It seeks to reduce situations of forced displacement by encouraging states and other institutions to create conditions that are conducive to the protection of human rights and the peaceful resolution of disputes, assists in the reintegration of returning refugees into their country of origin, and offers protection and assistance to refugees and others in an impartial manner, on the basis of their need irrespective of their race, religion, political opinion, gender, or legal status in the host nation. It pays particular attention to the needs of children and seeks to promote the equal rights of women and girls.

Domestic Advocacy Agencies and Organizations/NGOs and Nonprofits

American Bar Association

The ABA claims to be the largest voluntary professional association in the world, with more than 400,000 members. It provides law school accreditation, promotes education and information about the law, offers programs of assistance to lawyers and judges in their work, and sponsors initiatives to improve the legal system for the public. Its members defend refugees and persons charged with being in the nation illegally and advocates for legalization programs.

American Civil Liberties Union

Founded in 1920, the ACLU works nationally and with local chapters to protect the civil rights of citizens as guaranteed in the U.S. Constitution. It annually publishes many policy statements, pamphlets, studies, and reports on civil rights issues. Its newsletter, Civil Liberties Alert, is published semiannually. It has been a leading coalition partner in efforts to reform or amend the USA Patriot Act, and to rectify what it determines are civil rights abuses in procedural matters dealing with the process to remove illegal aliens in an expedited manner. It has been an active member of the coalition to promote a guest-worker program and legalization proposals more generally. Its sectors include LGBT rights, Civil Liberties, and Immigration.

American Conservative Union

The American Conservative Union is the oldest and largest of the numerous conservative lobbying organizations. Its purpose is to communicate effectively and advance the goals and principles of conservatism through one multi-issue, umbrella organization. ACU supports capitalism, belief in the doctrine of original intent of the framers of the Constitution, confidence in traditional moral values, and commitment to a strong national defense. Since 1994 it has sponsored "town meetings" to spearhead the conservative response to the health care reform issue, and since then has used the approach to support issues such as military protection and defending the homeland, and against more liberal immigration policy reforms. It rates the members of Congress according to their votes on issues of concern to conservatives; those ratings are used in a host of almanac and reference guides across the political spectrum. Its rating system has been copied by many other organizations. It publishes a significant amount of print, audio, and video material and television documentaries to promote public opinion on its issues of concern. Since 1974 it has hosted the Conservative Political Action Conference, where thousands of conservative activists and leaders from across the country meet to discuss issues and controversies and has become a factor in the Republican Party's presidential nomination process.

American Immigration Control Foundation

The AIC Foundation is a nonprofit research and educational organization whose stated primary goal is to inform Americans about the need for a reasonable immigration policy based on the nation's interests and needs. It is a large publisher of publications on America's immigration crisis. Founded in 1983, it is a prominent national voice for immigration control and is committed to educating citizens on what it views as the disastrous effects of uncontrolled immigration, and most particularly advocates for reform to better control illegal immigration. Besides its lobbying activity for immigration control, AIC conducts public education campaigns to influence public opinion of the issue, campaigning through direct mail, paid advertisements, opinion surveys, and public appearances by its spokesmen on radio and television. Its president is Robert Goldsborough, who also is a columnist with *Middle America News*.

American Immigration Law Foundation

It was founded in 1987 as a tax-exempt, nonprofit educational and service organization, and its stated mission is to promote understanding among the general public of immigration law and policy through education, policy analysis, and support to litigators. It has three core program areas: the Legal Action Center, the Public Education Program, and an Exchange Visitor Program.

American Immigration Lawyers Association

The American Immigration Lawyers Association is the national association of immigration lawyers established to promote justice, advocate for fair and reasonable immigration law and policy, advance the quality of immigration and nationality law and practice, and enhance the professional development of its members. Its members defend individuals charged with being in the United States illegally and in deportation hearings. It advocates against what it considers unfair or anti–civil liberty provisions in immigration law, particularly the USA Patriot Act and the Department of Homeland Security Act.

American Library Association

ALA is the oldest and largest library association in the world, with more than 64,000 members. Its stated mission is to promote the highest quality library and information service and public access to information. ALA offers professional services and publications to members and nonmembers. It entered the fray by joining in coalition with other organizations attempting to amend the USA Patriot Act.

American Refugee Committee International Headquarters USA

Begun in 1978, the ARC's stated mission is to work for the survival, health, and well-being of refugees, displaced persons, and those at risk, and it seeks to enable them to rebuild productive lives of dignity and purpose, striving always to respect the values of those served. ARC is an international, nonprofit, and nonsectarian organization that has provided multisector humanitarian assistance and training to millions of beneficiaries for more than 20 years.

Americans against Illegal Immigration

It claims to be the largest archive about illegal immigration and illegal immigrants, and the history of illegal immigration. It advocates strict enforcement of illegal immigration law.

Americans for Legal Immigration

Founded by William Gheen, it is a social media outreach for the Americans against Illegal Immigration.

Border Action Network

A human rights organization begun in 1999 and headquartered in Tucson, Arizona, it claims as its mission to establish safety, equity, dignity, understanding, and respect across cultures in border and immigrant communities.

Business Roundtable

The Business Roundtable is the association of chief executive officers of leading U.S. corporations with a combined workforce of more than 10 million employees in the United States. It is committed to advocating public policies that foster vigorous economic growth, a dynamic global economy, and a well-trained and productive U.S. workforce essential for future competitiveness. It is selective in the issues it studies; a principal criterion is the impact the problem will have on the economic well-being of the nation. Working in task forces on specific issues, it directs research, supervises the preparation of position papers, recommends policy, and lobbies Congress and the administration on selected issues. It supports proposals to establish an expanded guest-worker program, including "earned legalization" provisions with the proposed comprehensive immigration reform measures in the House and Senate committees.

California Coalition for Immigration Reform

CCIR is a Huntington Beach, California–based political advocacy group founded by Barbara Coe in 1994 primarily to fight against Proposition 187. Coe died in 2013. It has since joined in the coalition of groups forming what has become known as the Dreamer network.

Catholic Charities USA

Catholic Charities USA is a membership organization based in Alexandria, Virginia. It provides leadership, technical assistance, training, and other resources to enable local agencies to better devote their own resources to serving their communities. It promotes innovative strategies that address human needs and social injustices. It advocates policies that aim to reduce poverty, improve the lives of children and families, and strengthen communities. One of its major service programs involves refugee and immigration assistance. It has favored and advocated for enactment of comprehensive immigration reform.

Center for American Progress

Founded in 2003 by John Podesta, it is a progressive public policy research and advocacy think tank–type organization based in Washington, D.C. It advocates for comprehensive immigration reform.

Center for Democracy and Technology

The Center for Democracy and Technology works to promote democratic values and constitutional liberties in the digital age. With expertise in law, technology, and policy, the CDT seeks practical solutions to enhance free expression and privacy in global communications technologies. CDT states that it is dedicated to building a consensus among all parties interested in the future of the Internet and other new communications media. It has become a lobbying organization on the issue and has joined in coalition with other organizations concerned with civil liberty issues around the DHS, the USA Patriot Act, and Patriot Act II.

Center for Human Rights and Constitutional Law

The CHRCL is the organization that helps homeless 12- to 17-year-old inner-city youth to find an alternative to life on the streets through its Homeless Youth Project. It provides case management, job assistance, individual counseling, placement assistance, school placement, legal and medical referrals, life skills training, and aftercare. Of particular importance to immigrants, it assists in ESL classes, tutoring, clerical, recreation, outdoor activities, art, gardening, and a variety of other assignments. It does so without regard to the legal status of the immigrant being so served.

Center for the Applied Study of Prejudice and Ethnoviolence

The center examines responses to violence and intimidation based on prejudice—racial, ethnic, and so on. It issues a quarterly newsletter, *Forum*, as well as periodic reports and study papers. It is critical of efforts to control illegal immigration that it sees as often resulting from racial and ethnic prejudice against "undesirable" aliens.

Center for the Study of Hate Crimes and Extremism

A nonpartisan, domestic research and policy center that examines bigotry on both the regional and national levels, methods used to advocate extremism, and the use of terrorism to deny civil or human rights to people on the basis of race, ethnicity, religion, gender, sexual orientation, disability, or other relevant status characteristic. It sponsors public conferences, collaborates with international news media, and maintains an Internet site with information about and in cooperation with government organizations, human relations organizations, nonprofit organizations, and law enforcement.

Central American Resource Center

The CARC is a nonprofit immigration and human rights organization serving the refugee community on Long Island and throughout the southern portion of the state of New York. Founded in 1983, it works to protect the civil rights of immigrants, increase understanding between the native-born and newcomer communities, and raise awareness of the interaction of human rights disasters and immigration. It provides its services to persons without regard to their legal status.

Church World Service

Founded in 1946, the CWS is the relief, development, and refugee assistance ministry of 36 Protestant, Orthodox, and Anglican denominations in the United States. Working with indigenous organizations in more than 80 countries, it works worldwide to meet human needs and to foster self-reliance for all whose way is hard. One of its major programs is Immigration and Refugee Services. It advocates for more liberalized immigration policy and provides relief assistance to individuals without regard to their legal status. It supports "sanctuary" programs and provides emergency medical assistance to illegal immigrants. Critics allege that its sanctuary programs in fact promote and encourage illegal immigration. It works in coalition with other organizations to reform immigration law in a more fair and humanitarian way.

Coalition for Humane Immigrant Rights of Los Angeles

Founded in 1986 to lobby over IRCA, it is now an American political advocacy organization promoting immigrant rights and humane treatment of unauthorized immigrants. It helped form a national coalition of groups currently promoting enactment of the Dream Act, and supporting President Obama's executive actions regarding DACA and DAPA.

Colorado Alliance for Immigration Reform

This organization, largely a Web site to organize a coalition of groups and persons concerned about illegal immigration, is a nonprofit, Colorado-based organization that developed in response to the growing number of immigrants, and particularly illegal immigrants, who have dispersed to states beyond the traditional "gateway states." It is exemplary of similar coalitions that have sprung up in many states newly experiencing significant immigration influxes. CAIR promotes a proactive national policy to stabilize the population and conserve natural resources by insisting that Congress limit legal immigration (not to exceed 100,000 per year) and to crack down firmly on illegal immigration. It considers that both major political parties are supporting an "open borders" policy, which it adamantly opposes. It organizes protests and anti-immigration rallies focusing on the negative impacts of illegal immigration. It has been a leading supporter of former Colorado congressman Tom Tancredo. It sponsors "Defend Colorado Now"—a ballot initiative that would amend Colorado's constitution to require that persons who are trying to access certain public services be required to show that they are present in the United States legally—a Colorado version of California's Proposition 187. It advocates an immigration moratorium, no more amnesty programs, strict enforcement of immigration laws both at the borders and in the interior, enhanced employer sanctions, and, through the ballot-initiative process, ending government-sponsored benefits and entitlements for illegal immigrants. It promotes a U.S. constitutional amendment that would deny citizenship to children of illegal immigrants born in the United States. It has launched educational billboard campaigns and, most recently, the Colorado Alliance News, an all-volunteer news service, to promote its views on the immigration issue. Among its more notable directors is former Colorado governor Richard Lamm.

The Dream Is Now

http://www.thedreamisnow.org/
A Web site for the Dreamer movement.

Episcopal Migration Ministries

The EMM serves as the organizational arm of the Episcopal Church in all matters related to immigration and migration relief and assistance, and works in close consultation and coalition with other churches in pursuing humanitarian immigration policy and providing assistance and even sanctuary to persons accused of or suspected of being in the United States illegally.

Essential Worker Immigration Coalition

Supported by the U.S. Chamber of Commerce, the EWIC is a coalition of business groups, trade associations, and other organizations nationwide and across the industrial spectrum concerned about the shortage of both skilled and less skilled ("essential worker") labor. It lobbies the administration and the Congress to push forward immigration reform issues. It supports policies that facilitate the employment of essential workers by U.S. companies and organizations—that is, an expanded guest-worker program. It advocates reforming U.S. immigration policy to facilitate a sustainable workforce for the national economy while ensuring national security and prosperity.

Ethiopian Community Development Council

The ECDC's stated mission is to resettle refugees; promote cultural, educational, and socioeconomic development in the refugee and immigrant community in the United States; and conduct humanitarian and development programs in the Horn of Africa. It provides programs and services to assist newcomers to the United States to become productive members of their community; conducts outreach and educational activities to increase public awareness of refugee and immigrant issues; promotes civic participation by newcomers in the decision-making processes of local, state, and national levels; provides cross-cultural training to service providers; and assists in educational development and cultural preservation of the Ethiopian community. It does so without regard to the legal status of the immigrant or refugee being served.

Federal Immigration Reform and Enforcement Coalition

Largely a Web site approach to coalition building, FIRE is an offshoot of AIC. It claims to be a nationwide coalition of individuals and groups dedicated to influencing federal, state, and local laws to stop the flood of immigration and to promote policies to limit and control legal immigration. It pushes government to vigorous enforcement of immigration laws, the repatriation of illegal immigrants, and the removal of all incentives for individuals to illegally cross the borders through the enforcement and strengthening of existing laws penalizing those who employ or harbor illegal immigrants, and to inform public opinion as to the consequences of illegal immigration. It describes itself as a nonpartisan, direct-action, public education, and political campaigning coalition.

Federation for American Immigration Reform

Founded in 1979 by John Tanton, FAIR is a national, nonpartisan, nonprofit, public-interest membership organization of concerned citizens who share a common belief that the unforeseen mass immigration that has occurred largely since 1980 should be curtailed. It advocates a moratorium on all immigration except for spouses and minor children of U.S. citizens, and a limited number of refugees. In its view, a workable immigration policy is one that allows time to regain control of the U.S. borders and reduce overall levels of immigration to more traditional levels of about 300,000 a year. It believes that the United States can and must have an immigration policy that is nondiscriminatory while at the same time is designed to serve the social, economic, and environmental needs of the United States.

Free Congress Foundation

Free Congress is a politically conservative, culturally conservative think tank that is more of an advocacy organization that promotes the "Culture War" and advocates returning the nation and its policies to the traditional, Judeo-Christian, Western cultural heritage by stopping what it calls the long slide into the moral and cultural decay of "political correctness." It is strenuously opposed to illegal immigration and to any amnesty or legalization policy, favors strict enforcement of immigration law and English-only policy, and rejects multiculturalism.

Freedom Works

Founded in 1984, Freedom Works has full-time staffed offices in 10 states. It claims to be a coalition of some 700,000 volunteers nationwide. The organization is chaired by former U.S. House majority leader Dick Armey. It fights for lower taxes, less government, and more freedom. It has strongly backed a private business–based approach to a guest-worker program developed by the Krieble Foundation. It has developed into a serious force in the Republican Party's presidential nomination process, tilting such to the more extreme right of the political spectrum.

Hebrew Immigrant Aid Society

Founded in 1881, HIAS has assisted more than 4.5 million people in their quest for freedom, including the million Jewish refugees it helped to migrate to Israel and the thousands it helped resettle in Canada, Latin America, Australia, New Zealand, and elsewhere. As the oldest international migration and refugee resettlement agency in the United States, it played a major role in the rescue and relocation of Jewish survivors of the Holocaust and Jews from Morocco, Ethiopia, Egypt, and the communist countries of Eastern Europe. It advocates on behalf of refugees and migrants on the international, national, and community levels. It provides its services without regard to the legal status of the immigrant being assisted. It works in coalition with other church organizations of immigrant/refugee assistance and has lobbied on behalf of legislation aimed at liberal immigration reform in favor of legalization and guest-worker programs.

Heritage Foundation

The Heritage Foundation was founded in 1973 as a research and educational institute—one of the early think tanks. Its stated mission is to formulate and propose conservative public policies that are based upon the principles of free enterprise, limited government, individual freedom, traditional American values, and a strong national defense. On the illegal immigration issue, it promotes immigration reform that lessens total legal immigration levels, strengthens the enforcement of laws against illegal immigration, opposes amnesty, and increases border control to better secure the homeland against international terrorism. Since former senator Jim DeMint was selected to lead the foundation, it has shifted away from research and education and now is a more conservative advocacy group, lobbying and fund-raising for electoral politics on the right and often backing "Tea Party" challengers to establishment Republicans.

Human Rights Watch

Based in New York City, and cofounded by Aryeh Neier, Jeri Laber, and Robert Bernstein in 1978, it monitors countries for human rights violations. It received the UN Prize in the Field of Human Rights in 2008, and the Peabody Award in 2011.

Humane Borders

The mission statement of Humane Borders describes itself as an organization of people motivated by faith and committed to work to create a just and humane border environment. Its members respond with humanitarian assistance to those risking their lives and safety crossing the U.S. border with Mexico. It encourages the creation of public policies toward a humane, nonmilitarized border with legalized work opportunities for migrants in the United States and legitimate economic opportunities in migrants' countries of origin. It favors legalization and guest-worker programs. It lobbies and advocates in coalition with other organizations promoting more liberalized immigration policy.

League of United Latin American Citizens

LULAC is organized to promote the democratic principles of individual, political, and religious freedom, and the right to equal social and economic opportunities, and works in the cooperative endeavor toward the development of a U.S. society wherein the cultural resources, integrity, and dignity of every individual and group constitute basic assets of the American way of life. Among its goals are to be a service organization to actively promote and establish cooperative relations with civic and governmental institutions and agencies in the field of public service, to uphold the rights guaranteed to every individual by state and national laws, to ensure justice and equal treatment under those laws, and to oppose any infringement upon the constitutional political rights of an individual to vote and or be voted upon at local, state, and national levels. It brought the court case that overturned as unconstitutional many of the provisions of California's Proposition 187. It works in coalition with other organizations to oppose the USA Patriot Act and insists on amending some of its more egregious civil rights infringements. It favors legalization and a guest-worker program such as that contained in the Senate-passed (S.744) comprehensive immigration reform bill.

Lutheran Immigration and Refugee Service

The LIRS states as its mission to welcome the stranger, bringing new hope and new life through ministries and justice. It mobilizes action on behalf of uprooted people and sees that they receive fair and equal treatment, regardless of national origin, race, religion, culture, or legal status. It advocates for just and humane solutions to migration crises and their root causes, both national and international; works to turn solutions into reality; and encourages citizens to take part in shaping just and fair public policies, practices, and laws. It works in coalition with other mostly church-based immigration and refugee service organizations and lobbies to enact immigration reform that is more liberal. It favors legalization and a guest-worker provision. Some of the organization's member churches have supported the sanctuary movement.

Major Cities Chiefs of Police Association

An organization of chiefs of police of major American cities that formed in 1949, currently it meets three times per year and advocates for issues of concern to city police. It opposes the mandated use of local police to enforce federal immigration law. It supported President Obama's DACA and DAPA executive actions. Darrel Stephens is the association's executive director. In 2014, Chief Thomas Manger, the Montgomery County police chief, was elected to lead the association.

Mexican American Legal Defense Fund

Founded in 1968 in San Antonio, Texas, by Mario Obledo, and headquartered in Los Angeles, California, MALDEF is a leading nonprofit Latino litigation, advocacy, and educational outreach institution whose stated mission is to foster sound public policies, laws, and programs to safeguard the civil rights of the more than 40 million Latinos living in the United States and to empower the Latino community to fully participate in society. It advocates in coalition with other organizations to promote legalization, favors a guest-worker program, and is highly critical of what it holds are the civil rights infringements of the Patriot Act. It strongly opposed state initiatives like California's Proposition 187, and Arizona's anti-illegal immigrant law, and the congressional acts of 1996, which it held were racist, anti-Hispanic, and anti-immigrant. It has legally opposed English-only laws and initiatives as well. Its major sector is on civil liberties of Mexican Americans.

Minutemen

Its founder and president is Jim Gilchrist. It is an anti-immigrant organization that advocates reduced legal immigration, recommends stopping illegal immigration by strict border control, and organizes groups of members to voluntarily patrol the border areas "in support of the border patrol."

Minuteman Colorado

It is public policy and issues advocacy organization that aggressively addresses what it describes as the intensifying assaults that the American republic continues to endure.

Based in Denver, with Mike Zimmerle serving as its state director, it is part of the Minuteman Project alliance of "volunteer-patrol" groups.

Mothers against Illegal Aliens

Founded in 2006 by activist Michelle Dellacroce, MALA aims to "show every mother in American what is going on in our streets." It is a Phoenix-based, ultra right-wing organization that is particularly "anti-anchor babies." It joined in the Minuteman Civil Defense Corps rally in Arizona.

National Association for the Advancement of Colored People

Headquartered in Baltimore and founded by Archibald Grimlee, Henry Moskowitz, Ida B. Wells, and Lilliam Wald in 1909, NAACP is the oldest and best-known black civil rights advocacy organization. Its major sectors include antiracism and civil and political rights. It has formed coalitions with immigrant rights groups and lobbies for comprehensive, proimmigration reform.

National Conference of Catholic Bishops, Migration and Refugee Services, Office of Migration Policy and Public Affairs

Founded in 1966 and headquartered in Washington, D.C., it is the political advocacy arm of the Conference of Bishops and supports comprehensive immigration reform and immigrant rights.

National Council of La Raza

The NCLR is a private, nonprofit, nonpartisan, tax-exempt organization established in 1968 to reduce poverty and discrimination, and improve life opportunities for Hispanic Americans,

assisting the development of Hispanic community-based organizations in urban and rural areas nationwide. It conducts
applied research, policy analysis, and advocacy, providing a
Hispanic perspective on issues such as education, immigration,
housing, health, employment and training, and civil rights
enforcement, to increase policy maker and public understanding of Hispanic needs, and to encourage the adoption of programs and policies that equitably serve Hispanics.

Its Policy Analysis Center is a prominent Hispanic think
tank serving as a voice for Hispanic Americans in Washington,
D.C. It works in coalition with other Latino organizations and
lobby efforts to reform immigration law in a more humane
way. In 2014, it elected Janet Murguia as its president.

National Federation of Independent Business

The NFIB is the largest advocacy organization representing small and independent businesses in Washington, D.C.,
and all 50 state capitals. Its Education Foundation promotes
the importance of free enterprise and entrepreneurship. Its
Research Foundation researches policy-related small business
problems and affects public policy debate by making its findings widely available. Its Legal Foundation fights for small
businesses in the courts and seeks to educate small employers
on legal issues. It favors the guest-worker proposals of several
bills before the Congress and "earned legalization" provisions.

National Immigration Forum

Founded in 1982, NIF's stated mission is "to embrace and
uphold America's tradition as a nation of immigrants. The
Forum advocates and builds public support for public policies
that welcome immigrants and refugees and that are fair and
supportive to newcomers in our country." The forum works to
unite families torn apart by what it characterizes as unreason-
able and arbitrary restrictions. It advocates to secure fair treatment of refugees who have fled persecution; legalize the status
of hardworking immigrants caught in legal limbo; promote

citizenship as a pathway to full political participation (political incorporation); secure equitable access to social protections; and protect immigrants' fundamental constitutional rights, no matter their legal or undocumented status. It advocates to promote immigration policies that strengthen the U.S. economy by working with a diverse coalition of allies—immigrant, ethnic, religious, civil rights, labor, business groups, state and local governments, and other organizations—to forge and promote a new vision of immigration policy that is consistent with global realities, fosters economic growth, attracts needed workers to the United States, and protects the rights of workers and families. It works to help newcomers settle into their communities; to help them climb the socioeconomic ladder of U.S. society; to help localities weave immigrants into the fabric of community life; and to build bonds of mutual understanding between residents and newcomers. It supports President Obama's DACA and DAPA executive actions.

National Immigration Law Center

The National Immigration Law Center is a national support center whose mission is to protect and promote the rights and opportunities of low-income immigrants and their family members. Its staff specializes in immigration law and immigrant welfare. It conducts policy analysis and impact litigation and provides publications, technical services, and training to a broad constituency of legal aid agencies, community groups, and pro bono attorneys. It has offices in Los Angeles, Oakland, and Washington, D.C., and operates the Sacramento policy office for the California Immigrant Welfare Collaborative. It lobbies and works in coalition with other organizations favoring legalization and similar approaches to the illegal immigration problem.

National League of Cities

It serves as the national advocate for towns, villages, and more than 19,000 cities in the 49 states of the United States. It generally opposes any immigration measure that would involve unfunded mandates, especially on local police.

National Network for Immigrant and Refugee Rights

The NNIRR is a national organization composed of local coalitions and immigrant, refugee, community, religious, civil rights, and labor organizations and activists. It is a forum to share information and analysis, educate communities and the general public, and develop and coordinate plans of action on important immigrant and refugee issues. It promotes just immigration and refugee policy in the United States. It defends expanding the rights of all immigrants/refugees, regardless of their status. It seeks the enfranchisement of all immigrant and refugee in the United States through organizing and advocating for their full labor, environmental, civil, and human rights. It emphasizes the change in global, political, and economic structures exacerbating regional, national, and international patterns of migration, and builds support and cooperation to strengthen the rights, welfare, and safety of migrants.

National Organization for European American Rights

Founded in 2000, and led by David Duke, Grand Wizard of the Ku Klux Klan, NO FEAR is a loose alliance of white nationalist and white supremacist groups headquartered in Mandeville, Louisiana. It adamantly opposes any legalization provision, which it considers amnesty. It supports strict border control, reduced legal immigration, and the removal of all illegal immigrants.

New York Association for New Americans

The NYANA works to help those new to the United States, and those who have been in the country for some time, to fashion a roadmap for accomplishing their goals and dreams and to assist refugees and immigrants, their families, their sponsors, and companies that employ them, other institutions that serve them, and the communities in which they live. It serves immigrants without regard to their legal status.

No More Deaths

No More Deaths is a coalition of diverse individuals, faith communities, and human rights organizers who work for justice in the United States by mobilizing a response to the escalating numbers of deaths among illegal immigrants crossing the borders in the U.S. Southwest. The coalition has established a binational network of immigrant-friendly organizations and people in the Southwest and in northern Mexico who participate in interventions designed to stop migrant deaths, espousing the principle that humanitarian aid is never a crime. It establishes movable desert camps, supports the maintenance of water stations, and regularly launches what it terms "good Samaritan patrols" that search the desert for migrants at risk. A nonprofit organization, it advocates on behalf of migrant-related issues, including promoting public demonstrations such as days of fast in remembrance of the lives claimed along the borders and protesting the policies that cause those deaths. Several of its volunteers have been arrested for giving aid to illegal aliens, and the coalition protests to call on government to drop the charges against its members. It organizes clergy and others to contact elected officials, particularly members of Congress, in an attempt to influence immigration reform.

NumbersUSA

NumbersUSA is a nonprofit, nonpartisan, public-policy advocacy organization that seeks an environmentally sustainable and economically just society that protects individual liberties by advocating policies to stop mass illegal immigration. Its stated goals are to examine numerical levels of annual legal and illegal immigration, and to educate the public about the immigration-reduction recommendations from two national commissions of the 1990s: the 1995 Bipartisan U.S.

Commission on Immigration Reform (the Barbara Jordan Commission) and the 1996 President's Council on Sustainable Development. It specifically advocates the elimination of chain migration and of the visa lottery. It views the elimination of those two immigration categories as the best way to protect vulnerable U.S. workers and their families. It promotes itself as proenvironment, proworker, proliberty, and proimmigrant. Its founders are John Tanton and Roy Beck. It networks with Americans of all races and includes many immigrants and their spouses, children, and parents. It advocates for illegal immigration reform and against any guest-worker type of program. It seeks to reduce overall legal immigration and advocates the reduction and eventual elimination of all illegal immigration. It advocates stricter border control measures, such as expansion of the Border Patrol and of the fences along the southern border.

Office of Migration and Refugee Services, U.S. Conference of Catholic Bishops

Since the turn of the 20th century, the Catholic Church in the United States has engaged in the resettlement of refugees, advocating on behalf of immigrants and people on the move, and providing pastoral care and services to newcomers from all over the world. Since 1970 alone it has assisted in resettlement of more than 1 million refugees. The MRS is committed to its resettlement, pastoral care, and advocacy roles on behalf of immigrants, migrants, and refugees. It assists the bishops in the development and advocacy of policy positions at the national and international levels, which address the needs and conditions of immigrants, refugees, and other people on the move. It works with the federal government and with local churches in resettling refugees admitted to the United States into caring and supportive communities. It serves its clientele without regard to their legal status and has worked in coalition with other church organizations in the sanctuary movement and for passage of comprehensive immigration reform.

Rights for All People

Rights for All People is a recently formed coalition to organize immigrants and their allies to achieve justice, dignity, and human rights for immigrants in Colorado. It was formed in response to the passage of anti-immigrant, anti–civil rights initiatives, such as Proposition 187 in California and "Defend Colorado Now." Committed to the struggle for the rights of immigrants, the coalition espouses that the protection of immigrant rights is directly connected to preserving the rights of all people. Its primary strategy is to promote those rights by organizing with immigrants in a broad-based advocacy coalition. It sponsors direct action protests and marshals public opinion against specific legislation—such as the CLEAR Act. It counters by promoting legislation that would allow driver's licenses for undocumented immigrants (backing Colorado senate bill SB67 in 2002).

The Social Contract Press

Another organization founded by John Tanton, it is an American publisher favoring reduction of U.S. legal immigration and advocated reforms to stop illegal immigration.

Southern Poverty Law Center

A civil rights advocacy organization headquartered in Montgomery, Alabama, it was founded in 1971 by Joe Levin, Julian Bond, and Morris Dees. Its sectors are: antipoverty, antifascism, and fund-raising, and it is an advocate for comprehensive immigration reform. Its current president is J. Richard Cohen.

The Stein Report

Founded by Marc Stein, a project of the Federation for American Immigration Reform, it is the social media, Web-based outlet for FAIR.

Tolstoy Foundation

The foundation describes itself as an organization that for more than a half-century has been committed to its founder,

Alexandra Tolstoy, whose empathy for the plight of peoples of her homeland and abhorrence of all forms of oppression and human suffering remain at the heart of the foundation's charitable activities today. Its stated mission is to promote respect for human dignity, freedom of choice, building of self-reliance through education and practical training, and assistance and relief to the distressed, children, the aged, the sick, and the forgotten at home and abroad. It is dedicated to enhancing the quality of life of its elderly population, providing a home and congenial surroundings to its residents, and caring for their physical, spiritual, and intellectual needs. It seeks to preserve the cultural traditions, the heritage, and the resources of the Russian diaspora, and now has come full circle from its history of assisting new immigrants in their assimilation process to helping the peoples of Russia and the former Soviet Union acquire the knowledge and skills necessary to achieve self-reliance in their own homeland.

United We Dream

United We Dream began in 2005, organized to fight for the dignity and fair treatment of immigrant youth regardless of legal status. The largest immigrant-youth led organization in the United States, it is a voice for a nonpartisan network of 55 affiliated organizations with over 100,000 immigrant youth and their allies in 26 states with its headquarters in Washington, D.C. It is especially noted for fighting for the Deferred Action programs of DACA and DAPA

U.S. Chamber of Commerce

Constituting the largest umbrella organization for business in the United States, the U.S. Chamber represents more than 3 million businesses organized into 2,800 state and local chambers and 830 business associations. Its business members are from all sizes and sectors of the economy—from Fortune 500 companies to small, one-person operations. Its staff consists of lobbyists, policy specialists, and lawyers who promote an economic, political, and social system based on individual incentive, initiative, opportunity, and responsibility. The U.S. Chamber founded the Americans for Better Borders coalition. Believing that the borders can and should be a line of defense against international terrorists but also allowing for legitimate commerce and travel, the coalition promotes the efficient allocation of technology, personnel, and infrastructure resources to achieve those goals. The coalition unites regional business organizations, companies, and national trade associations in all sectors of the economy to ensure the efficient flow of exports and tourism across the borders while addressing national security concerns. The chamber promoted a workable compromise on the Illegal Immigration Reform and Immigrant Responsibility Act of 1996. The Americans for Better Borders Coalition was founded in 1998. It lobbied the Congress on the establishment of the DHS. It currently endorses and promotes passage of the Senate proposal with its more comprehensive immigration reform provisions and an extensive guest-worker program plan that the U.S. Chamber considers essential to any effective immigration reform.

U.S. Committee for Refugees

USCR describes its mission as defending the rights of all uprooted people regardless of their nationality, race, religion, ideology, or social group. It believes that once the consciences of men and women are aroused, great deeds can be accomplished. It bases its work on the following principles: (1) refugees have basic human rights, and no person with a well-founded fear of persecution should be forcibly returned to his or her homeland; (2) asylum seekers have the right to a fair and impartial hearing to determine their refugee status; and (3) all uprooted victims of human conflict, regardless of whether they cross a border, have the right to humane treatment as well as adequate protection and assistance.

V-DARE

V-DARE, the Virginia-based outlet for its leader Peter Brimelow, begun in 1999. It describes itself as a national non-profit educational organization dedicated to preserving the historical unity of Americans into the 21st century. It monitors development on a broad range of economic, domestic, defense, and foreign policy issues related to the American nation-state, which it maintains can survive as the political expression of a distinct American people, in the face of emerging threats of mass immigration, multiculturalism, multilingualism, and affirmative action. It filed an amicus brief in *Hamdi v. Rumsfeld*, challenging the assumption an enemy combatant Saudi citizen is a U.S. citizen solely because he was a native-born son of a temporary worker.

It filed another amicus brief in *The Barton Case*, which overturned Mrs. Barton's conviction and 45-day jail sentence for "expressing her opinion that immigrants should learn English." It also filed an amicus brief in *Alexander v. Sandoval*, wherein the U.S. Supreme Court upheld Alabama's law, passed by citizen referendum, requiring applications for driver's licenses be made in English only.

Voices of Citizens Together/American Patrol

America Patrol is West Texas's largest and most experienced aerial patrol service. Its purpose is to "fight for U.S. sovereignty" by demanding apprehensions and the removal of all illegal immigrants and the restoration of border security

Immigration Research Centers and Think Tanks

American Assembly

The assembly's major objectives are to focus attention and stimulate information on a range of critical U.S. policy topics, both domestic and international; to provide government officials, community and civic leadership, and the general public with factual background information and the range of policy options on a given issue; and to facilitate communications among decision makers and the public and private sectors.

Bell Policy Center

The Bell Policy Center is a research center located in Colorado and committed to making Colorado a state of opportunity for all. Its stated goal is to reinvigorate the debate on issues affecting the well-being of Coloradoans and to promote policies that open gateways to opportunity. It conducts nonpartisan research on issues of concern, shares its research with policy makers, uses its staff and a network of supporters and consultants to inform public opinion and to encourage responsible public dialogue and debate, and makes policy recommendations and advocates for changes that will increase opportunities for individuals and families. It has recently issued study briefs on the impact of immigration on Colorado as well as information sheets on immigration bills before the state legislature and the U.S. Congress. It favors a guest-worker program and maintains that immigration drives economic growth in the nation as a whole and in Colorado. Its recent study found that wages and employment of native-born workers were not significantly affected by immigration, that 90 percent of undocumented immigrant men are working, and that immigration adds about $10 billion to the U.S. economy annually.

Brookings Institution, Center on Urban and Metropolitan Policy

Founded in 1916 by Peter Assoy, Robert Rubin, and Robert Brookings, the Brookings Institution is an independent, nonpartisan organization devoted to research, analysis, education, and publication focused on public policy issues in the areas of economics, foreign policy, and governance. Its stated goal is to improve the performance of U.S. institutions and the quality of public policy by using social science to analyze emerging issues and to offer practical approaches to those issues in language aimed at the general public. It does so through three research programs—Economic Studies, Foreign Policy Studies, and Governance Studies—as well as through the Center for Public Policy Education and the Brookings Institution Press, which publishes about 50 books a year. Its research is conducted to inform the public debate, not to advocate or advance a political agenda. It began in 1927. It is financed largely by endowment and through support by philanthropic foundations, corporations, and private individuals. It is consistently ranked as the most influential, most quoted, and most trusted think tank.

Cato Institute

The Cato Institute was founded in 1977 as a public policy research foundation headquartered in Washington, D.C. Named for *Cato's Letters*, a series of libertarian pamphlets that helped lay the philosophical foundation of the American Revolution, the institute describes its mission as seeking to broaden the parameters of public policy debate to allow consideration of the traditional American principles of limited government, individual liberty, free markets, and peace. To pursue that goal, the institute strives to achieve greater involvement of the intelligent, concerned lay public in questions of policy and the proper role of government. It is a nonprofit, tax-exempt educational foundation.

Center for Equal Opportunity

The center is a think tank devoted to the promotion of color-blind equal opportunity and racial harmony. It seeks to counter what it holds to be the divisive impact of race-conscious public policies. It focuses on three issues in particular: racial preferences, immigration and assimilation, and multicultural education. The center promotes the assimilation of legal immigrants into society and conducts research on their economic and social impact on the United States. It advocates against bilingual education, holding that such programs promote a racial ideology that risks balkanization of a multiracial society. It was founded and is headed by Linda Chavez.

Center for Immigration Studies

The CIS is an independent, nonpartisan, nonprofit research organization founded in 1985. It is the nation's only think tank devoted exclusively to research and policy analysis of the economic, social, demographic, fiscal, and other impacts of immigration on the United States. Its stated mission is to expand the base of knowledge and understanding of the need for an immigration policy that gives first concern to the broad national interest. It is animated by a proimmigrant, low-immigration vision that seeks fewer immigrants but a warmer welcome for those admitted. The center also publishes *Immigration Review.* It is led by Mark Kirkorian.

Center for Migration Studies

The CMS of New York was founded in 1964. It is one of the premier institutes for migration studies in the United States. Its stated mission is to facilitate the study of sociodemographic, historical, economic, political, legislative, and pastoral aspects of human migration and refugee movements. In 1969 it was incorporated as an educational nonprofit institute. It brings an independent perspective to the interdisciplinary study of international migration and refugees without the institutional constraints of government analysts and special interest groups, or the profit considerations of private research firms. It claims to be the only institute in the United States devoted exclusively to understanding and educating the public on the causes and consequences of human mobility at both origin and destination counties. It generates and facilitates the dissemination of new knowledge and the fostering of effective policies. It publishes the leading scholarly journal in the field, the *International Migration Review.*

Immigration History Research Center

Founded in 1965, the Immigration History Research Center is an international resource on American immigration and ethnic history. The IHRC collects, preserves, and makes available archival and published resources documenting immigration and ethnicity on a national scope and is particularly rich for ethnic groups that originated in Eastern, Central, and Southern Europe and the Near East. It sponsors academic programs and publishes bibliographic and scholarly works.

Manhattan Institute

The Manhattan Institute claims to have been an important force shaping American political culture for more than 25 years. It supports and publishes research on a host of challenging public policy issues, including welfare, crime, the legal system, urban life, education, and immigration—both legal and illegal. It publishes or supports the research for books, does book reviews and interviews, presents public speeches by its fellows, writes op-ed pieces for major public news outlets, and publishes the quarterly *City Journal*. It sponsors forums and conferences devoted to its research issues.

Migration Policy Institute

MPI is an independent, nonpartisan, nonprofit think tank in Washington, D.C., dedicated to the study of the movement of people worldwide. It provides analysis, development, and evaluation of migration and refugee policies at the local, national, and international levels. It aims to meet the rising demand for pragmatic and thoughtful responses to the challenges and opportunities that large-scale migration, whether voluntary or forced, presents to communities and institutions in an increasingly integrated world. Founded in 2001 by Kathleen Newland and Demetrios G. Papademetriou, MPI grew out of the International Migration Policy Program at the Carnegie Endowment for International Peace.

National Immigration Forum

The purpose of the NIF is to embrace and uphold America's tradition as a nation of immigrants. The forum advocates and builds public support for public policies that welcome immigrants and refugees and that are fair and supportive to newcomers in the United States.

National Network for Immigrant and Refugee Rights

A national organization composed of local coalitions and immigrant, refugee, community, religious, civil rights, and labor organizations and activists, the network serves as a forum to share information and analysis, to educate communities and the general public, and to develop and coordinate plans of action on important immigrant and refugee issues. It works to promote a just immigration and refugee policy in the United States and to defend and expand the rights of all immigrants and refugees, regardless of immigrant status, advocating for their full labor, environmental, civil, and human rights.

Pew Hispanic Center

Founded in 2001, the PHC is a nonpartisan research organization supported by the Pew Charitable Trusts. Its mission is to improve understanding of the U.S. Hispanic population and to chronicle Latinos' growing impact on the entire nation. Timeliness, relevance, and scientific rigor characterize its work. It does not advocate for or take positions on policy issues. Demography, immigration, and remittances are its major research foci on illegal immigration.

Prejudice Institute

The Prejudice Institute describes itself as a resource for activists, lawyers, and social scientists. It is devoted to policy research and education on all dimensions of prejudice, discrimination, and ethnoviolence.

Public Policy Institute of California

The PPIC is a private, nonprofit organization dedicated to improving public policy in California through independent, objective, nonpartisan research. It was established in 1994 with an endowment from William R. Hewlett. Its research focuses on three program areas: population, economy, and governance and public finance. Its publications include reports, research briefs, surveys, fact sheets, special papers, and demographic bulletins. It also communicates its research and analysis through conferences, forums, luncheons, and other targeted outreach efforts.

RAND Corporation

RAND (a contraction of the terms "research and development") was the first organization to be called a think tank. Established in 1946 by the U.S. Air Force, today RAND is a nonprofit institution that helps improve policy and decision making through research and analysis whose areas of expertise include child policy, civil and criminal justice, community and U.S. regional studies, drug policy, education, health, immigration, infrastructure, international policy, methodology, national security, population and aging, science and technology, and terrorism. On occasion its findings are considered so compelling that it advances specific policy recommendations. It serves the public interest by widely disseminating its research findings.

Tolerance.org

Tolerance.org is a Web project of the Southern Poverty Law Center, a national civil rights organization. Its stated mission is to create a national community committed to human rights by centralizing e-mail addresses and inviting users to view special features and stories on the Web site. It promotes and disseminates scholarship on all aspects of prejudice and discrimination, promoting tolerance, exposing hate groups and hate news, providing assistance on litigation and legal matters, and publishing antihate and protolerance tracts such as: "Ten Ways to Fight Hate," "101 Tools for Tolerance," and "Center Information Packet."

Urban Institute

One of the oldest of the think tanks, the Urban Institute researches policy matters in which it measures effects; compares options; shows which stakeholders get the most and the least; tests conventional wisdom; reveals trends; and makes costs, benefits, and risks explicit on a broad array of public policy issues, employing the right methodologies and quantitative modeling, survey design, and statistical analyses. It publishes an extensive list of books that follow standard academic peer-review procedures for an audience of program administrators, other researchers and university students, the news media, nonprofit organizations, stakeholders in the private sector, and that important segment of the public engaged in policy debates through the media.

References

Barone, Michael, and Chuck McCutcheon, eds. 2014. *The Almanac of American Politics*. Chicago: University of Chicago Press.

Diller, Daniel C., and Stephen L. Robertson. 2001. *The Presidents, First Ladies, and Vice Presidents: White House Biographies, 1789–2001*. Washington, DC: Congressional Quarterly Press.

Graff, Henry A., ed. 1997. *The Presidents: A Reference History*. New York: Charles Scribner's Sons.

Hamilton, Neil A. 2001. *Presidents: A Biographical Dictionary*. New York: Facts on File.

Jacobson, Doranne. *Presidents and First Ladies of the United States*. New York: Smithmack, 1995.

LeMay, Michael. *Illegal Immigration: A Reference Handbook*, 1st ed. Westport, CT: Praeger Press, 2007.

LeMay, Michael. *Transforming America: Perspectives on Immigration, vol. 3: Immigration and Superpower Status, 1945 to Date*. Santa Barbara, CA: ABC-CLIO, 2013.

U.S. Citizenship and Immigration Services. 2006. http://www.uscis.gov/.htm.

U.S. Department of Justice. 2006. http://www.usdoj.gov.

Web Sites

www.bennet.senate.gov/p=biography

www.govtrack.us/congress/members/michael-bennet/412330

www.black.house.gov/Home/About-Me

www.boehner.house.gov/

www.speaker.gov/

www.bishop.house.gov/biography

www.azcentral.com/story/news/. . . /03/arizona . . . brewer/632

www.nytimes.com/ . . . / jan-brewer-arizona-governor-won't-seek-re-election

www.gov.ca/m_about-php

www.carper.senate.gov/biography

www.governor.ny.gov/

www.andrewcuomo.com/

www.carper.senate.gov/biography

www.splc.org/who-we-are/leadership/richard-cohen

www.conyers.house.gov/index.cfm/biography

www.congress.gov/member/john-cornyn11692

www.uschamber.com/thomas-donohue

www.flake.senate.gov/biography

www.thesocialcontract.com/president

www.alipac.us/William_Gheen/

www.williamgheen.com/biography_william_gheen/

www.gowdy.house.gov/biography

www.grassley.senate.gov/biography

www.judgepedia.org/Andrew_Hanen

www.hatch.senate.gov/public/index.cfm/

www.hinojosa.house.gov/biography

www.fairus.org/issues/
huddle-1996-study-of-the-costs-of-illegal-immigration

www.unitedwedream.org/christina-jimenez-managing-director

www.dhs.gov/Home-about-DHS

www.ronjohnson.senate.gov/about

www.cmsny.org/tag/donald-kerwin/about-us/staff

www.klobuchar.senate.gov/biography

www.peterking.house.gov/about/full-biography

www.cis.org/krikorian

www.govtrack.us/congress/members/jon_kyl300062

www.leahy.senate/gov/biography

www.logren.house.gov/biography

www.mccain.senate.gov/about-biography

www.mccaskill.senate.gov/about-claire

www.mcconnell.senate.gov/public/index.cfm?p=Biography

www.mccaul.house.gov/about/full-biography

www.menendez.senate.gov/biography

www.candicemiller.house.gov/about-full-biography

www.nclr.org/janet-murgia

www.migrationpolicy.org/about/staff/
demetrios-papademetriou

www.pelosi.house.gov/full-biography

www.pewresearch.org/staff/jeffrey-s-passel/

www.immigration.procon.org/source/biographies

www.rickperry.org/about/

www.reid.senate.gov/about-Senator-Harry-Reid
www.rubio.senate.gov/About-Marco
www.schumer.gov/biography
www.govtrack.us/congress/members/charles_schumer/30087
www.sensenbrenner,house.gov/about-jim-biography
www.sessions.senate.gov/biography
www.americasvoiceonline.org/experts/frank_sharry
www.chrissmith.house.gov/about-chris
www.lamarsmith.house.gov/about
www.annenburg.usc.edu/. . . .media/faculty/roberto_suro
www.thesocialcontract.com/answering_our_critics/
  tanton_resume
www.numbersusa.org/about
www.benniethompson.house.gov/about-bennie
www/cmsny.org/about-us/staff
www.vitter.senate.gov/about-david
www.wyden.senate.gov/meet-ron/biography

Introduction

Public policy has been defined as "a purposive course of action followed by an actor or set of actors in dealing with a problem or matter of concern" (Anderson 1979: 3). Chapter 4 presented biographical sketches of the major actors involved. In its first section, this chapter presents data on illegal immigration–related trends in table and graphic formats. In its second section it presents summaries of the "actions"—some key legislative and judicial decisions. These laws and cases, taken together, constitute the "course" of immigration policy and its frequent reforms aimed at controlling illegal immigration.

Data

Table 5.1   Comparison of Legal and Illegal Immigration Trends over Time

This table shows the number of legal immigrants to the United States, 1992–2013; the number of illegal apprehensions at the borders, 1992–2013; and the number of Mexican alien apprehensions, 2000–2013.

President Barack Obama meets with a group of "Dreamers" in the Oval Office of the White House in Washington on February 4, 2015. During an Oval Office meeting, the president spoke with six of the young immigrants who would be subject to eventual deportation under a bill passed by the House. New legislation would overturn Obama's executive actions, DAPA and DACA, limiting deportations for millions here illegally and giving them the ability to work. (AP Photo/Evan Vucci)

FY	Total Legal Immigrants to the United States	Total Alien Apprehensions	Mexican Alien Apprehensions
1992	973,977	1,199,560	—
1993	904,191	1,263,490	—
1994	804,416	1,031,666	—
1995	720,461	1,324,202	—
1996	915,900	1,549,876	—
1997	718,378	1,412,953	—
1998	654,451	1,555,778	—
1999	646,568	1,579,010	—
2000	849,807	1,678,438	1,636,883
2001	1,064,318	1,266,214	1,224,047
2002	1,059,902	955,310	917,993
2003	703,542	931,557	882,012
2004	957,883	1,160,395	1,086,006
2005	1,122,373	1,189,075	1,023,905
2006	1,266,129	1,089,092	981,066
2007	1,052,415	876,704	808,688
2008	1.107,126	723,825	661,766
2009	1,120,818	556,041	503,386
2010	1,042,625	439,382	404,385
2011	1,062,040	340,252	286,154
2012	1,031,631	364,765	265,755
2013	990,553	420,789	267,734

Source: Adapted from Department of Homeland Security, 2011, "Persons Obtaining Permanent Resident Status, Fiscal Years 1820–2010." *Yearbook of Immigration Statistics*. Washington, DC: Department of Homeland Security. Updated by annual reports, 2011–2014. Online at http://www.dhs.gov/sites/default/files/publications/ois_1pr_fr_2013.pdf.

Table 5.2   Estimated Unauthorized Mexican-Born Immigrant Population Compared to All Unauthorized Immigrants, Assorted Years, 1995–2012

This table presents the estimated unauthorized Mexican-born immigrant population in the United States compared to all unauthorized immigrants, for assorted years, 1995–2012.

Year	From Mexico (Millions)	All Unauthorized (Millions)
1995	2.9	5.7
2000	4.5	7.9
2005	6.3	11.1
2007	6.9	12.2
2008	6.4	11.3
2009	6.3	11.4
2010	6.2	11.5
2011	6.2	11.2
2012	5.9	11.3

Source: Data from Pew Research Center, based on augmented American Community Survey, 1998–2000. Online at http://www.pewhispanic.org/2014/11/18/unauthorized_immigrant_total_rise_fall. http://www.pewhispanic.org/2014/09/03/as_growth_stalls_unauthorized_population_becomes_more_stable.

Table 5.3   Estimated Unauthorized Immigrants in the U.S. Labor Force, Assorted Years, 1995–2012

This table indicates the total number of estimated unauthorized immigrants in the labor force of the United States, 1995 to 2012, by which year it was exceeding 8 million. The table demonstrates dramatically that the employer sanctions approach enacted by IRCA, 1986, simply failed to achieve its goal of demagnetizing the draw of the U.S. labor market to unauthorized immigrants.

Year	Estimated Millions in U.S. Labor Force
1995	3.6
2000	5.6
2005	7.3
2006	8.2

(continued)

Table 5.3   (continued)

Year	Estimated Millions in U.S. Labor Force
2009	8.1
2011	8.3
2012	8.2

Source: Adapted from graphs and data from the Pew Research Center, estimates based on augmented American Community Survey data. http://www.pewhispanic.org/2014/11/18/unauthorized_immigrant_totals_rise_fall. Accessed March 10, 2015.

Table 5.4   Unaccompanied Alien Children Encountered, by Fiscal Year, Country of Origin, 2009–2014

This table presents the dramatic rise in the number of children unaccompanied by adults who arrived at U.S. borders from Mexico and Central America and promptly turned themselves in to Border Patrol authorities. The "crisis" nature of the influx prompted several legislative proposals to deal with the problem.

Country	2009	2010	2011	2012	2013	2014
El Salvador	1,221	1,910	1,394	3,314	5,990	16,404
Guatemala	1,115	1,517	1,56	3,835	8,068	17,057
Honduras	968	1.017	974	2,997	6,747	18,244
Mexico	16,114	13,724	11,768	13,974	17,240	15,634
Total	19,418	18,168	15,701	24,120	38,045	67,339

Source: Data from U.S. Customs and Border Patrol, http://www.cbp.gov/newsroom/stats/southwest-border-unaccompanied-children. Accessed March 10, 2015.

Table 5.5   Trends in Removals, 2011–2013

This table shows the rise in the number of removals of undocumented aliens for the years 2011–2013. Expedited removals increased significantly during the Obama administration's first term and continued, as the table shows, into his second term as well.

Year	2011 (%)	2012 (%)	2013 (%)
Expedited	122,236 (31.6)	163,308 (39.0)	193,032 (44.0)
Reinstatements	124,784 (32.2)	146,044 (34.9)	170,247 (38.8)
All others	140,114 (36.2)	109,045 (26.1)	75,142 (17.1)
TOTAL	387,134 (100)	418,397(100)	438,421 (100)

Source: DHS, Yearbook of Immigration Statistics, 2013. http://www.dhs.gov/sites/default/files/publications/ois_enforcement_ar_2013.pdf.

Table 5.6   Gallup Poll Trend Line, "Do You Think Immigration Is a Good Thing or a Bad Thing for the U.S. Today?," 2001–2014

This table shows Gallup Poll public opinion data of whether Americans think immigration is a good or a bad thing for the U.S. today, for 2001 to 2014.

Year	%Good Thing	%Bad Thing	%Mixed
2001	62	31	5
2002	52	42	4
2003	58	36	4
2004	61	34	3
2005	67	28	4
2007	60	33	3
2008	64	30	4
2009	58	36	3
2010	57	36	4
2011	59	37	2
2012	66	29	3
2013	72	25	2
2014	63	33	3

Source: Data from Gallup Polls, http://www.gallup.com/poll/1660/immigration.aspx.

Table 5.7   Gallup Poll Trend Line, 2001–2014, "Should Immigration Be Kept at Its Present Level, Increased, or Decreased?"

This table gives an overall depiction of Gallup Poll public opinion data as to whether immigration should be kept at its present level, increased, or decreased, presenting the trends for 2001 to 2014.

Year	%Kept at Present Level	%Increased	%Decreased
2001	42	14	41
2002	36	12	49
2003	37	13	47
2004	33	14	49
2005	34	16	46
2006	42	17	39
2007	35	16	45
2008	39	18	39

(continued)

Table 5.7   (*continued*)

Year	%Kept at Present Level	%Increased	%Decreased
2009	32	14	50
2010	34	17	45
2011	35	18	43
2012	42	21	35
2013	40	23	35
2014	33	22	41

Source: Data from Gallup Polls, http://www.gallup.com/poll/1660/immigration_aspx.

Table 5.8a   Gallup Poll Trend Line, 2006–2014, "What Should Be the Main Focus of U.S. Government in Dealing with Illegal Immigration?"

These tables show Gallup Public Opinion Poll data from 2006–2014, about the focus of government policy in dealing with illegal immigrants residing in the United States.

Year	%Halting Flow of Illegals	%Dealing With Those in U.S. Illegally	%No Opinion
2006	52	43	4
2010	53	45	3
2011	50	45	3
2012	55	43	2
2013	46	55	4
2014	41	53	6

Table 5.8b   Gallup Poll Trend Line, 2006–2011, "What Should U.S. Policy Be Toward Illegal Immigrants Residing in the United States?"

	% Deport All	Remain in U.S./ Allowed to Work	Remain in U.S./ Path to Citizenship	Na
2006	16	17	66	1
March 2007	24	15	59	2
June 2011	21	13	64	3

Source: Data from Gallup Polls, http://www.gallup.com/poll/1660/immigration_aspx.

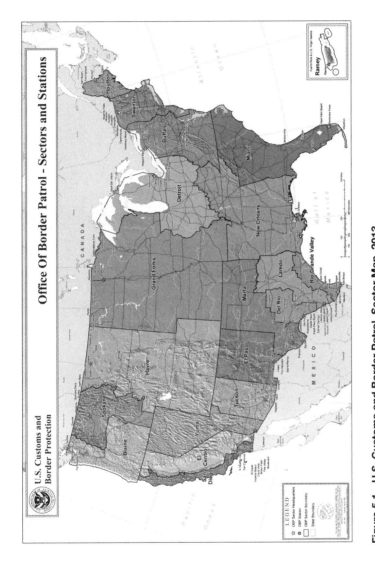

Figure 5.1   U.S. Customs and Border Patrol, Sector Map, 2013

Source: U.S. Customs and Border Patrol. Online at http://ecso.swf.usace.army.mil/maps/SectorP.pdf.

U.S. DEPARTMENT OF HOMELAND SECURITY

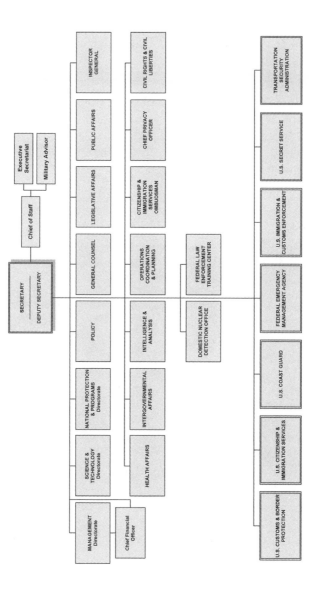

Figure 5.2   Department of Homeland Security Organizational Chart

Source: Department of Homeland Security. Online at http://www.dhs.gov/xlibrary/assets/dhs-orgchart.pdf

Documents

Key Illegal Immigration Legislative Actions, 1981–2013

Executive Summary Recommendations of the Select Commission on Immigration and Refugee Policy, 1981

Of great importance to the reform of immigration policy was the report of the Select Commission on Immigration and Refugee Policy (SCIRP). SCIRP was a joint presidential and congressionally appointed commission that began its work in the final days of the Carter administration in 1979. It studied thoroughly immigration law and, more particularly, the problem of illegal immigration. It issued its final report in 1981. Its recommendations informed subsequent legislative action by Congress throughout the 1980s and 1990s. The next document presents some of the major recommendations of the SCIRP's final report.

The Select Commission recommends:

1. The United States work with other nations and principal international organizations to collect information and research on migratory flows and treatment of international migration.

2. The United States expand bilateral consultation with other governments, especially Mexico and other regional neighbors, regarding migration.

3. Border patrol funding levels be raised to provide for a substantial increase in the number and training of personnel, replacement sensor systems . . . and other needed equipment.

4. That regional border enforcement posts be established to coordinate work with the INS, the U.S. Customs Service, the DEA, and the U.S. Coast Guard in the interdiction of both undocumented/illegal migrants and illicit goods, specifically narcotics.

5. That high priority be given to the training of INS officers to familiarize them with the rights of aliens and U.S.

citizens and to help them deal with persons of other cultural backgrounds.

6. That legislation be passed making it illegal for employers to hire undocumented workers.

7. That a program to legalize illegal/undocumented aliens now in the United States be adopted.

8. That eligibility for legalization be determined by interrelated measurements of residence—date of entry and length of continuous residence—and by specified groups of excludability that are appropriate to the legalization program.

9. That voluntary agencies and community organizations be given a significant role in the legalization program

10. An annual ceiling of 350,000 numerically limited immigrant visas with an additional 100,000 visas available for the first five years to . . . allow backlogs to be cleared.

11. That a substantial number of visas be set aside for reunifying spouses and unmarried sons and daughters, and it should be given top priority in the numerically limited family reunification. . . .

12. That country ceilings apply to all numerically limited family reunification preferences. . . .

13. That "special" immigrants remain a numerically exempt group but be placed within the independent category.

14. Creation of a small, numerically limited subcategory within the independent category to provide for the immigration of certain investors.

15. That specific labor market criteria be established by the selection of independent immigrants. . . .

16. A fixed percentage limit to the independent immigration from any one country.

17. That U.S. allocation of refugee numbers include both geographic considerations and specific refugee characteristics. . . .

18. That state and local governments be involved in planning for initial refugee resettlement and that . . . a federal program of impact aid [be established] to minimize the financial impact of refugees on local services. . . .

19. That refugee achievement of self-sufficiency and adjustment to living in the United States be reaffirmed as the goal of resettlement.

Source: The Select Commission on Immigration and Refugee Policy, *Final Report* (Washington, DC: U.S. Government Printing Office, March 1, 1981), xv–xxxii.

The Immigration Reform and Control Act of 1986

The Immigration Reform and Control Act of 1986, commonly known as IRCA, had a lengthy and tangled history. In 1986 a joint Conference Committee finally agreed on a package that could be enacted into law. The next document offers portions of the major provisions of IRCA. Much of it is still relevant today, and reaction to its amnesty program drives Republican opposition to anything resembling amnesty in current proposals.

Title I—Control of Illegal Immigration

SEC. 101. CONTROL OF UNLAWFUL EMPLOYMENT OF ALIENS

In General, It is unlawful for a person or other entity to hire, or to recruit or refer for a fee, for employment in the United States—

(A) an alien, knowing the alien is an unauthorized alien . . .

(B) an individual without complying with the requirements of subsection (b).

Continuing employment—It is unlawful for a person or other entity, after hiring an alien for employment in accordance with paragraph (1), to continue to employ the alien in the United States knowing the alien is (or has become) an unauthorized alien with respect to such employment.

Defense—A person or entity that establishes that it has complied in good faith with the requirements of subsection (b) with respect to the hiring, recruiting, or referral for employment of an alien in the United States has established an affirmative defense that the person or entity has not violated paragraph (1)(A) with respect to such hiring, recruiting, or referral.

Use of Labor through Contract—A person or other entity who uses a contract, subcontract, or exchange, entered into, renegotiated, or extended after the date of the enactment of this section, to obtain the labor of an alien in the United States knowing that the alien is an unauthorized alien, with respect to performing such labor, shall be considered to have hired the alien for employment in the United States in violation of paragraph (1)(A).

Use of State Employment Agency Documentation—A person or entity shall be deemed to have complied with the requirements of subsection (b) with respect to the hiring of an individual who was referred for such employment by a State employment agency.

Employment Verification System—The requirements referred to [above] are, in the case of a person or other entity hiring, recruiting, or referring an individual for employment in the United States, the requirements specified in the following three paragraphs:

(1) Attestation after Examination of Documentation—

(A) In General—The person or entity must attest, under penalty of perjury and on a form established by the Attorney General by regulation, that it has verified that the individual is not an unauthorized alien by examining—

(i) a document described in subparagraph (B), or

(ii) a document described in subparagraph (C) and (D).

(B) Documents Establishing Both Employment Authorization and Identity—A document described in this
subparagraph is an individual's—

(i) United States passport;

(ii) certificate of United States Citizenship;

(iii) certificate of naturalization;

(iv) unexpired foreign passport, if the passport has an
appropriate, unexpired endorsement of the Attorney
General authorizing the individual's employment in
the United States; or

(v) resident alien card or other alien registration, if said card
contains a photograph of the individual, and is evidence
of authorization of employment in the United States.

(C) Documents Evidencing Employment Authorization—
A document described [above] is

(i) a social security account number card;

(ii) certificate of birth in the United States or establishing United States nationality at birth;

(iii) other documents evidencing authorization of
employment in the United States which the Attorney
General finds, by regulation, to be acceptable for the
purposes of this section.

(D) Documents Establishing Identity of an Individual—A
document described in this subparagraph is an individual's

(i) driver's license or similar document issued for the
purpose of identification by a State, if it contains a
photograph of the individual;

(ii) in the case of individuals under 16 years of age or
in a State which does not provide for issuance of an
identification document,

(iii) documentation of personal identity of such type as
the Attorney General finds, by regulation, provides a
reliable means of identification. . . .

(3) Definition of Unauthorized Alien—the term "unauthorized alien" means, with respect to the employment of an alien at a particular time, that the alien is not at that time either (A) an alien lawfully admitted for permanent residence, or (B) authorized to be so employed by this Act or by the Attorney General.

Deferral of Enforcement with Respect to Seasonal Agricultural Services—

(A) In General—it is unlawful for a person or entity (including a farm labor contractor) or an agent of such a person or entity, to recruit an unauthorized alien (other than an alien described in clause [ii]) who is outside the United States to enter the United States to perform seasonal agricultural services.

(ii) Exception—Clause (i) shall not apply to an alien who the person or entity reasonably believes to meet the requirements of section 210(a)(2) of this Act (relating to the performance of seasonal agricultural services).

General Accounting Office Reports—
IN GENERAL—

Beginning one year after the date of enactment of this Act, and at intervals of one year thereafter for a period of three years after such date, the Comptroller General of the United States shall prepare and transmit to the Congress and to the task force established under subsection (k) a report describing the results of a review of the implementation and enforcement of this section during the preceding twelve-month period, for the purpose of determining if—

(A) such provisions have been carried out satisfactorily;

(B) a pattern of discrimination has resulted against citizens or nationals of the United States or against eligible workers seeking employment; and

(C) an unnecessary regulatory burden has been created for employers hiring such workers.

REVIEW BY TASK FORCE—

(1) Establishment of Task Force—The Attorney General, jointly with the Chairman of the Commission on Civil Rights and the Chairman of the Equal Employment Opportunity Commission, shall establish a task force to review each report of the Comptroller General.

(2) Recommendations to Congress—If the report transmitted includes a determination that the implementation of this section has resulted in a pattern of discrimination in employment (against other than unauthorized aliens) on the basis of national origin, the task force shall, taking into consideration any recommendations in the report, report to Congress recommendations for such legislation as may be appropriate to deter or remedy such discrimination. . . .

TERMINATION DATE FOR EMPLOYER SANCTIONS—

(1) If Report of Widespread Discrimination and Congressional Approval—The provisions of this section shall terminate 30 days after receipt of the last report required to be transmitted under subsection (j), if—

(A) the Comptroller General determines, and so reports . . . that a widespread pattern of discrimination has resulted against citizens or nationals of the United States or against eligible workers seeking employment solely from the implementation of this section; and

(B) there is enacted, within such period of 30 calendar days, a joint resolution stating in substance that the Congress approves the findings of the Comptroller General contained in such report.

(2) Senate Procedures for Consideration—Any joint resolution referred to in clause (B) of paragraph (1) shall be considered in the Senate in accordance with subsection (n). . . .

Increased Authorization of Appropriations for INS and EOIR—In addition to any other amounts authorized to be appropriated, in order to carry out this Act, there are authorized to be appropriated to the Department of Justice—

(1) for the [INS], for FY 1987, $12,000,000, and for FY 1988, $15,000,000 . . . to provide for an increase in the border patrol personnel . . . so that the average level of such personnel in each fiscal year 1987 and 1988 is at least 50 per cent higher than such level for fiscal year 1986.

Title II—Legalization

SEC. 201. LEGALIZATION OF STATUS.

Temporary Resident Status—

The Attorney General shall adjust the status of an alien to that of an alien lawfully admitted for temporary residence if the alien meets the following requirements:

(1) Timely Application—

  (A) During Application Period—Except as provided in subparagraph (B), the alien must apply for such adjustment during the 12-month period beginning on a date (not later than 180 days after the date of enactment of this section) designated by the Attorney General. . . .

  (2) Continuous Lawful Residence Since 1982—

  (A) In General—The alien must establish that he entered the United States before January 1, 1982, and that he has resided continuously in the United States in an unlawful status since such date and through the date the application is filed under this subsection.

  (B) Nonimmigrants—In the case of an alien who entered the United States as a nonimmigrant before January 1, 1982, the alien must establish that the alien's period of authorized stay as a nonimmigrant expired before such date through the passage of time or the alien's unlawful status was known to the Government as of such date.

*Subsequent Adjustment to Permanent Residence and
Nature of Temporary Resident Status—*

(1) Adjustment to Permanent Residence—The Attorney General shall adjust the status of any alien provided lawful temporary resident status under subsection (a) to that of an alien lawfully admitted for permanent residence if the alien meets the following requirements:

(A) Timely Application After One Year's Residence—The alien must apply for such adjustment during the one-year period beginning with the nineteenth month that begins after the date the alien was granted such temporary status.

(B) Continuous Residence—The alien must establish that he has continuously resided in the United States since the date the alien was granted such temporary resident status.

(C) Admissible as Immigrant—The alien must establish that he or she—

(i) is admissible to the United States as an immigrant . . . and

(ii) has not been convicted of any felony or three or more misdemeanors committed in the United States.

Basic Citizenship Skills—The alien must demonstrate that he or she either—

(I) meets the requirements of section 312 (relating to minimal understanding of ordinary English and a knowledge and understanding of the history and government of the United States), or (II) is satisfactorily pursuing a course of study (recognized by the Attorney General) to achieve an understanding of English and such knowledge and understanding of the history and government of the United States. . . .

Temporary Disqualification of Newly Legalized Aliens from Receiving Certain Public Welfare Assistance—

(1) In General—During the five-year period beginning on the date an alien was granted lawful temporary resident status under subsection (a) except as provided in paragraphs (2) and (3), the alien is not eligible for—

(i) any program of financial assistance furnished under Federal law;

(ii) medical assistance under a State plan approved under Title XIX of the Social Security Act; and

(iii) assistance under the Food Stamp Act of 1977; and State or political subdivision therein may, to the extent consistent with paragraph (A) and paragraphs (2) and (3), provide that an alien is not eligible for the programs of financial assistance or for medical assistance described in subparagraph (A) (ii) furnished under the law of that State or political subdivision. . . .

Title III—Reform of Legal Immigration Part A—Temporary Agricultural Workers

SEC. 301. H-2A AGRICULTURAL WORKERS

(a) Providing New "H-2A" Nonimmigrant Classification for Temporary Agricultural Labor—Paragraph (15) (H) of section 101 (a) (8 USC 1101(a)) is amended by striking out "to perform temporary services or labor," in clause (ii) and inserting in lieu thereof, "(a) to perform agricultural labor or services, as defined by the Secretary of Labor in regulations and including agricultural labor defined in section 3121(g) of the Internal Revenue Code of 1954 and agriculture as defined in section 3(f) of the Fair Labor Standards Act of 1938 . . . or a temporary or seasonal nature, or (b) to perform other temporary service or labor."

Source: Immigration Reform and Control Act (IRCA), Pub.L. 99–603, 100 Stat. 3445, enacted November 6, 1986

Summaries of Laws on Immigration

In 1996, Congress passed two measures that essentially enacted the provisions of Proposition 187. Congress enacted a welfare reform act that contained several legal and illegal immigrant–related provisions similar to those in Proposition 187. The illegal immigration provisions are shown in the next document.

Immigration Provisions of the Welfare Reform Act (HR 3734—PL 104–193)

The welfare reform law imposed restrictions on both legal and illegal immigrants, including provisions to:

Illegal Aliens

Restrictions. Restrict the federal benefits for which illegal aliens and legal nonimmigrants, such as travelers and students, could qualify. The benefits denied were those provided by a federal agency or federal funds for:

- Any grant, contract, loan, professional license or commercial license.

- Any retirement, welfare, health, disability, food assistance or unemployment benefit.

Exceptions. Allow illegal aliens and legal nonimmigrants to receive:

- Emergency medical services under Medicaid, but denied coverage for prenatal or delivery assistance that was not an emergency, and short-term, noncash emergency disaster relief.

- Immunizations and testing for treatment for the symptoms of communicable diseases.

- Noncash programs identified by the attorney general that were delivered by community agencies such as soup kitchens, counseling, and short-term shelter that were not conditioned on the individual's income or resources and were necessary for the protection of life and safety.

- Certain housing benefits (for existing recipients only).
- Licenses and benefits directly related to work for which a nonimmigrant had been authorized to enter the United States.
- Certain Social Security retirement benefits protected by treaty or statute.

State and local programs. Prohibit states from providing state or local benefits to most illegal aliens, unless a state law was enacted after August 22, 1996, the day the bill was enacted, that explicitly made illegal aliens eligible for the aid. However, illegal aliens were entitled to receive a school lunch and/or breakfast if they were eligible for a free public education under state or local law and a state could opt to provide certain other benefits related to child nutrition and emergency food assistance.

From 1994 through 1996, Congress grappled with bills that would have reformed immigration law more generally—not just dealing with problems of illegal immigration. A sufficient consensus to enact broad-scale legal immigration reform could not be reached. Congress cleared a measure to restrict illegal immigration only after folding its provisions into the omnibus fiscal 1997 spending bill that President Clinton signed into law on September 30, 1996. The full measure is over 200 pages long. The next document summarizes the illegal immigration section of the omnibus spending bill.

Illegal Immigration Provisions of the Omnibus Spending Bill (HR 3610—PL 104–208)

Border Controls
- Authorized funding to increase the number of Border Patrol agents by 1,000 per year through fiscal 2001, doubling the total force from 5,000 to 10,000, and to increase the number of clerical workers and other support personnel at the border by 300 per year through fiscal 2001. The law

ordered the INS to relocate as many agents as possible to border areas with the largest number of illegal immigrants, and to coordinate relocation plans with local law enforcement agencies. The INS was required to report to Congress on these activities within six months of enactment.

- Authorized funding of 900 additional INS agents to investigate and prosecute cases of smuggling, harboring or employing illegal aliens; and 300 new agents to investigate people who overstay their visas.

- Authorized $12 million for the second and third tiers of a triple fence along a 14-mile strip at the U.S.-Mexico border south of San Diego, and for roads surrounding the fence. The project was exempt from the strictures of the 1973 Endangered Species Act and the 1969 Environmental Policy Act if either would prevent expeditious construction and allowed the attorney general to acquire land for the fence.

- Required the INS to develop alien identification cards that include a biometric identifier, such as a fingerprint, that could be read by machine, and for future cards that could use such devices as retina scanners.

- Created a penalty up to five years in prison for fleeing through an INS checkpoint, and deportation of those convicted.

- Ordered the attorney general, within two years, to create a data base of information gathered from the documents people filled out as they legally entered and left the country which would allow the INS to match entry and exit records to identify people who overstayed their visas.

- Required the INS to establish "preinspection" stations at five of the ten foreign airports that were the departure points for the largest number of inadmissible immigrants to screen people who did not have proper documents.

- Allowed the INS to enter into agreements with state and local governments for help in investigating, arresting, detaining, and transporting illegal immigrants.

DOCUMENT FRAUD AND ALIEN SMUGGLING

- Granted wiretap authority to the criminal division of the Justice Department for investigating cases of immigration document fraud.

- Created felonies for alien smuggling for up to ten years in prison for the first and second offenses, and fifteen years for subsequent offenses; and making it a crime with up to five years in prison for employers who knowingly hired ten people or more who were smuggled into the United States.

- Created twenty-five positions for assistant U.S. attorneys to prosecute cases of alien smuggling and document fraud.

- Granted broad authority for the INS to conduct undercover operations to track organized illegal immigration rings that allowed the INS to create or acquire companies, deposit funds in bank accounts without regard to federal regulations, and use profits from such front companies.

- Increased the penalty for document fraud from five years to ten or fifteen years in most cases; and if fraud was used in facilitating a drug trafficking crime, a new penalty of twenty years in prison, and if involving terrorism, a new penalty of twenty-five years.

- Created a civil penalty for hiring someone to make a false application for public benefits such as food stamps, and created a criminal penalty for "knowingly and willfully" failing to disclose it, punishable by up to fifteen years.

- Created a criminal penalty of up to five years in prison for falsely claiming U.S. citizenship.

- Created a criminal penalty for up to one year in prison for unlawfully voting in a federal election.

- Allowed courts, in imposing sentences against violators of immigration statutes, to seize vehicles, boats, airplanes, and real estate if they were used in the commission of a crime or profit from the proceeds of a crime.

- Increased the penalty from five years in prison to ten years for employers who kept workers in a state of involuntary servitude.

- Allowed INS agents to subpoena witnesses and to videotape testimony at deportation proceedings.

DETENTION AND DEPORTATION

- Barred any alien who had been deported from reentry into the United States for five years; and up to ten years if the alien left while deportation proceedings were in progress or attempted to reenter the country unlawfully; and barred repeat offenders for two years, and people convicted of aggravated felonies.

- Denied legal status to anyone who resided in the United States unlawfully for at least 180 days; and persons so convicted could not gain legal status for three years. People in the country illegally for a year or more could not become legal for ten years, except for minors or persons with a pending application for asylum, or were battered women and children, or were people granted protection under the family unity provision of the 1990 Act, or spouses and minor children granted amnesty under the Immigration Reform and Control Act of 1986 to stay in the United States even if they entered illegally, while their application for legal status was pending.

- Allowed people who arrived in the United States without legitimate documentation to be detained and deported without hearing unless they could demonstrate a credible fear of persecution back home. An asylum officer was to screen each case and if decided there was no credible fear, could summarily deport the applicant. The applicant could request a review by an immigration judge within seven days, during which time the applicant had to remain in detention.

- Required the detention of most illegal aliens serving criminal sentences after their prison terms were completed. The attorney general could release certain illegal immigrants from detention centers if there was insufficient space and if he determined their release did not pose a security risk or a risk of fleeing, or who came from countries that would not take them back.

- Streamlined deportation by replacing multiple proceedings with one, allowing proceedings by telephone or teleconference after ten-day notice of a hearing.
- Required aliens be deported within ninety days of a deportation order, with mandatory detention during that period. Violent criminals would have to complete their prison terms before being deported; some nonviolent criminal aliens could be deported before their term was up.
- Limited judicial review of deportation orders. The state department could discontinue all visas for countries that declined to take back their deported nationals.
- Authorized $5 million for a criminal alien tracking center using criminal alien data base authorized in the 1994 crime law (PL 103–322) to be used to assist local governments in identifying criminals who might be deportable.
- Advised the president to negotiate bilateral prisoner transfer treaties to allow criminals to serve their terms in their home countries. The secretary of state and attorney general were to report to Congress by April 1, 1997, on the potential for such treaties.
- Made a potential immigrant who did not have proof of proper vaccinations inadmissible.
- Added stalking, domestic violence, and child abuse to the crimes that made someone deportable.
- Permanently barred from entry anyone who renounced his or her citizenship to avoid taxes.
- Allowed the attorney general to authorize local law enforcement officials to perform the duties of an immigration officer in the event of a mass influx of immigrants.
- Broadened authority of judges to issue deportation orders; allowing someone deported as part of probation or a plea agreement.

- Created a pilot program on the use of closed military bases as INS detention centers.

EMPLOYEE VERIFICATION

- Ordered the attorney general to set up three pilot programs—a basic pilot program, a Citizen Attestation Program, and a Machine-Readable Document Pilot Program—to test the effectiveness of workplace verification systems. Participation in the pilot programs by employers would be voluntary; and the attorney general was to choose the states where each program would be tested, though in some cases employers in nonselected states could participate. All federal departments and agencies within the chosen states were required to participate in the program.

- Allowed participating employers to contact the INS via telephone, fax, or e-mail, to check job applicant's immigration status. INS was to maintain a database of names, Social Security numbers, and other information useful to verify an applicant's eligibility to work; and the INS was to respond to inquiries within three days, and if the tentative response was that the person was not legal, the INS had ten days to confirm that determination. The program was to be tested in five of the seven states with the largest number of illegal immigrants.

- Created a similar program that would allow applicants to bypass the check if they attested that they were U.S. citizens. The penalty for false claims of such was set at five years in prison.

- Allowed employers to scan a card into a machine to verify the owner's Social Security number with the INS data base. These were to be placed in states selected by the attorney general in which driver's licenses or other state documents included Social Security numbers that could be read by machine.

- Made it harder for the government to sue employers who used immigration laws to discriminate against certain workers, job applicants, or other individuals by placing the burden on the government to show that the employer "acted for the purpose, or with the intent to discriminate" against the individual.

PUBLIC BENEFITS

- Allowed any consular agent to deny an immigrant visa on the basis that the person was likely to become a public charge.
- Allowed states to create pilot programs to explore the feasibility of denying driver's licenses to illegal immigrants. The attorney general was to report to Congress on such after three years.
- Clarified that Social Security benefits were not to be paid to illegal immigrants.
- Ordered the General Accounting Office to study the use of student aid by illegal immigrants and to report on such to Congress within one year of enactment.
- Required the GAO to report to Congress within 180 days on the unlawful use of means-tested benefits—such as food stamps and cash welfare—by illegal immigrants.
- Amended the new welfare law to permit certain illegal immigrants who were victims of domestic violence to qualify for public benefits.
- Amended the welfare law so that nonprofit charitable organizations were no longer required to verify the immigration status of applicants to determine their eligibility for benefits.
- Allowed judges to double the monetary penalty and triple the prison terms for anyone who forged or counterfeited any U.S. seal to make a false application for public benefits.
- Allowed reimbursement to states and localities for emergency medical care of illegal immigrants, if the care was not already reimbursed via existing federal programs.

- Required the secretary of Housing and Urban Development to deny financial assistance through subsidized housing programs to families in which all members were illegal immigrants. If families were split between legal and illegal immigrants, HUD could adjust the size of the benefit to match the percentage of family members who were in the United States legally.

OTHER PROVISIONS

- Created a crime punishable by prison for performing female genital mutilation.
- Required "international matchmaking organizations" to disseminate to their clients information about U.S. immigration laws under penalty of a $20,000 fine for failure to do so; and requiring the attorney general to prepare a report to Congress on the mail-order bride business within a year of enactment.
- Required the INS to report by the end of 1996 whether or not the United States had an adequate number of temporary agricultural workers.
- Set national standards for birth certificates, driver's licenses, and other identification documents. The Department of Transportation was to set standards for IDs, which had to include Social Security numbers, and agencies issuing them had to keep those numbers on file and confirm their accuracy with the Social Security Administration. The standards were intended to make such documents more tamper-resistant; were to be issued within one year; and to be complied with by October 1, 2000.
- Required the Social Security Administration to develop a prototype tamperproof identity card.

In response to the 9/11 international terrorist attacks, Congress passed the USA Patriot Act, a bill of 288 pages. Its key immigration-related provisions broadened the definition of terrorism, expanded grounds for inadmissibility to include aliens suspected of terrorist activity or who publicly endorsed such, and required the attorney general to detain aliens whom he certified as threats to national security. The following document presents its key provisions relating to illegal immigration.

USA Patriot Act of 2001—HR 3162, October 24, 2001
Title IV—Protecting the Border.

SUBTITLE A—PROTECTING THE NORTHERN BORDER

Sec. 401—Ensures adequate personnel on the northern border.

Sec. 403—Grants access by the Department of State and the INS to certain identifying records of visa applicants and applicants for admission to the United States.

Sec. 405—Establishes an integrated automated fingerprint identification system for ports of entry and overseas consular posts.

SUBTITLE B—ENHANCED IMMIGRATION PROVISIONS

Sec. 412—Mandates detention of suspected terrorists; suspends habeas corpus under certain conditions; and limits judicial review.

Sec. 413—Ensures multilateral cooperation against terrorists.

Sec. 414—Provides for increased integrity and security of visas.

Sec. 415—Mandates the participation of the Office of Homeland Security on the Entry-Exit Task Force.

Sec. 416—Establishes a foreign student monitoring program.

Sec. 417—Calls for machine-readable passports.

Title X—Miscellaneous

Sec. 1006—Provides for the inadmissibility of aliens engaged in money laundering.

On November 19, 2002, Congress passed the Department of Homeland Security (DHS) Act. It is in excess of 400 printed pages. It merged 22 federal agencies, the most extensive reorganization of the federal bureaucracy since the creation of the Department of Defense after World War II. It creates within DHS two bureaus, each headed by an undersecretary: Border and Transportation Security, and the Bureau of Citizenship and Immigration Services. Key provisions from Title IV of the Act are highlighted next.

H.R. 5005—Homeland Security Act of November 19, 2002
Title IV—Border and Transportation Security.
SUBTITLE A—GENERAL PROVISIONS
Sec. 401. Creates the Under Secretary for Border and Transportation Security.
Sec. 402. Responsibilities—Transfers functions of the INS to the DHS.

The Secretary, acting through the Under Secretary for Border and Transportation Security, shall be responsible for the following:

(1) Preventing the entry of terrorists and the instruments of terrorism into the U.S.

(2) Securing the borders, territorial waters, ports, terminals, waterways, and air, land and sea transportation systems of the United States, including managing and coordinating those functions transferred to the Department at ports of entry.

(3) Carrying out the immigration enforcement functions vested by statute in, or performed by, the Commissioner of Immigration and Naturalization (or any officer, employee, or component of the Immigration and Naturalization Service) immediately before the date on which the transfer of functions specified under section 441 takes effect [March 1, 2003].

(4) Establishing and administering rules, in accordance with section 428, governing the granting of visas or other forms of permissions, including parole, to enter the United States to individuals who are not a citizen or an alien lawfully admitted for permanent residence in the United States.

(5) Establishing national immigration enforcement policies and priorities.

Subtitle B—Immigration and Nationality Functions
CHAPTER 1—IMMIGRATION ENFORCEMENT

Sec. 411. Details the transfer of functions of the Border Patrol, INS, to the Under Secretary for Border and Transportation Security in the DHS.

Sec. 412. Establishes a Bureau of Border Security headed by a Director.

Sec. 415. Calls for a report to Congress on improving enforcement functions.

CHAPTER 2—CITIZENSHIP AND IMMIGRATION SERVICES

Subchapter A—Transfer of Functions

Sec. 421. Establishes a Bureau of Citizenship and Immigration Services headed by a Director

Sec. 422. Establishes a Citizenship and Immigration Services Ombudsman office.

Sec. 425. Establishes an Office of Immigration Statistics within Bureau of Justice Statistics.

Sec. 426. Concerns preservation of the Attorney General's authority.

SUBCHAPTER B—OTHER PROVISIONS

Sec. 432. Calls for elimination of backlogs.

Sec. 433. Requires a report to Congress on efforts at improving immigration services.

Sec. 435. Calls for the application of Internet-based technologies.

CHAPTER 3—GENERAL PROVISIONS

Sec. 41. Abolishes the INS as of March 1, 2003.

Sec. 45. Requires reports and implementation plans to Congress.

Sec. 46. Details immigration functions.

The Dream Act, as it is commonly referred to, is a bill proposed in various versions from 2001 through 2012. Its name is from the acronym for the formal title of the proposed bill: Development, Relief, and Education for Alien Minors. In summary, the various bills, if enacted, would provide conditional permanent residence status to certain immigrants of good moral character who graduated from U.S. high schools, arrived in the country as minor children (under age 16), and lived in the United States continuously for at least five years prior to the bill's enactment. In most versions of the bill, such minors were required to complete two years military service or to attend a two- or four-year institution of higher learning. They would be granted temporary residency for six years and would qualify for permanent status if they had acquired a degree from an institution of higher learning, had completed at least two years, in good standing, of a program for a bachelor's or higher degree, or have served in the armed services for at least two years and been honorably discharged.

Proponents argue it should not be considered an "amnesty program," and if enacted, the law would produce a variety of social and economic benefits. Critics argue it would be an amnesty program and would reward and thus encourage more illegal immigration, invite fraud, and shield gang members from deportation.

Versions of the bill by various sponsors were introduced in subsequent years but to date have failed to pass one or both houses of Congress. As of 2013, 15 states have enacted some sort of their own version of the Dream Act: Texas, California, Illinois, Utah, Nebraska, Kansas, New Mexico, New Jersey, New York, Washington, Wisconsin, Massachusetts, Maryland, Minnesota, and

Oregon. It is worth noting that the Maryland Dream Act was approved by a statewide ballot, winning 59 percent of the vote, in 2012.

The Dream Act (various proposed bills):

In virtually all its variations in Congress, Dream Act beneficiaries are designated as:

- Not have entered the United States on a non-immigrant Visa (no overstayers).
- Can provide proof of having arrived in the United States before age 16.
- Have proof of having resided in the United States for five consecutive years since their date of arrival.
- Be between the ages of 12 and 35 at the time of the bill's enactment.
- Have graduated from an American high school, obtained a GED, or been admitted to an institution of higher education.
- Be of good moral character.

Since 2007, several senior officials of the DOD have argued in favor of including a provision promising resident status to members of the military as a means of boosting recruitment.

Legislative versions of the Dream Act, proposed in the U.S. Congress:

- In 2001, HR 1582, sponsored by Rep. Luis Gutierrez (D-IL), with 34 co-sponsors.
- Later, in May, 2001, a more limited version was introduced, entitled "Student Adjustment Act of 2001." HR 1918. In the Senate, Orrin Hatch introduced a similar bill, S. 1291.

Since 2001, some version of the Dream Act has been introduced as:

In the U.S. Senate:

- S. 1545, 108th Congress, 2004
- S. 2075, 109th Congress, 2006

- S. 744, 110th Congress, 2008
- S. 2205, 110th Congress, 2010

In the U.S. House of Representatives:

- H.R. 1684, 108th Congress, 2004
- H.R. 5131, 109th Congress, 2006
- H.R. 1275, 110th Congress, 2010

The gist of the Dream Act has been folded into other immigration-related bills as well:

- The Comprehensive Immigration Reform Act of 2006, S. 2611, 109th Congress; and again in the 2007 version, S. 1348. Senator Durbin included a version of the bill in a 2008 Department of Defense Authorization bill, S. 2619.
- In 2007, Senators Dick Durbin, Charles Hagel, and Richard Lugar re-introduced the bill as S. 2205. Other Republican senators insisted the bill require as filibuster-proof count of 60 affirmative votes, and the measure failed, as it has in years since then.
- In 2009 it was reintroduced in both chambers, during the 111th Congress, sponsored by Senators Dick Durbin (D-IL), Richard Lugar (R-IN), Harry Reid (D-NV), Mel Martinez (R-FL), Patrick Leahy (D-VT), Joseph Lieberman (I-CT), Ted Kennedy (D-MA), and Russ Feingold (D-WI). In the House it was sponsored by Rep. Howard Berman (D-CA) and to date has be co-sponsored by 128 representatives and 39 senators, but again failed to reach the 60 vote threshold.
- In 2010, the 111th Congress considered new versions of the bill with various amendments to address concerns voiced by opponents. In 2011, a version was incorporated into the National Defense Authorization Act, but a Senate filibuster of the bill was maintained, 56–43.
- In 2011, then Senate Majority Leader Harry Reid introduced his version of the Dream Act, with some bi-partisan

support (Sen. John Cornyn, TX, and John Kyl and John McCain, AZ, and Lindsey Graham, SC) but the Republican senators withheld their votes objecting it should not be approved without first increasing border enforcement. In 2011, California enacted a version of the Dream Act, and in August, Illinois authorized a privately funded scholarship plan for children of immigrants whether legal or illegal.

• In 2012, President Barack Obama issued his executive actions announcing the Justice Department would stop deporting young illegal aliens who matched criteria previously included under Dream Act proposals.

On December 17, 2004, 108th Congress enacted Public Law 108–458, entitled "The Intelligence Reform and Terrorism Prevention Act of 2004." The full bill runs hundreds of pages, and has a total of eight titles, each of which has numerous subtitles and many sections. The following is the table of contents for the titles and sections most related to border protection, immigration, and visa matters, a few sections related to terrorism prevention that relate to illegal immigration, and implementation of certain sections of the 9/11 Commission's recommendations.

Title V—Border Protection, Immigration, and Visa Matters

SUBTITLE A—ADVANCED TECHNOLOGY NORTHERN BORDER SECURITY PILOT PROGRAM

Sec. 5102. Program requirements.

Sec. 5103. Administrative provisions.

Sec. 5104. Report.

Sec. 5105. Authorization of appropriations.

SUBTITLE B—BORDER AND IMMIGRATION ENFORCEMENT

Sec. 5201. Border surveillance.

Sec. 5202. Increase in full-time Border Patrol agents.

Sec. 5203. Increase in full-time immigration and customs enforcement investigators.

Sec. 5204. Increase in detention bed space.

SUBTITLE C—VISA REQUIREMENTS

Sec. 5301. In-person interviews of visa applicants.

Sec. 5302. Visa application requirements.

Sec. 5304. Revocation of visas and other travel documentation.

SUBTITLE D—IMMIGRATION REFORM

Sec. 5401. Bringing in and harboring certain aliens.

Sec. 5402. Deportation of aliens who have received military-type training from terrorist organizations.

Sec. 5403. Study and report on terrorists in the asylum system.

SUBTITLE E—TREATMENT OF ALIENS WHO COMMIT ACTS OF TORTURE, EXTRAJUDICIAL KILLINGS, OR OTHER ATROCITIES ABROAD

Sec. 5501. Inadmissibility and deportability of aliens who have committed acts of torture or extrajudicial killings abroad.

Sec. 5502. Inadmissibility and deportability of foreign government officials who have committed particularly severe violations of religious freedom.

Sec. 5503. Waiver of inadmissibility.

Sec. 5504. Bar to good moral character for aliens who have committed acts of torture, extrajudicial killings, or severe violations of religious freedom.

Sec. 5505. Establishment of the Office of Special Investigations.

Title VI—Terrorism Prevention. . .

SUBTITLE D—ADDITIONAL ENFORCEMENT TOOLS

Sec. 6301. Bureau of Engraving and Printing security printing.

Sec. 6302. Reporting of certain cross-border transmittal of funds.

Sec. 6303. Terrorism financing.

Subtitle E—Criminal History Background Checks

Sec. 6402. Reviews of criminal records of applicants for private security officer employment.

Sec. 6403. Criminal history background checks.

Title VII—Implementation of 9/11 Commission Recommendations

SUBTITLE B—TERRORIST TRAVEL AND EFFECTIVE SCREENING

Sec. 7201. Counterterrorist travel intelligence.

Sec. 7202. Establishment of human smuggling and trafficking center.

Sec. 7204. International agreements to track and curtail terrorist travel through the use of fraudulently obtained documents.

Sec. 7205. International standards of transliteration of names into Roman alphabet for international travel documents and name-based watchlist system.

Sec. 7206. Immigration security initiative.

Sec. 7207. Certification regarding technology for visa waiver participants.

Sec. 7208. Biometric entry and exit data system.

Sec. 7209. Travel documents.

Sec. 7210. Exchange of terrorist information and increased preinspection at foreign airports.

Sec. 7211. Minimun standards for birth certificates.

Sec. 7212. Driver's licenses and personal identification cards.

Sec. 7213. Social security cards and numbers.

Sec. 7215. Terrorist travel program.

Sec. 7216. Increase in penalties for fraud and related activity.

Sec. 7217. Study on allegedly lost or stolen passports.

Sec. 7218. Establishment of visa and passport security program in the Department of State.

Title VIII—Other Matters

SUBTITLE B—DEPARTMENT OF HOMELAND SECURITY MATTERS

Sec. 8201. Homeland Security geospatial information.

Subtitle C—Homeland Security Civil Rights and Civil Liberties Protection

Sec. 8302. Mission of the Department of Homeland Security.

Sec. 8303. Officer for Civil Rights and Civil Liberties.

Sec. 8304. Protection of Civil Rights and Civil Liberties by Office of Inspector General.

Title 1—Reform of the Intelligence Community

National Security Intelligence Reform Act of 2004, 50 USC 401 note. 118 STAT. 3644, Public Law 108–458—December 17, 2004, President, Congress, 50 USC 403.

Subtitle A—Establishment of Director of National Intelligence

Sec. 102 (a) DIRECTOR OF NATIONAL INTELLIGENCE.

(1) There is a Director of National Intelligence who shall be appointed by the President, by and with the advice and consent of the Senate. Any individual nominated for appointment as Director of National Intelligence shall have extensive national security expertise.

(2) The Director of National Intelligence shall not be located within the Executive Office of the President.

(b) Principal Responsibility—Subject to the authority, direction, and control of the President, the Director of National Intelligence shall—

(1) serve as head of the intelligence community;

(2) act as the principal adviser to the President, to the National Security Council, and the Homeland Security Council for intelligence matters related to the national security;

(3) consistent with section 1018 of the National Security Intelligence Reform Act of 2004, oversee and direct the implementation of the National Intelligence Program.

(c) Prohibition of Dual Service—the individual serving in the position Director of National Intelligence shall not, while so serving, also serve as the Director of the Central Intelligence Agency or as the head of any other element of the intelligence community.

In 2005, Congress passed the law commonly known as the Real ID Act, Title II, H.R.1268: The Emergency Supplemental Appropriations Act for Defense, the Global War on Terror, and Tsunami Relief, 2005 (Enrolled and agreed to or passed by both House and Senate).

Title II—Improved Security for Drivers' Licenses and Personal

IDENTIFICATION CARDS.

Section. 202—MINIMUM DOCUMENT REQUIREMENTS AND ISSUANCE STANDARDS FOR FEDERAL RECOGNITION.

(a) Minimum Standards for Federal Use—

(1) IN GENERAL—beginning 3 years after the date of enactment of this division, a Federal agency may not accept, for any official purpose, a driver's license or identification card issued by a State to

any person unless the State is meeting the requirements of this section.

(2) STATE CERTIFICATIONS—The Secretary shall determine whether a State is meeting the requirements of this section based on certifications made by the State to the Secretary. Such certifications shall be made at such times and in such manner as the Secretary, in consultation with the Secretary of Transportation, may prescribe by regulation.

(b) Minimum Document Requirements.—To meet the requirements of this section, a State shall include, at a minimum, the following information and features on each driver's license and identification card issued to a person by the State:

(1) The person's full legal name.

(2) The person's date of birth.

(3) The person's gender.

(4) The person's driver's license or identification card number.

(5) A digital photograph of the person.

(6) The person's address of principle residence.

(7) The person's signature.

(8) Physical security features designed to prevent tampering, counterfeiting, or duplication of the document for fraudulent purposes.

(9) A common machine-readable technology, with defined minimum data elements.

(c) Minimum Issuance Standards—

(1) IN GENERAL—To meet the requirements of this section, a State shall require, at a minimum, presentation and verification of the following information before issuing a driver's license or identification card to a person:

(A) A photo identification document, except that a non-photo identity document is acceptable if it includes both the person's full legal name and date of birth.

(B) Documentation showing the person's date of birth.

(C) Proof of the person's Social Security account number or verification that the person is not eligible for a social security account number.

(D) Documentation showing a person's name and address of physical residence.

(2) SPECIAL REQUIREMENTS—

(A) IN GENERAL—To meet the requirements of this section, a State shall comply with the minimum standards of this paragraph:

(B) EVIDENCE OF LAWFUL STATUS—A State shall require, before issuing a valid driver's license or identification card to a person, valid documentary evidence that the person:

(1) is a citizen or national of the United States;

(2) is an alien lawfully admitted for permanent resident status or temporary residence in the United States;

(3) has conditional permanent resident status in the United States;

(4) has an approved application for asylum in the United States or has entered into the United States in refugee status;

(5) has a valid, unexpired nonimmigrant visa or nonimmigrant visa status for entry into the United States;

(6) has a pending application for asylum in the United States;

(7) has a pending or approved application for temporary protected status in the United States;

(8) has approved deferred action status; or

(9) has a pending application for adjustment of status to that of an alien lawfully admitted for permanent resident status in the United States.

(C) Temporary Driver's Licenses and Identification Cards

(1) IN GENERAL—If a person presents evidence under any clauses (5) through (9) of subparagraph B, the State may only issue a temporary driver's license or temporary identification card to such person.

(2) EXPIRATION DATE—a temporary driver's license or temporary identification card issued pursuant to this subparagraph shall be valid only during the period of time of the applicant's authorized stay in the United States or, if there is no definite end to the period of the authorized stay, a period of one year.

(3) DISPLAY OF EXPIRATION DATE—a temporary driver's license or temporary identification card issued pursuant to this subparagraph shall clearly indicate that it is temporary and shall state the date upon which it expires.

(4) RENEWAL—temporary driver's license or temporary identification card issued pursuant to this subparagraph may be renewed only upon presentation of valid documentary evidence that the status by which the

applicant qualified for the temporary driver's license or temporary identification card has been extended by the Secretary of Homeland Security.

(3) VERIFICATION OF DOCUMENTS—to meet the requirements of this section, a State shall implement the following procedures:

(A) Before issuing a driver's license or identification card to a person, the State shall verify, with the issuing agency, the issuance, validity, and completeness of each document required to be presented by the person under paragraph (1) or (2).

(B) The State shall not accept any foreign document, other than an official passport, to satisfy a requirement of paragraph (1) or (2).

(C) Not later than September 11, 2005, the State shall enter into a memorandum of understanding with the Secretary of Homeland Security to routinely utilize the automated system known as Systematic Alien Verification of Entitlement, as provided for by section 404 of the Illegal Immigration Reform and Immigrant Responsibility Act of 1996 (110 Stat. 3009–664), to verify the legal presence status of a person, other than a United States citizen, applying for a driver's license or identification card.

(D) Other requirements—To meet the requirements of this section, a State shall adopt the following practices in the issuance of driver's licenses and identification cards:

(1) Employ technology to capture a digital image of identity source of documents so that the images may be retained in electronic storage in a transferable format.

(2) Retain paper copies of source documents for a minimum of 7 years or images of source documents presented for a minimum of 10 years.

(3) Subject each person applying for a driver's license or identification card to mandatory facial image capture.

(4) Establish an effective procedure to confirm or verify a renewing applicant's information.

(5) Confirm with the Social Security Administration a social security account number presented by a person using the full social security account number. In the event that a social security account number is already registered to or associated with another person to which any State has issued a driver's license or identification card, the State shall resolve the discrepancy and take appropriate action.

(6) Refuse to issue a driver's license or identification card to a person holding a driver's license issued by another State without confirmation that the person is terminating or has terminated the driver's license.

(7) Ensure the physical security of locations where driver's licenses and identification cards are produced and the security of document materials and papers from which driver's licenses and identification cards are produced.

(8) Subject all persons authorized to manufacture or produce driver's licenses and identification cards to appropriate security clearance requirements.

(9) Establish fraudulent document recognition training programs for appropriate employees engaged in the issuance of driver's licenses or identification cards.

(10) Limit the period of validity of all driver's licenses and identification cards that are not temporary to a period that does not exceed 8 years.

(11) In any case in which State issues a driver's license or identification card that does not satisfy the requirements of this section, ensure that such license or identification card—

    (a) clearly states on its face that it is may not be accepted by any Federal agency for federal identification or any other official purpose; and

    (b) uses a unique design or color indicator to alert Federal agency or other law enforcement personnel that it may not be accepted for such purpose.

(12) Provide electronic access to all other States to information contained in the motor vehicle database of the State.

(13) Maintain a State motor vehicle database that contains, at a minimum—

    (a) all data fields printed on driver's licenses and identification cards issued by the State; and

    (b) motor vehicle drivers' histories, including motor vehicle violations, suspensions, and points on licenses.

SECTION 203. TRAFFICKING IN AUTHENTIFICATION FEATURES FOR USE IN FALSE IDENTIFICATION DOCUMENTS.

(a) Criminal penalty—Section 1028(a)(8) of title 18, United States Code, is amended by striking "false authentication features" and inserting "false or actual authentication features," (1) IN GENERAL—The Secretary shall enter, into the appropriate aviation security screening database, appropriate information regarding any person convicted of using a false driver's license at an airport (as such term is defined in section 40102 of title 49, United States Code). (2) FALSE DEFINED—In this subsection, the term "false" has the same meaning such term has under section 1028(d) of title 18, United States Code.

SECTION 204. GRANTS TO STATES.

(a) In General—The Secretary may make grants to a State to assist the State in conforming to the minimum standards set forth in this title.

(b) Authorization of Appropriations—There are authorized to be appropriated to the Secretary for each of the fiscal years 2005 through 2009 such sums as may be necessary to carry out this title.

SECTION 205. AUTHORITY.

(a) Participation of Secretary of Transportation and States—All authority to issue regulations, set standards, and issue grants under this title shall be carried out by the Secretary, in consultation with the Secretary of Transportation and the States.

(b) Extension of Deadlines—The Secretary may grant to a State an extension of time to meet the requirements of section 202(a)(1) if the State provides adequate justification for noncompliance.

SECTION 207. LIMITATION ON STATUTORY CONSTRUCTION.

Nothing in this title shall be construed to affect the authorities or responsibilities of the Secretary of Transportation or the States under chapter 303 of title 49, United States Code.

In 2006, Congress passed the Secure Fence Act, which provided for the construction of a fence along the U.S. southwestern border

(with Mexico) as a "hard" method to secure greater control of the border.
The Secure Fence Act of 2006. (H.R. 6061) An Act to Establish Operational Control Over the International and Maritime Borders of the United States.

SECTION 2: ACHIEVING OPERATIONAL CONTROL ON THE BORDER.

(a) IN GENERAL—Not later than 18 months after the date of the enactment of this Act, the Secretary of Homeland Security shall take all actions the Secretary determines necessary and appropriate to achieve and maintain operational control over the entire international land and maritime borders of the United States, to include the following—

   (1) systematic surveillance of the international land and maritime borders of the United States through more effective use of personnel and technology, such as unmanned aerial vehicles, ground-based sensors, satellites, radar coverage, and cameras; and

   (2) physical infrastructure enhancements to prevent unlawful entry by aliens into the United States and facilitate access to the international land and maritime borders by United States Customs and Border Protection, such as additional checkpoints, all weather access roads, and vehicle barriers.

(b) OPERATIONAL CONTROL DEFINED.—In this section, the term "operational control" means the prevention of all unlawful entries into the United States, including entry by terrorists, narcotics, other unlawful aliens, instruments of terrorism, narcotics, and other contraband.

(c) REPORT.—Not later than one year after the date of the enactment of this Act and annually thereafter, the Secretary shall submit to Congress a report on the progress made toward achieving and maintaining operational control over the entire international land and maritime borders of the United States in accordance with this section.

SECTION 3. CONSTRUCTION OF FENCING AND SECURITY IMPROVEMENTS IN BORDER AREA FROM PACIFIC OCEAN TO GULF OF MEXICO.

Section 102(b) of the Illegal Immigration Reform and Immigrant Responsibility Act of 1996 (Public Law 104–208; 8 U.S.C. 1103 note) is amended—

(a) REINFORCED FENCING.—In carrying out subsection (a), the Secretary of Homeland Security shall provide for at least 2 layers of reinforced fencing, the installation of additional physical barriers, roads, lighting, cameras, and sensors—

   (i)   extending from 10 miles west of the Tecate, California, port of entry to 10 miles east of Tecate, California, port of entry;

   (ii) extending from 10 miles west of Calexico, California, port of entry to 5 miles east of the Douglas, Arizona, port of entry;

   (iii) extending from 5 miles west of Columbus, New Mexico, port of entry to 10 miles east of El Paso, Texas;

   (iv) extending from 5 miles northwest of the Del Rio, Texas, port of entry to 5 miles southwest of the Eagle Pass, Texas, port of entry; and

   (v)   extending 15 miles to the Brownsville, Texas, port of entry.

(b) PRIORITY AREAS.—With respect to the border described—

   (i)   In subparagraph (A)(ii), the Secretary shall ensure that an interlocking surveillance camera system is installed along such area by Mary 30, 2007, and that fence construction is completed by May 30, 2008; and

   (ii) In subparagraph (A)(v), the Secretary shall ensure that fence construction from 15 miles northwest of the Laredo, Texas, port of entry to 15 miles southeast of the Laredo, Texas, port of entry is completed by December 31, 2008.

(c) EXCEPTION—If the topography of a specific area has an elevation grade that exceeds 10 percent, the Secretary may use other means to secure such area, including the use of surveillance and barrier tools.

SECTION 4. NORTHERN BORDER STUDY.

(A) IN GENERAL.—The Secretary of Homeland Security shall conduct a study on the feasibility of a state-of-the-art infrastructure security system along the northern international land and maritime border of the United States and shall include in the study—

(1) the necessity of implementing such a system;

(2) the feasibility of implementing such a system;

(3) the economic impact implementing such a system will have along the northern border.

(B) REPORT.—Not later than one year after the date of the enactment of this Act, the Secretary of Homeland Security shall submit to the Committee on Homeland Security of the House and Representatives and the Committee on Homeland Security and Government Affairs of the Senate a report that contains the results of the study conducted under subsection (A)

SECTION 5. EVALUATION AND REPORT RELATING TO CUSTOMS AUTHORITY TO STOP CERTAIN FLEEING VEHICLES.

(A) EVALUATION.—Not later than 30 days after the date of the enactment of this Act, the Secretary of Homeland Security shall—

(1) evaluate the authority of personnel of United States Customs and Border Protection to stop vehicles that enter the United States illegally and refuse to stop when ordered to do so by such personnel, compare such Customs authority with the authority of the Coast Guard to stop vessels under section 637 of title 14, United States Code, and make an assessment as to whether such Customs authority should be expanded;

(2) review the equipment and technology available to United States Customs and Border Protection personnel to stop vehicles described in paragraph (1) and make an assessment as to whether or not better equipment or technology is available or should be developed; and

(3) evaluate the training provided to United States Customs and Border Protection personnel to stop vehicles described in paragraph (1).

(B) REPORT.—Not later than 60 days after the date of the enactment of this Act, the Secretary of Homeland Security shall submit to the Committee on Homeland Security of the House of Representatives and the Committee on Homeland Security and Governmental Affairs of the Senate a report that contains the results of the evaluation conducted under subsection (a).

In June 2013, a group of 19 conservative Republicans in the House of Representatives introduced a bill, the Strengthen and Fortify Enforcement Act (the SAFE Act), designed to "harden" the border to maintain control of the border and stop illegal immigration. The bill's table of contents indicating its titles and sections makes clear its total reliance on a "crack-down" approach to border security and law enforcement.

H.R. 2278. The SAFE Act, 2013.

TITLE 1—IMMIGRATION LAW ENFORCEMENT BY STATES AND LOCALITIES

Sec. 102. Immigration law by States and localities.

TITLE III—REMOVAL OF CRIMINAL ALIENS

Sec. 302. Precluding admissibility of aliens convicted of aggravated felonies or other serious offenses.

Sec. 303. Espionage clarification.

Sec. 304. Prohibition of the sale of firearms to, or the possession of firearms by, certain aliens.

Sec. 305. Uniform statute of limitations for certain immigration, naturalization, and peonage offenses.

Sec. 308. Precluding refugee or asylee adjustment of status for aggravated felons.

Sec. 309. Inadmissibility and deportability of drunk drivers.

Sec. 310. Detention of dangerous aliens.

Sec. 311. Grounds of inadmissibility and deportability for alien gang members.

Sec. 312. Extension of identity theft offenses.

Sec. 313. Laundering of monetary instruments.

Sec. 314. Increases criminal penalties relating to alien smuggling and related offenses.

Sec. 315. Penalties for illegal entry.

Sec. 316. Illegal entry.

Sec. 317. Reform of passport, visa, and immigration fraud offenses.

Sec. 319. Expedited removal for aliens inadmissible on criminal or security grounds.

Sec. 320. Increased penalties barring the admission of convicted sex offenders failing to register and requiring deportation of sex offenders failing to register.

Sec. 321. Protecting immigrants from convicted sex offenders.

Sec. 322. Clarification of crimes of violence and crimes involving moral turpitude.

Sec. 323. Penalties for failure to obey removal orders.

TITLE IV—VISA SECURITY

Sec. 401. Cancellation of additional visas.

Sec. 402. Visa information sharing.

Sec. 403. Restricting waiver of visa interviews.

Sec. 404. Authorizing the Department of State to not interview certain ineligible visa applicants.

Sec. 405. Visa refusal and revocation.

Sec. 406. Funding for the visa security program.

Sec. 407. Expeditious expansion of visa security program to high-risk posts.

Sec. 408. Expedited clearance and placement of Department of Homeland Security personnel at overseas embassies and consular posts.

Sec. 409. Increased criminal penalties for student visa integrity.

Sec. 410. Accreditation requirements.

Sec. 411. Visa fraud.

Sec. 412. Background checks.

Sec. 413. Flight schools not certified by FAA.

Sec. 414. Revocation of accreditation.

Sec. 415. Report on risk assessment.

TITLE V—AID TO U.S. IMMIGRATION AND CUSTOMS ENFORCEMENT OFFICERS

Sec. 501. ICE immigration enforcement agents.

Sec. 502. ICE detention enforcement officers.

Sec. 503. Ensuring the safety of ICE officers and agents.

Sec. 504. ICE Advisory Council.

Sec. 505. Pilot program for electronic field processing.

Sec. 506. Additional ICE deportation officers and support staff.

Sec. 507. Additonal ICE prosecutors.

TITLE VI—MISCELLANEOUS ENFORCEMENT PROVISIONS

Sec. 601. Encouraging aliens to depart voluntarily.

Sec. 602. Deterring aliens ordered removed from remaining in the United States unlawfuly.

Sec. 603. Reinstatement of removal orders.

Sec. 605. Reports to Congress on the exercise and abuse of prosecutorial discretion.

Sec. 606. Waiver of Federal laws with respect to border security actions on Department of the Interior and Department of Agriculture lands.

TITLE 1—IMMIGRATION LAW ENFORCEMENT BY STATES AND LOCALITIES

(c) SEVERABILITY.—If any provision of this title, or the application of such provision to any person or circumstance, is held invalid, the remainder of this title, and the application of such provision to other persons not similarly situated or to other circumstances, shall not be affected by such invalidation.

Also in 2013, the Senate passed a comprehensive immigration reform bill, S. 744. The following summarizes some key sections of the bill, sponsored by Sen. Charles Schumer (D-NY) and passed Senate on June 27, 2013.

S. 744. THE BORDER SECURITY, ECONOMIC OPPORTUNITY, AND IMMIGRATION MOBILIZATION ACT.

Sec. 2. States passage of Act recognizes that the primary tenet of its success depends on securing U.S. sovereignty and establishing a coherent and just system for integrating those who seek to join American society.

Sec. 3. Prohibits the Secretary of Homeland Security from processing applications for registered provisional immigrant status (RPI) until the Secretary has submitted to Congress the notice of commencement of implementation of the Comprehensive Southern Border Security Strategy and the Southern Border Fencing Strategy.

Sec. 4. Establishes a Southern Border Security Commission.

Sec. 5. Directs the Secretary to implement a Comprehensive Southern Border Security Strategy for achieving and maintaining effective control between and at the ports of entry in all border sectors along the Southern border; and a Southern Border Fencing Strategy as to where 700 miles of fencing and technology should be deployed.

Sec. 6. Establishes in the Treasury the Comprehensive Immigration Reform Trust Fund.

Title 1: Border Security. Directs the Secretary to increase the number of trained full-time active U.S. Border Patrol agents deployed to the Southern Border to 38,405 by September 30, 2021, and increase the number of CBP officers by 3,500 by September 30, 2017; and increase trained CBP Air and Marine unmanned aircraft systems crew, marine agent, and personnel by 160; and their flight hours to 130,000 annually by September 30, 2015.

Sec. 1103. Authorizes the governor of a state, with approval of the Secretary of Defense (DOD), to order National Guard personnel to perform operations in the Southwest border region.

Sec. 1104. Directs the Secretary to increase the number of crossing prosecutions in the Tucson sector to up to 210 prosecutions per day by increasing funding for additional attorneys and support staff, interpreters and U.S. marshals. Directs the Secretary to enhance border infrastructure by additional Border Patrol stations, upgrading and establishing additional Border Patrol operating bases, and establishing a grant program with DOT to construct transportation improvements at international border crossings. Authorizes FY 2014–2018 appropriations for such.

Directs the President to appoint additional district judges for Arizona, California, and Texas.

Increases fee for filing a civil action in U.S. district court to $360.

Sec. 1105. Directs USDA and Secretary of Interior to provide CBP personnel with immediate access to federal lands in the Southwest Border region in Arizona for security activities.

Sec. 1106. Requires CBP to deploy additional mobile, video, and portable surveillance systems, and unarmed, unmanned drone vehicles in the Southwest Border region to provide 24-hour surveillance.

Sec. 1107. Directs the Secretary to establish a two-year grant program to improve communications in the border region and authorizes appropriations for such.

Sec. 1108. Directs Attorney General (DOJ) to reimburse state, county, tribal, and municipal governments for costs associated with the prosecution and pre-trial detention of federally initiated criminal cases and authorizes FY2014–2018 appropriations.

Sec. 1110. Authorizes appropriations for the state criminal assistance program (SCAAP) through FY 2015.

Sec. 1112. Directs the Secretary to provide appropriate training for CBP officers, Border Patrol officers, ICE agents, U.S. Air and Marine Division agents, agriculture specialists stationed within 100 miles of any U.S. land or marine border, or at any U.S. port of entry; and to establish CBP child custody guidelines.

Sec. 1113. Establishes a DHS Border Oversight Task Force and authorizes FY2014-FY2017 appropriations.

Sec. 1114. Establishes an Ombudsman for Immigration Related Concerns in the DHS.

Sec. 1115. Directs the Secretary to consider safety and family concerns in any action of repatriation of individuals apprehended for immigration violations and provides for training for CBP personnel.

Sec. 1116. Revises maximum distances in a Northern Border sector or district which DHS personnel have the authority to board and search and search vehicles for aliens.

Sec. 1120. Human Trafficking Reporting Act of 2013.

Sec. 1133. DHS to report to Congress every six months on removals.

Sec. 1201. Directs the Secretary to initiate certain expedited removal proceedings relating to border security.

Title II: Immigrant Visas—Registration and Adjustment of Registered Provisional Immigrants.

Sec. 2101. After certification by the Secretary DHS about national security and law enforcement clearances, to grant RPI status to certain aliens unlawfully in the U.S. (enacting provisions of the Dream Act).

Sec. 2102. Essentially, establishes a process for the earned legalization of certain aliens unlawfully in the U.S. Makes those authorized RPIs ineligible for any federal means-tested benefit. Authorizes RPIs to be issued a Social Security number and to enlist in the Armed Forces.

Prohibits an RPI alien from applying for lawful permanent status until the Secretary of State certifies that immigrant visas have become available for all approved petitions filed before the date of enactment of this Act.

States that an RPI alien may only adjust status under the merit-based system provided for by the Act.

Sec. 2013. Authorizes enactment of the DREAM ACT of 2013.

Sec. 2105. Sets a criminal penalty of up to $10,000 for a person who knowingly uses, publishes or permits the improper use of RPI application information.

Sec. 2106. Authorizes USCIS to establish a program to award grants to eligible nonprofit organizations to assist RPI applicants

Subtitle B: Agriculture Worker Program. Enacts the Agriculture Worker Program Act of 2013 with all its various provisions, including making a blue card alien ineligible for any federal means-tested benefit.

Sec. 2212. Requires payment of a $400 fine, and payment of any federal tax liability.

Sec. 2232. Establishes a nonimmigrant agricultural (W-3 and W-4 visa) worker program; and among its many provisions, excludes W-3 and W-4 workers from any need-based federal financial assistance program.

Subtitle C: Future Immigration.

Sec. 2301. Establishes a merit-based points immigration admission system with 120,000 admissions per year with increases based on certain specified admission and employment conditions to a maximum admission cap of 250,000, allows recapture of unused visas, and allows lawful permanent resident status for such entrants.

Sec. 2303. Repeals the diversity immigrant program as of October 1, 2014.

Sec. 2304. Sets forth worldwide levels of employment and family-based immigrants.

Sec. 2305. Includes spouses or minor child of a lawful permanent alien in the definition of "immediate family."

Sec. 2306. Eliminates the per-country limit for employment-based immigrants and increases the per-country limit for family tied immigrants.

Sec. 2307. Revises certain provisions of the family-based immigrant visa allocation system; including elimination of the visa category for brothers and sisters of U.S. citizens.

Sec. 2318. Extends the Iraqi and the Afghan special immigrant visa program.

Title IV: Reforms to Nonimmigrant Visa Programs-Subtitle A: Employment-based Nonimmigrant Visas.
Several sections revise and change the caps for H-1B to a cap of 115,000 per fiscal year; and a minimum of 115,000 visas to a maximum of 180,000 visas in subsequent years.

Limits the exemption from H-1B numerical limitations to STEM occupations and increases the annual STEM allocation to 25,000.

Subtitle B: H-1B Visa Fraud and Abuse Protection. Several sections that revise H-1B provisions to deal with fraud and abuse.

Subtitle C: L Visa Fraud and Abuse Protection. Includes several sections to address L visa fraud and abuse concerns.

Subtitle D: Other Nonimmigrant Visas. Includes numerous sections to revise nonimmigrant visas

Subtitle F: Reforms to the H-2B Visa Program. Includes numerous sections to revise and reform the H-2B visa program.

Subtitle G: W Nonimmigrant Visas. Establishes a Bureau of Immigration and Labor Market Research to supplement W-visa recruitment methods, conduct survey every three months on the need for W-visa cap of construction worker unemployment and report to Congress on employment-based immigrant and nonimmigrant visa programs.

Subtitle H: Investing in New Venture, Entrepreneurial Startups, and Technologies. Contains several sections to establish a nonimmigrant X-visa for qualified entrepreneur who invest certain amounts in U.S. business and which create certain numbers of jobs and generate at least $250,000 in annual revenues to the U.S. A provision of which establishes a $1,000 X-visa fee.

Subtitle I: Student and Exchange Visitor Programs. Contains a dozen or so provisions regarding student visa integrity.
These executive actions were projected to affect 4.4 million persons. DAPA program implementation was temporarily blocked by a federal district court in Texas which issued an order to cease accepting applications for DAPA or expanded DACA until a higher court issues an order that allows the initiatives to go forward.

Deferred Action is an administrative relief from deportation that has been around for a long time. The president's executive action authorizes the DHS to allow certain non-U.S. citizens to remain in the United States temporarily, granted on a case-by-case basis.

The Deferred Action for Childhood Arrivals (DACA) Program and the Deferred Action for Parents of Americans and Lawful Permanent Residents (DAPA).

PERSONS ELIGIBLE FOR DAPA INCLUDE:

-A parent of a U.S. citizen or lawful permanent resident.

-Have continuously lived in the U.S. since January 1, 2010.

-Have been present in U.S. on November 20, 2014.

-Not have a lawful immigration status as of November 20, 2014—meaning one entered the country undocumented or if lawfully entered, must have stayed beyond the expiration of the temporary visa.

-Have not been convicted of certain criminal offenses, including felonies and some misdemeanors.

DACA APPLICANTS MUST:

-Have come before their 16th birthday.

-Lived in the U.S. continuously since January 1, 2010.

-Be present in U.S. on June 15, 2012 and every day since.

-Have graduated or obtained a GED certificate, or be in school on the date the person submits an application.

-Pays an application fee of $465, which consists of a $380 fee for employment authorization, and an $85 fee for fingerprints.

Sources: All summaries by author.

References

Anderson, James. 1979. *Public Policy Making*. New York: Holt, Rinehart and Winston.

Information Plus. 2006. *Immigration and Illegal Aliens: Burden or Blessing?* Detroit: Thomson/Gale.

LeMay, Michael. 2004. *U.S. Immigration: A Reference Handbook*. Santa Barbara, CA: ABC-CLIO.

LeMay, Michael, and Elliott Robert Barkan. 1999. *U.S. Immigration and Naturalization Laws and Issues: A Documentary History*. Westport, CT: Greenwood.

LeMay, Michael, ed. 2013. *Transforming America: Perspectives on Immigration*, 3 vols. Santa Barbara, CA: ABC-CLIO.

Introduction

This chapter lists and briefly discusses the major sources of information the reader is encouraged to consult. It begins with print sources, first from the agencies and organizations involved in immigration policy and particularly those concerned with illegal immigration policy reforms.

Scholarly books on the subject follow, with more than 100 such cited and annotated. The major scholarly journals in the field are then covered and described. Major governmental reports are listed and described.

Finally, the chapter discusses nonprint sources; more than 50 films and videos produced since 2000 and available for viewing. These nonprint sources often dramatically depict the issues and people involved, putting real "faces" to the numbers and statistics

Immigration and Customs Enforcement officers escort an arrestee in an apartment building, in the Bronx borough of New York, during a series of early-morning raids on March 3, 2015. Immigrant and Customs Enforcement say an increasing number of cities and counties across the United States are limiting cooperation with the agency and putting its officers in dangerous situations as they track down foreign-born criminals. Instead, more of its force is out on the streets, eating up resources and conducting investigations because cities like New York and states like California have passed legislation that limits many of the detention requests issued by immigration authorities. Customs Enforcement finds it easier to apprehend illegal immigrants as they attempt to cross the border than to enforce immigration law and deport undocumented immigrants once they have entered the United States. (AP Photo/Richard Drew) *so often referred to in debates over the illegal immigration contro-versy. They highlight the human interest aspect of the issue.*

Selected Print Resources

Books

Aleinikoff, T. Alexander, and Douglas Klusmeyer, eds. 2000. *From Migrants to Citizens: Membership in a Changing World.* Washington, DC: Brookings Institution Press. It is scholarly discussion of the incorporation of immigrants with discussion of naturalization law and policy.

Aleinikoff, T. Alexander, and Douglas Klusmeyer, eds. 2001. *Citizenship Today: Global Perspectives and Practices.* Washington, DC: Brookings Institution Press. A Carnegie Endowment for International Peace book by leading immigration lawyer experts in the subject.

Aleinikoff, T. Alexander, and Douglas Klusmeyer, eds. 2002. *Citizenship Policies for an Age of Migration.* Washington, DC: Brookings Institution Press. A Carnegie Endowment for International Peace book by two leading immigration lawyers focusing on naturalization policy in a global context.

Allport, Alan and John E. Ferguson, Jr., eds. 2009. *Immigration Policy*, 2nd ed. New York: Chelsea House/Facts on File. This book uses a point/counterpoint approach to a discussion of the complex topic of immigration. It covers controversies like the cost/benefits of illegal immigration and English as an official language, among a wide range of issues covered.

Anderson, Stewart. 2010. *Immigration.* Westport, CT: Greenwood Press. This volume takes a comprehensive look at U.S. immigration policy and its impact on the nation, with a historic overview and a guide to how immigration works in practice for businesses and economics.

Andreas, Peter. 2000. *Border Games: Policing the U.S.-Mexico Divide.* Ithaca, NY: Cornell University Press. It is an extensive study of the difficulty of enacting and implementing policy to control illegal immigration, focusing on the southern border.

Andreas, Peter, and Timothy Snyder, eds. 2000. *The Wall around the West: State Borders and Immigration Controls in North America and Europe.* Lanham, MD: Rowman & Littlefield. A balanced but critical examination of the increasing barriers being enacted to control immigration flows into Canada, the United States, and the major immigration-receiving nations of Europe, particularly the European Union countries.

Arnold, Kathleen R., ed. 2011. *Anti-Immigration in the United States: A Historical Encyclopedia.* Santa Barbara, CA: ABC-CLIO. This two-volume set is one of the first to address American anti-immigration sentiment. Organized alphabetically, it covers major historical periods and relevant concepts, leading figures and groups in the anti-immigration movement.

Arreola, Daniel D., ed. 2004. *Hispanic Spaces, Latino Places: Community and Cultural Diversity in Contemporary America.* Austin: University of Texas Press. It is a collection of original essays on Hispanic migration to the U.S. Southwest. Numerous scholars examine a panorama of issues and sectors of society affected by the influx, and how those communities affect the incorporation of new Hispanic immigrants.

Baker, Susan Gonzales. 1990. *The Cautious Welcome: The Legalization Program of the Immigration Reform and Control Act.* Santa Monica, CA: Rand Corporation and the Urban Institute Press. It is a critical examination of IRCA's legalization programs and the difficulties and failures in its implementation.

Bakken, Gordon M. and Alexandra Kindell. 2006. *Encyclopedia of Immigration and Migration in the American West,* 2 vol. Thousand Oaks, CA: Sage Publications. This two-volume encyclopedia looks at the ethnic groups crossing the plains, landing at ports, and crossing borders. It contains focused biographies, community histories, economic enterprise analyses, and a variety of demographic data.

Barone, Michael. 2013. *Shaping Our Nation: How Surges of Migration Transformed America and Its Politics.* New York: Crown Forum/Random House. The author examines the history of immigration and how past surges in immigration influenced American culture, society, and politics.

Barone, Michael and Chuck McClutcheon. 2014. *The Almanac of American Politics.* Chicago: University of Chicago Press. The "gold standard" almanac of the Congress, updated every two years with a new congress, it covers all the members, their districts, the politics involved in each, and aspects of the workings of Congress, committee assignments, and caucus memberships.

Barstram, David, Maristsa V. Poros, and Pierre Monfort. 2014. *Key Concepts in Migration.* Thousand Oaks, CA: Sage Publications. This volume uses a key concepts approach to the study of immigration. It considers three dozen concepts at the heart of migration studies. It is a valuable reference resource for students and scholars alike.

Bean, Frank B., and Stephanie Bell-Rose, eds. 1999. *Immigration and Opportunity: Race, Ethnicity, and Employment in the U.S.* New York: Russell Sage. An extensive collection of essays from leading sociologists and demographers that provides a systematic account of the sundry ways in which immigration impacts the labor market experiences of the native-born.

Bean, Frank, Barry Edmonston, and Jeffrey Passell. 1990. *Undocumented Migration to the U.S.* Santa Monica, CA: Rand Corporation and the Urban Institute Press. It is a thorough and scholarly look at illegal immigration focusing on that across the southern U.S. border.

Bean, Frank D., and Gillian Stevens. 2003. *America's New-comers: Immigrant Incorporation and the Dynamics of Diversity.* New York: Russell Sage. A demographer and a language specialist examine the factors influencing the gradual incorporation of immigrants and their children and what aspects influence the rate of incorporation.

Bean, Frank, George Vernez, and Charles B. Keely. 1989. *Opening and Closing the Doors.* Santa Monica, CA, and Washington, DC: Rand Corporation and the Urban Institute Press. One of the more important books in a series of excellent books and monographs published as a result of a joint Rand Corporation/Urban Institute major research project examining immigration policy particularly as to the impact of the Immigration Reform and Control Act of 1986 (IRCA).

Beck, Roy H. 1996. *The Case against Immigration.* New York: Norton. It is a thorough articulation of all the arguments and data that can be marshaled against high levels of immigration.

Boeri, Tito, et al., eds. 2002. *Immigration Policy and the Welfare State.* New York: Oxford University Press. This book draws together and unifies analysis of immigration into the major EU countries and the United States, covering the major trends and dramatic developments of the 1990s. It emphasizes the influence of the welfare state on immigration incentives, and examines other influences on both legal and illegal migration and on their market outcomes on these two continents.

Borjas, George. 1997. *Friends and Strangers: The Effects of Immigration on the U.S. Economy.* New York: Basic. A noted scholar examines and critically evaluates the economic impact of high levels of legal and illegal immigration to the United States.

Brewer, Stuart. 2006. *Borderland and Bridges: A History of U.S.-Latin American Relations.* Westport, CT: Praeger Securities

International. Brewer examines the complex relationship between the United States and Latin America with an introduction to the most important events in the diplomatic, military, social, and economic history of the relationship.

Briggs, Vernon M., Jr., and Stephen Moore. 1994. *Still an Open Door? U.S. Immigration Policy and the American Economy.* Washington, DC: American University Press. It is another volume of noted scholars of the economic impact of immigration, stressing the negative effects of large-scale immigration and the negative effects of illegal migration.

Brubaker, William Roger, ed. 1989. *Immigration and the Politics of Citizenship in Europe and North America.* New York: University Press of America and the German Marshall Fund of the United States. It is an interesting collection of essays on naturalization, citizenship, and the impact of immigration on the politics of the United States and of the EU nations. Focus is on legal immigration.

Calavita, Kitty. 1992. *Inside the State: The Bracero Program, Immigration, and the INS.* New York: Routledge. One of the best examinations of the Bracero Program, with insights into temporary worker programs and the problems associated with that approach.

Camarota, Steven A. 1999. *Immigrants in the United States–1998: A Snapshot of America's Foreign-Born Population.* Washington, DC: Center for Immigration Studies. An extensive demographic-data look at immigrants in the United States and the degree to which they are assimilating into the socioeconomic structures of society.

Chavez, Leo R. 1992. *Shadowed Lives: Undocumented Immigrants in American Society.* New York: Harcourt Brace Jovanovich. It is a sharply focused examination of all the problems and negative impacts, and discrimination facing undocumented aliens.

Chiswick, Barry R. 2005. *The Economics of Immigration: Selected Papers of Barry S. Chiswick.* Cheltenham, UK:

Edward Edgar Publishing. A thorough collection of the writings of Barry Chiswick, widely considered one of the leading scholars of the economics of immigration, and of the complexity of measuring the costs and benefits of legal immigration.

Cieslik, Thomas, David Felsen, and Akis Kalaitzdis. 2008. *Immigration: A Documentary and Reference Guide.* Westport, CT: Greenwood Press. These three respected authorities on immigration and international affairs examine the contemporary realities of immigration enmeshed as it is in economics, human rights, and national security issues.

Conover, Ted. 1987. *Coyotes: A Journey through the Secret World of America's Illegal Aliens.* New York: Vintage. A reporter's "inside" look at the illegal alien smuggling problem and how it operates and largely avoids border control.

Craig, Richard B. 1971. *The Bracero Program: Interest Groups and Foreign Policy.* Austin: University of Texas Press. One of the early scholarly analyses of the Bracero Program, focusing on interest groups for and against and how they shaped the program and its implementation and relation to foreign policy concerns.

Crane, Keith, et al. 1990. *The Effects of Employer Sanctions on the Flow of Undocumented Immigrants to the United States.* Santa Monica, CA: Rand Corporation and the Urban Institute Press. One of an excellent series of studies by the Rand Corporation and the Urban Institute studying the impact of IRCA and especially the effects of the employer sanctions approach to control illegal immigration.

Crockoff, James D. 1986. *Outlaws in the Promised Land: Mexican Immigrant Workers and America's Future.* New York: Grove. It provides a critical view of the illegal immigration flow, the exploitation of undocumented workers, and the economic effects of illegal immigration on the U.S. economy.

Daniels, Roger. 1990. *Coming to America: A History of Immigration and Ethnicity in American Life.* New York: Harper.

It is a brief but insightful history of immigration and ethnicity and their impact on U.S. society by a noted immigration historian.

Daniels, Roger. 2005. *Guarding the Golden Door: American Immigration Policy and Immigration since 1882.* New York: Hill and Wang. One of the leading authorities and immigration historians, Daniels gives a detailed analysis of immigration policy and how and why it changed over time, from 1882 to 2000.

Daniels, Roger, and Otis L. Graham. 2003. *Debating American Immigration, 1882–Present.* Lanham, MD: Rowman & Littlefield. Two noted historians of immigration debate the American immigration experience.

Erler, Edward, and Margaret Stock. 2012. *The Cost to Americans and America of Ending Birthright Citizenship.* Arlington, VA: National Foundation for American Policy. It is a critical examination of the philosophical, ideological, and legal aspects of the birthright citizenship issue.

Etzioni, Amitai, and Jason H. Marsh, eds. 2003. *Rights v. Public Safety after 9/11: America in the Age of Terrorism.* Lanham, MD: Rowman & Littlefield. It provides a timely scholarly debate on the issues of civil rights, homeland defense, and public safety.

Faist, Thomas. 2000. *The Volume and Dynamics of International Migration and Transnational Social Spaces.* New York: Oxford University Press. This volume offers an innovative theoretical account of the causes, nature, and extent of the movement of international migrants between affluent and poorer countries and provides a conceptual framework for migration decision making and the dynamics of international movement of peoples.

Ferris, Elizabeth G., ed. 1985. *Refugees and World Politics.* New York: Praeger. A thorough collection of essays on the refugee crisis up to the early 1980s, it is an important source for world refugee numbers to that point in time, and most of the issues and many of the problems remain relevant today.

Fix, Michael, ed. 1991. *The Paper Curtain: Employer Sanctions Implementation, Impact, and Reform.* Washington, DC: Urban Institute. An objective, scholarly examination of the employer sanctions program of IRCA, the problems involved in its implementation, why it largely failed to achieve its aims, and some suggested reform approaches.

Foner, Nancy, and George M. Frederickson. 2004. *Not Just Black and White: Historical and Contemporary Perspectives on Immigration, Race, and Ethnicity in the United States.* New York: Russell Sage. It is an examination of the complexity of racial and ethnic politics in America, and how that complexity impacts immigration and immigration policy.

Foner, Nancy, Ruben Rumbant, and Steven J. Gold, eds. 2000. *Immigration Research for a New Century: Multidisciplinary Perspectives.* New York: Russell Sage. A thorough examination of current research on the post-1965 wave of immigrants presenting the work of a new generation of immigration scholars from the various social science disciplines.

Francis, Samuel T. 2001. *America Extinguished: Mass Immigration and the Disintegration of American Culture.* Monterey, VA: Americans for Immigration Control. A collection of editorial essays by Samuel Francis of AIC, it presents all of AIC's arguments and perspectives on the cultural wars, the dire affects, and reasons to oppose mass immigration, legal and illegal.

French, Laurence A. 2010. *Running the Border Gauntlet: The Mexican Migrant Controversy.* Santa Barbara, CA: Praeger Press. This book traces the long history of racial, political, religious, and class conflicts resulting from America's contentious immigration policies in a lucid narrative account accessible to college students and the general public.

Gans, Judith, Elaine M. Replogie, and Daniel J. Tichenor. 2012. *Debates on U.S. Immigration.* Thousand Oaks, CA: Sage Publications. This is an issue-based solid reference guide that examines immigration policy in the United States and the impassioned debates about the scope and nature of restrictionist policy. It has an introductory essay and then uses a collection of point/counterpoint articles exploring the multiple sides of this complex issue.

Gerstle, Gary, and John Mollenkopf, eds. 2001. *E Pluribus Unum? Contemporary and Historical Perspectives on Immigrant Political Incorporation.* New York: Russell Sage. It is a path-breaking volume that brings together historians and social scientists exploring the dynamics of political incorporation (assimilation) of the 20th century's two great immigration waves. From political machines to education, transnational loyalties, and racial exclusion, these essays provide insights into the way immigration has changed culture and politics in the United States.

Gjerde, Jon, ed. 1998. *Major Problems in American Immigration and Ethnic History.* Boston: Houghton Mifflin. A collection of essays from leading scholars about a wide variety of problems emerging from large-scale immigration flows to the United States.

Glazer, Nathan, ed. 1985. *Clamor at the Gates: The New American Immigration.* San Francisco: ICS Press. One of the most noted scholars of immigration focuses on the "new" wave of post-1965 immigration and examines the demographics of the wave.

Hamermesh, Daniel S., and Frank Bean, eds. 1998. *Help or Hindrance? The Economic Implications of Immigration for African Americans.* New York: Russell Sage. The debate over how, and the degree to which, immigration adversely impacts African Americans is thoroughly examined in essays edited by two leading scholars/demographers of the U.S. immigration.

Hammamoto, Darrell Y., and Rodolfo Torres, eds. 1997. *New American Destinies: A Reader in Contemporary Asian and Latino Immigration.* New York: Routledge. A collection of scholarly essays focusing on the changed nature in the flow of immigrants since 1965 and the shift in that flow from Northwestern Europeans to Latin Americans and Asians.

Haugen, David M. 2009. *Immigration.* Detroit: Greenhaven Press. Using an opposing viewpoints approach, Haugen explores immigration through a wide range of views by respected experts in the pro-con format.

Hayes, Patrick, ed. 2012. *The Making of Modern Immigration: An Encyclopedia of People and Ideas.* Santa Barbara, CA: ABC-CLIO. It is a library reference volume that examines the legal immigration system to the United States.

Hero, Rodney, and Christina Wolbrecht, eds. 2005. *The Politics of Democratic Inclusion.* Philadelphia: Temple University Press. It is a collection of original essays from a variety of scholars on the subject of immigrant incorporation and what aids or hinders the process.

Hirschman, Charles, Joshua DeWind, and Philip Kasinitz, eds. 1999. *The Handbook of International Migration.* New York: Russell Sage. An extensive collection of essays on the basics of international migration flows.

Huddle, Donald. 1993. *The Costs of Immigration.* Washington, DC: Carrying Capacity Network. Huddle's study was among the first careful scholarly attempts to measure the impact of immigration using an economist's cost-benefit analysis approach. Controversial as it was for those interested in measuring immigration's costs, it spurred a host of other studies.

Information Plus. 2006. *Immigration and Illegal Aliens: Burdens or Blessings?* Farmington Hills, MI: Thomson/Gale. The latest in a series of brief but thorough monographs that examine the "illegal alien issue" from a variety of perspectives and present many graphs, figures, and tables of data that touch upon every aspect of the "illegal alien immigration" issue.

Pros and cons of all sides of the issue and a solid historical perspective are included in every volume in the series.

Information Plus. 2014. *American Immigration: An Encyclopedia of Political, Social, and Cultural Changes.* Farmington Hills, MI: Thomson/Gale. A library reference volume with narrative history, tables, figures, and analysis of immigration to the United States, focusing on current immigration issues, laws, and policies.

Jones-Correa, Michael, ed. 2001. *Governing American Cities.* New York: Russell Sage. Focusing on the newest wave of immigration, this volume looks at its impact on the nation's major metropolitan areas. The volume provides what is clearly among the best analyses of how immigration has reshaped urban politics in the United States. It covers especially New York, Los Angeles, and Miami. It provides valuable insight into the new American urban melting pot by offering sophisticated theoretical perspectives on intergroup coalitions and conflicts. It provides rich details and analysis of class and generational dynamics as those forces influence the political behavior of diverse immigrant groups.

Kastoryano, Riva. 2000. *Negotiating Identities: States and Immigrants in France and Germany.* Princeton: Princeton University Press. Immigration is even more hotly debated in Europe than in the United States. This pivotal work of action and discourse analysis draws on extensive field interviews with politicians, immigrant leaders, and militants to analyze interactions between the state and immigrants in France and Germany.

Kirstein, Peter N. 1977. *Anglo over Bracero: A History of the Mexican Worker in the United States from Roosevelt to Nixon.* San Francisco: R. and E. Research Associates. It is a thorough, historical examination of the Bracero Program.

Kiser, George C., and Martha W. Kiser. 1979. *Mexican Workers in the United States.* Albuquerque: University of New Mexico

Press. It is another thorough and scholarly historical analysis of the Bracero Program.

Kivisto, Peter, and Thomas Faist. 2010. *Beyond a Border: The Causes and Consequences of Contemporary Immigration.* Thousand Oaks, CA: Sage Publications. It is a comprehensive look at legal and illegal immigration to America with a focus on both push and pull factors.

Koehn, Peter. 1991. *Refugees from Revolution: U.S. Policy and Third World Migration.* Boulder, CO: Westview. An examination of how U.S. policy responds to refugee flows and immigration waves induced by the political turmoil in "Third World" countries.

Krauss, Erich, and Alex Pacheco. 2004. *On the Line: Inside the U.S. Border Patrol.* New York: Citadel/Kensington. An "insider's" look, journalistic in style, at the Border Patrol, its difficult tasks, resource problems, successes, and shortcomings.

Kraut, Alan. 1994. *Silent Travelers: Germs, Genes and the "Immigrant Menace."* Baltimore, MD: Johns Hopkins University Press. An interesting examination of the problem of mass migration and disease spread, intentional or unintentional, from epidemics to pandemics.

Kretsedemas, Philip, and Ana Aparico, eds. 2004. *Immigrants, Welfare Reform and the Poverty of Policy.* Westport, CT: Praeger Press. A comprehensive, scholarly examination of the linkage between immigration and welfare reform, with a focus on the 1996 acts covering welfare reform, which denied access to welfare programs to illegal immigrants.

Kyle, David, and Rey Koslowski. 2001. *Global Human Smuggling: Comparative Perspectives.* Baltimore, MD: Johns Hopkins University Press. A careful examination of human smuggling in historical and comparative perspectives, it examines the emergence of international law and of a global moral order of human rights while at the same time exploring the economic and political facets of illegal trafficking in humans. It is a comprehensive examination of illegal immigration and those who profit most from it.

Lamm, R. D., and G. Imhoff. 1985. *The Immigration Time Bomb: The Fragmenting of America.* New York: Truman Tally/E. P. Dutton. Published prior to the enactment of IRCA, this book marshals all the arguments and data to show the cost or detrimental effects of large-scale immigration, in particular, those used to promote policy reforms to "control" the illegal immigration flow. The arguments offered here continue to inform former governor Lamm's positions against illegal immigration today.

LeMay, Michael. 1987. *From Open Door to Dutch Door: An Analysis of U.S. Immigration Policy since 1820.* New York: Praeger. A historical overview of immigration policy making since 1820, it presents the "immigration waves" and distinguishes four phases of immigration policy that dominated historical eras in reaction to preceding waves, employing a "door" analogy to characterize each phase or era of immigration policy.

LeMay, Michael. 1994. *Anatomy of a Public Policy: The Reform of Contemporary American Immigration Law.* Westport, CT: Praeger. A detailed "case study" examination of the Immigration Reform and Control Act of 1986 and the Immigration Act of 1990. It examines the political movement to enact IRCA and IMMACT of 1990, using roll-call analysis and interviews with key political actors to explain why the laws were passed and what key provisions each contained.

LeMay, Michael. 2004. *U.S. Immigration: A Reference Handbook.* Santa Barbara, CA: ABC-CLIO. It is a library reference volume examining legal immigration from 1965 to 2004 in the standard format of the *Contemporary World Issues* series of volumes.

LeMay, Michael, ed. 1989. *The Gatekeepers: Comparative Immigration Policies.* New York: Praeger. It is a collection of six original essays, each examining the immigration policy and the reforms thereof of six leading immigration-receiving nations.

LeMay, Michael, ed. 2013. *Transforming America: Perspectives on Immigration*, 3 vol. Santa Barbara, CA: ABC-CLIO. A three-volume series of chapters by some 30 authors from various disciplinary perspectives, it covers immigration from 1820 to 2012 in a thorough view of immigration to the United States in all its complexities.

LeMay, Michael, and Elliott Robert Barkan, eds. 1999. *U.S. Immigration and Naturalization Laws and Issues: A Documentary History.* Westport, CT: Greenwood. This unique volume summarizes 150 documents covering all major laws and court cases concerning U.S. immigration and naturalization law from colonial times to 1996.

Light, Paul C. 2002. *Homeland Security Will Be Hard to Manage.* Washington, DC: Brookings Institution. Written just after the enactment of the law establishing the new Department of Homeland Security, this expert in bureaucratic management offers insights and accurate foresight as to the difficulties the new DHS will face as its managers attempt to merge the operations, procedures, and political/bureaucratic cultures of so many diverse agencies into the new mega-department.

Loescher, Gil, and Ann Dull Loescher. 1994. *The Global Refugee Crisis.* Santa Barbara, CA: ABC-CLIO. Another in a series of volumes on contemporary issues viewed in a global perspective, this volume thoroughly examines the current global refugee crisis in the "research handbook" format of the series.

Loucky, James, Jeanne M. Armstrong, and Larry J. Estrada, eds. 2006. *Immigration in America Today: An Encyclopedia.* Westport, CT: Greenwood Press. This book offers an interdisciplinary overview of complex immigration-related issues with alphabetically arranged entries that define key terms and concepts, provide a historical background, and suggest future trends.

Lutton, Wayne, and John Tanton. 1994. *The Immigration Invasion.* Petoskey, MI: Social Contact. An "indictment" of immigration, discussing all of the problems that can be viewed as the cause and marshaling every conceivable argument against it.

Lynch, James P., and Rita J. Simon. 2003. *Immigration the World Over: Statutes, Policies, and Practices.* Lanham, MD: Rowman & Littlefield. It is a current and thorough, though necessarily somewhat brief, presentation of immigration policies and practices of the major immigration-receiving countries of the world in a comparative perspective.

Majaridge, Dale. 1996. *The Coming White Minority: California's Eruptions and America's Future.* New York: Random House. An argument for all of the ills that can (will) befall the United States as the rest of the nation experiences California's high level of immigration, both legal and illegal.

Martinez, Oscar J. 1994. *Border People: Life and Society in U.S.-Mexico Borderlands.* Tucson: University of Arizona Press. This is a sociological examination of life in the borderlands. It shows how the flow of immigrants affects people living in and working across the Mexican-U.S. border in all aspects of their daily lives.

Massey, Douglas, Jorge Durand, and Nolan Malone. 2002. *Beyond Smoke and Mirrors: Mexican Immigration in an Era of Economic Integration.* New York: Russell Sage. The authors provide a fresh perspective of Mexican migration history by systematically tracing the predictable consequences of highly unsystematic policy regimes. They provide an incisive analysis of the current policy dilemma by marshaling new and compelling evidence to expose the flagrant contradiction of allowing the free flow of goods and capital but not people, and they argue for much-needed policy reforms.

Massey, Douglas, et al. 1987. *Return to Aztlan: The Social Process of International Migration from Western Mexico.* Berkeley: University of California Press. It is a thorough and many-viewed examination of Mexican immigration—both legal and illegal—to the southwestern United States (the mythical Aztlan of the title).

Marshall, Ray. 2007. *Immigrants for Shared Prosperity—A Framework for Comprehensive Reform.* Washington, DC: Economic Policy Institute. Former U.S. secretary of labor proposes and explains what provisions need to be included in any comprehensive immigration reform package, and why comprehensive immigration reform is essential to the future of the United States and the vibrancy of its economy.

McCarthy, Kevin F., and George Vernez. 1997. *Immigration in a Changing Economy: California's Experience.* Santa Monica, CA: Rand Corporation. Another in a series of volumes and studies that emerged from the massive Rand Corporation study of immigration policy post-IRCA, this volume is an authoritative case study of the impact of immigration on California's economy and politics.

McDowell, Lorraine, and Paul T. Hill. 1990. *Newcomers in America's Schools.* Santa Monica, CA: Rand Corporation. One of the volumes of careful research that the Rand Corporation published on the impact of the new immigration flow, it focuses on the effects of large-scale legal and illegal immigration on California's schools.

Merino, Noel. 2012. *Illegal Immigration.* Boston: Cengage/Greenhaven. Merino presents a thorough discussion of illegal immigration in a reference-volume format.

Miller, Debra. 2014. *Immigration.* Boston: Cengage/Greenhaven. This is an exhaustive examination of legal immigration in a library reference-volume format.

Morris, Milton. 1985. *Immigration: The Beleaguered Bureaucracy.* Washington, DC: Brookings Institution. Then a senior fellow at Brookings, author Morris addresses the concerns over contemporary immigration by focusing on the character and performance of the INS and the State Department's Bureau of Consular Affairs. His focus is on the problems resulting from serious shortcomings in administration: inadequate funding, unclear objectives, and faulty structures and procedures.

Motomura, Hiroshi. 2006. *Americans in Waiting: The Lost Story of Immigration and Citizenship in the United States.* New York: Oxford University Press. Professor Motomura provides an in-depth look at Chinese and Japanese Americans and their struggles to secure citizenship rights from a nation that had institutional racism infusing its immigration and naturalization policy and law.

Motomura, Hiroshi. 2014. *Immigration Outside the Law.* New York: Oxford University Press. An immigration history scholar examines the complex issue of unauthorized immigration.

Muller, Thomas, and Thomas Espanshade. 1985. *The Fourth Wave.* Washington, DC: Urban Institute. This groundbreaking book was among the first and most thoroughly analytical examinations of the post-1965 wave of immigrants to the United States. It contributed significantly to renewing the scholarly debate over large-scale immigration and its costs and benefits to the United States.

National Research Council. 1997. *The New Americans: Economic, Demographic, and Fiscal Effects of Immigration.* Washington, DC: NRC/National Academy Press. Continuing to contribute to the now extensive literature examining the new (post-1965) wave of immigration and the degree to which the new immigrants are incorporating into U.S. society socially, politically and economically, it is in many ways *The Fourth Wave* circa 1997.

Navarro, Armando. 2005. *American Political Experience in Occupied Aztlan.* Lanham, MD: Alamira Press. A critical look at the Hispanic/Latino, and especially Mexican immigrants' struggle with American politics and their minority status as a result of racial attitudes.

Nevins, Joseph. 2002. *Operation Gatekeeper: The Rise of "Illegal Aliens" and the Making of the U.S.-Mexican Boundary.* New York: Routledge. A comprehensive look at the illegal immigration problem, flow, and resulting impact of the U.S.-Mexican border sector.

O'Hanlon, Michael E., et al. 2002. *Protecting the American Homeland: A Preliminary Analysis.* Washington, DC: Brookings Institution. The authors offer a four-tier plan for efforts of the Bush administration and Congress. This book includes a rationale and recommendations on spending and projected costs to the private sector, and the restructuring of federal agencies associated with establishing a Department of Homeland Security. Its recommendations include the restructuring of the INS and the Border Patrol as well as visa and naturalization activities into the new DHS.

Papademetriou, Demetrios, Alexander Aleinikoff, and D. W. Meyers. 1999. *Reorganizing the U.S. Immigration Function: Toward a New Framework for Accountability.* Washington, DC: Carnegie Endowment for International Peace. This volume presents the Carnegie Endowment "plan" for restructuring the INS and reforming immigration policy. Many of its ideas and concerns are reflected in the new DHS approach. Its analysis presents a good picture of "what was wrong" with the INS and with U.S. immigration policy, justifying the concern that it "was broken and needed fixing" in such a way that a major reorganization was necessary rather than the incremental "tinkering" with reform that characterized efforts during the 1990s.

Papademetriou, Demetrios, and Mark Miller, eds. 1984. *The Unavoidable Issue.* Philadelphia: Institute for the Study of Human Issues. This volume is an impressive array of essays discussing all of the major issues of U.S. immigration policy and the need for reforms in policy; it is a particularly good review of the topic for the 1965 to 1980 period.

Passel, Jeffrey. 1994. *Immigrants and Taxes: A Reappraisal of Huddle's "The Cost of Immigration."* Washington, DC:

Urban Institute. A major and important "reappraisal" of how to measure the costs of immigration, it rebuts Huddle's approach and finds a considerable difference in such costs, essentially concluding that immigration is a positive benefit rather than a significant cost to the U.S. economy.

Passel, Jeffrey S. and Rebecca L. Clark. 1994. *How Much Do Immigrants Really Cost?* Washington, DC: Urban Institute. Another extensive "rebut" of Huddle's analysis, it helped to fuel the academic debate over how to measure the costs and benefits of immigration, both legal and illegal, that raged during the 1990s as a result of the Huddle thesis.

Payan, Tony. 2006. *The Three U.S.-Mexico Border Wars: Drugs, Immigration and Homeland Security.* Westport, CT: Praeger Securities International. This book examines the post-9/11 attack responses to the most affected area—the U.S.-Mexico border. It analyzes the comprehensive security strategy in place on the border and the effects of those three "wars" on drugs, immigration enforcement, and the war on terror.

Perea, Juan F. 1997. *Immigrants Out! The New Nativism and the Anti-Immigrant Impulses in the United States.* New York: New York University Press. A collection of 18 original essays by leading immigration scholars, this volume uses interdisciplinary perspectives to examine the current surge in nativism in light of past waves. It examines the relationship between the races and the perception of a national immigration crisis.

Portes, Alejandro, ed. 1996. *The New Second Generation.* New York: Russell Sage. It details the transformation of the postimmigrant generation during the current age of diversity in the United States.

Portes, Alejandro, ed. 1998. *The Economic Sociology of Immigration.* New York: Russell Sage. It is a culminating volume presenting the new scholarship on the "incorporation" of the second-generation immigrants—politically, socially, and economically.

Portes, Alejandro, and Ruben G. Rumbaut. 2001. *Legacies: The Story of the Immigrant Second Generation*. Berkeley: University of California Press; New York: Russell Sage. This study reports on a series of surveys of immigrant children and their parents conducted between 1992 and 1996 in Miami, Florida, and San Diego, California. It uses interview data and school records to provide an overview of the "New Americans," emphasizes segmented assimilation and its determinants, how to measure "making it" in the United States, immigrants' outlooks on the United States, language and ethnic identities, the role of schools and education on the psychology of the second generation, and the causes and consequences of school achievement or failure.

Portes, Alejandro, and Ruben G. Rumbaut, eds. 2001. *Ethnicities: Children of Immigrants in America*. New York: Russell Sage. These two volumes present the findings of an extensive examination of the "political incorporation" of second-generation immigrants. Whether in the summary volume above or in this collection of essays, the authors detail that while assimilation was in their view in the past a relatively homogeneous linear process, now it is a segmented one.

Powell, John. 2005. *Encyclopedia of North American Immigration*. New York: Facts on File. This narrative history shows how, for good or bad, immigration has shaped and transformed the nation. It covers the magnitude and diversity of migration to North America. It is a solid, one-volume encyclopedia with more than 300 A–Z entries, and an extensive bibliography of resources for further research.

Power, J. Gerard, and Teresa Byrd, eds. 1998. *U.S. Mexico Border Health: Issues for Regional and Migrant Populations*. Thousand Oaks, CA: Sage Publications. The editors have compiled a wide range of studies involving health care and promotion on the U.S.-Mexico border.

Pozzetta, George, ed. 1991. *Contemporary Immigration and American Society*. New York: Garland. The volume is the last in a series of 20 relating to immigration history. It is somewhat spotty and varied in its quality and relevance to contemporary society. It covers many groups that one would expect to see: Filipinos, Mexicans, Koreans, Haitians, Hispanics, Cubans, and Vietnamese. Yet some that one might look for are puzzlingly absent: Cambodians, Laotians, Chinese, Indians, Canadians, and Russians. No attention is paid to the influx during the 1980s from Ireland or Eastern Europe. The collection contains 23 articles drawn from 17 journals that provide a useful cross-disciplinary perspective. By selecting sources only from previously published articles rather than original essays, the volume's impact is limited in terms of contributing significantly to the literature. Devoid of any post-IRCA perspective, it is limited too in its contribution toward new methodologies and interpretations relevant to contemporary U.S. society.

Reimers, David. 1985. *Still the Golden Door: The Third World Comes to America*, 2nd ed. New York: Columbia University Press. One of the foremost immigrant historians in the United States examines post-1965 and particularly post-1980s immigration, including the impact of IRCA (1986) and IMMACT (1990) and the unforeseen consequences of those laws. It assesses these laws as less restrictive in their impact than opponents of the laws suggest.

Russell, James C. 2004. *Breach of Faith: American Churches and the Immigration Crisis.* Raleigh, NC: Representative Government Press. A polemical perspective on the role Christian churches play in the illegal immigration problem, it presents the view of the conservative right on the cultural wars engendered by the process.

Salzman, H., et al. 2013. *Guestworkers in the High-Skill U.S. Labor Market: An Analysis of Supply, Employment and Wage Trends.* Washington, DC: Economic Policy Institute. Economists use a rich cache of economic data in table and figures to examine the need for and impact of guest-worker programs like the STEM approach.

Sergeant, Harriet. 2001. *Immigration and Asylum in the U.K.* London: Chameleon. This volume presents the results of a study of the Center for Policy Studies on the issues of immigration and asylum and how they impact the United Kingdom. It is a scholarly and objective examination of the issue.

Simcox, David. 1985. *Measuring the Fallout: The Cost of the IRCA Amnesty after 10 Years.* Washington, DC: Center for Immigration Studies. An extensive examination of the costs attributable to the legalization program of IRCA, it underscores the CIS's calls for strictly limiting immigration and its opposition to another amnesty.

Simcox, David. 1997. *U.S. Immigration in the 1980s: Reappraisal and Reform.* Boulder, CO: Westview/Center for Immigration Studies. This collection of 16 original essays by outstanding immigration scholars from various fields surveys current literature on immigration and its effects on the United States and on the problems or advantages that immigration brings to a rapidly changing society. Its major topics include effects on U.S. workers, national unity, California as the nation's immigrant laboratory, demographics of displacement, and approaches to a more rational, enforceable immigration policy.

Smith, James P., and Barry Edmonston, eds. 1998. *The New Americans: Studies on the Economic, Demographic, and Fiscal Effects of Immigration.* Washington, DC: National Academy Press. It offers a comprehensive and objective analysis of the new immigration, both legal and illegal, and the broad-ranging effects of the issue.

Stedman, Stephen J., and Fred Tanner, eds. 2003. *Refugee Manipulations: War, Politics and the Abuse of Human Suffering.* Washington, DC: Brookings Institution Press. Examines why and the ways in which armed groups manipulate refugees and how and why international actors assist in their manipulation.

Suarez-Orozco, Marcelo, ed. 1998. *Crossings: Mexican Immigration in Interdisciplinary Perspectives.* Cambridge: Harvard University Press. Scholars from numerous disciplines examine the multifaceted effects of Mexican immigrant labor, predominantly undocumented labor, on the United States and on the immigrants themselves.

Tomasi, Lydio, ed. *In Defense of the Alien.* New York: Center for Migration Studies. Annual. These volumes are a series providing the collected essays and papers presented at the Center for Migration Studies' annual National Conference on Immigration Law held in Washington, D.C. Each volume presents essays from leading government officials, lawyers, scholars, and immigration policy practitioners focused around the issues and topics discussed at the annual national convention.

Torr, James D. 2004. *Homeland Security.* San Diego: Greenhaven. It provides a highly critical but comprehensive examination of the homeland security issue, and its myriad ramifications. Torr is very skeptical as to the effectiveness of the "super-agency" approach to the massive new department, focusing on the largely unanticipated managerial problems of the new department.

Ueda, Reed. 1994. *Postwar Immigrant America: A Social History.* Boston: Bedford/St. Martin's. Using an interdisciplinary focus and joining history and several social science perspectives, this volume probes the impact of arriving ethnic groups on the historical foundations of the United States, stressing how the new Asian and Hispanic immigrants revitalized political and civic institutions inherited from the Founders and reshaped the debate over how democracy could encompass ethnic groups with greater inclusiveness and egalitarianism. It uses demographic and quantitative analysis applied to the rise of worldwide immigration as well as sociology and demography to understand the development of group life. Political science and law illuminate the relationship of immigration to U.S. government and its ethnic policies.

Warner, Judith A. 2008. *Battleground Immigration,* 2 vol. Westport, CT: Greenwood Press. The political battles over legal and undocumented immigrants within U.S. borders have characterized much of American politics since 1965, This book examines the most critical issues surrounding immigration, including its effects on the economy, education, and employment. It assesses the viability of the foreign-born in the United States with an emphasis on post-9/11 security and border control issues.

Warner, Judith A. 2010. *U.S. Border Security: A Reference Handbook.* Santa Barbara, CA: ABC-CLIO. Warner examines thoroughly the challenges facing U.S. Customs and Border Patrol over the 2,000-mile U.S.-Mexico border. It contrasts the border security issues pre- and post-9/11, the controversial topics of illegal immigration, counterterrorism, drugs and weapons trafficking, and human smuggling; their impact on border security; and the effects of the war on terrorism on civil and human rights.

Wolbrecht, Christina, and Rodney E. Hero. 2005. *The Politics of Democratic Inclusion.* Philadelphia: Temple University Press. This is an innovative examination of the complexity of the incorporation process for immigrants, explaining the "inclusion" or "incorporation" approach to the issue instead of the linear "assimilation" approach.

Wolfe, Alan. 2002. *One Nation, After All.* New York: Penguin Putnam. A "tour" through what middle-class Americans think about God, country, family, racism, welfare, immigration, homosexuality, the Right, the Left, and each other.

Wood, Andrew G., ed. 2008. *The Borderlands: An Encyclopedia of Culture and Politics on the U.S. Mexico Divide.* Westport, CT: Greenwood Press. This volume presents a broad collection of essays from multidisciplinary backgrounds. It uses the encyclopedia approach to examine the complex issues around migration flows, legal and illegal, across the U.S.-Mexico borders.

Yang, Philip O. 1995. *Post-1965 Immigration to the United States: Structural Determinants.* Westport, CT: Praeger. Yang examines why countries differ in the scale of legal permanent immigration in the period since 1965 by investigating the structural determinants of cross-national variation during this time. He seeks the integration and development of international migration theories. He discusses the policy implications of how the United States should regulate and control immigration.

Yans-McLaughlin, Virginia, ed. 1990. *Immigration Reconsidered: History, Sociology, and Politics.* New York: Oxford University Press. A collection of 11 original essays by scholars presenting at a conference in New York City in 1986, this volume covers various topics: immigration patterns, ethnicity and social structure, the study of new immigration, and new approaches to the study of immigration, and the politics of immigration policy and its reform.

Zhou, Min, and Carl Bankston III. 1999. *Growing Up American: How Vietnamese Children Adapt to Life in the United States.* New York: Russell Sage. This book examines the single largest group of refugee children—the Vietnamese—as they experienced growing up in the United States. Chapters examine such topics as the scattering by the war, resettlement, reconstruction of an ethnic community, social networks, language and adaptation, experiences in adaptation in U.S. schools, bicultural conflicts, gender role changes, and delinquency.

Zimmerman, Klaus F. 2002. *European Migration: What Do We Know?* New York: Oxford University Press. It is a thorough assessment of the current situation regarding migration in a comprehensive range of European countries. It includes chapters on the United States, Canada, and New Zealand for comparative purposes. Each country "case study" is written by a local expert, and the overall editor is one of Europe's leading scholars on the economics of immigration.

Zolberg, Aristide. 2008. *A Nation by Design: Immigration Policy in the Fashioning of America.* Cambridge, MA: Russell Sage Foundation at Harvard University Press. The late Harvard professor explores American immigration policy from the colonial period to the present, discussing how it has been used as a tool of nation building. It covers policy at the local and state levels and profiles the vacillating currents of opinion on immigration throughout American history. It examines legal, illegal, and asylum-seeking immigration.

Zolberg, Aristide, Astri Suhrki, and Sergio Aguayo. 1989. *Escape from Violence: Conflict and the Refugee Crisis in the Developing World.* New York: Oxford University Press. It is a cogent treatment of the causes of refugee flows, emphasizing domestic and international causes and regional differentiations around the globe. Case studies are rich in detail; analysis is systematic and comprehensive.

Zucker, Norman, and Naomi Flink Zucker. 1987. *The Guarded Gate: The Reality of American Refugee Policy.* San Diego: Harcourt Brace, Jovanovich. It is a critical assessment of U.S. asylum policy, stressing the political elements of the asylum debate. Emphasis is on U.S. government asylum policy rather than refugee policy broadly construed.

Zuniga, Victor, and Ruben Hernandez-Leon, eds. 2005. *New Destinations: Mexican Immigration to the United States.* New York: Russell Sage. An eclectic array of essays on the new Mexican immigration to the United States, it includes both legal and illegal immigration matters. It looks at several U.S. communities where they settle and how they are shaping and shaped by their new areas of settlement. It uses census data to discern the historical evolution of Mexican immigration to the United States, discussing the demographic, economic, and legal factors that led to recent moves to areas beyond where their predecessors had settled, concluding that undocumented aliens did a better job than did their documented peers in integrating into the local culture. It looks at paternalism and xenophobic aspects of local residents toward the new immigrants and the strong work ethic of the migrants, and provides hopeful examples of progress. It is the first scholarly assessment of the new settlements and experiences in the Midwest, Northeast, and the deep South, and of America's largest immigrant group enriched by the perspectives from demographers, sociologists, folklorists, anthropologists, and political scientists.

Leading Scholarly Journals

American Demographics

Published 10 times per year, this peer-reviewed journal is an outlet for multidisciplinary articles dealing with all topics related to demography as well as occasional articles and reflective essays on migration, legal and illegal immigration, and an annual resource guide.

American Journal of Sociology

A scholarly, peer-reviewed quarterly journal of sociology, with frequent articles concerning assimilation and integration, social trends, and policies regarding migration and legal and illegal immigration, it also has book reviews on immigration-related topics.

Citizenship Studies

This quarterly journal publishes internationally recognized scholarly work on contemporary issues in citizenship, human rights, and democratic processes from an interdisciplinary perspective covering politics, sociology, history, and cultural studies.

Columbia Law Review

It is a law review published eight times per year and frequently has case reviews and analytical articles and original essays dealing with immigration law matters.

Demography

This peer-reviewed journal of the Population Association of America publishes scholarly research of interest to demographers from a multidisciplinary perspective, with emphasis on social sciences, geography, history, biology, statistics, business, epidemiology, and public health. It publishes specialized research papers and historical and comparative studies.

Ethnic and Racial Studies

It is a bimonthly journal for the analysis of race, ethnicity, and nationalism in the present global environment. It is an interdisciplinary forum for research and theoretical analysis, using disciplines of sociology, social policy, anthropology, political science, economics, geography, international relations, history, social psychology, and cultural studies.

Ethnohistory

A quarterly publication of the *Journal of the American Society for Ethnohistory*, it contains articles of original research, commentaries, review essays, and book reviews.

Ethnology

This international journal of culture and social anthropology publishes original research articles by scientists of any country regarding cultural anthropology with substantive data. Topics of interest relate to ethnicity, social integration, and migration adaptation.

Foreign Affairs

This bimonthly magazine publishes articles and original essays on topics related to foreign policy, including policy related to both legal and illegal migration, by both scholars and practitioners in the field. It regularly publishes related book reviews.

Georgetown Immigration Law Journal

This quarterly law review is the most specifically related law journal dealing with U.S. immigration law, its current developments, and reform-related matters concerning all three branches of the U.S. government, and frequently focusing on illegal immigration. It contains case reviews, articles, notes and commentaries, and workshop reports devoted to the topic.

Geographical Journal

This quarterly academic journal of the Royal Geographical Society publishes research reports and review articles of refereed articles related to all subjects concerning geography, often dealing with international migration matters.

Geographical Review

The quarterly journal of the American Geographical Society, it publishes research on all topics related to geography: hence, occasional ones deal with legal and illegal migration and immigration reform, and with the incorporation of immigrants. It also publishes related book reviews.

Harvard Law Review

This law review is published eight times per year. It contains original articles, case reviews, essays, commentaries, and book reviews occasionally on topics related to U.S. immigration law and its reform.

Identities

Identities explores the relationship of racial, ethnic, and national identities and power hierarchies within national and global arenas. Its interdisciplinary focus uses social, political, and cultural analyses of the processes of domination, struggle, and resistance. It stresses class structures and gender relations integral to both maintaining and challenging subordination.

INS Reporter

It is a quarterly publication that provides brief surveys of recent developments in U.S. immigration law.

INS Statistical Yearbook

It was an annual publication giving statistical data in text, graphic, and tabular form. The latest "official" numbers on U.S. immigration, the yearbook is now published by the DHS.

International Migration

This quarterly is an intergovernmental publication featuring documents, conference reports, and articles dealing with international migration topics.

International Migration Review

The leading quarterly journal in the field of migration, *IMR* contains current research articles, book reviews, documents, and bibliographies.

International Organizations

This journal is published quarterly by MIT Press for the World Peace Foundation. It contains articles on all aspects of world politics and international political economy.

International Review of the Red Cross

This journal, published six times annually, contains articles on international humanitarian law and policy matters.

International Social Sciences Journal

This quarterly journal is published by Blackwell Publishers for UNESCO. It regularly contains articles concerning international migration and its impact on societies and social systems, and other topics related to UNESCO.

International Studies Quarterly

This is another scholarly quarterly journal published by Blackwell Publishers (as above).

International Studies Review

This quarterly journal is another published by Blackwell, with contact information as listed earlier. The journal is published for the International Studies Association. It contains original scholarly articles of research, review essays, book reviews, and an annual special issue on a theme.

Journal of American Studies

Published three times per year, this multidisciplinary, scholarly refereed journal is multinational with an emphasis on articles on politics, economics, and geography, and with book reviews that will often relate to immigration matters.

Journal of Economic History

This journal publishes original scholarship on the study of economic aspects of the human past from a diversity of perspectives, most notably history and economics.

Journal of Economic Issues

This is a scholarly economics journal covering all aspects of economic issues, with occasional original research on immigration and migration with a focus on economic impact, labor market issues, and so on. Each issue has book reviews of related matters as well.

Journal of Economic Perspectives

This journal of the American Economic Association publishes occasional symposium issues and, regularly, original scholarly articles, features, and economic analysis on a variety of public policy issues, including both legal and illegal immigration, and reviews of related books.

Journal of Ethnic and Migration Studies

Published by the Sussex Center for Migration Research at the University of Sussex, the journal presents quality research on all forms of migration and its consequences, with articles on ethnicity, ethnic relations and ethnic conflict, race and racism, multiculturalism and pluralism, nationalism and transnationalism, citizenship and integration, identity and hybridity, globalization and cosmopolitanism, policy debates, and theoretical papers.

Journal of Intercultural Studies

This journal presents international research related to intercultural studies across national and disciplinary boundaries. One issue per year is thematic. It examines common issues across a range of disciplinary perspectives. Peer-reviewed research, theoretical papers, and book reviews are included in each issue.

Journal of International Refugee Law

This quarterly publishes articles on refugee law and policy matters, including legislation, documentation, and abstracts of recent publications in the field.

Journal of Migration and Human Security

A publication of the Center for Migration Studies of New York, it is an online, peer-reviewed public policy academic journal focusing on the broad scope of social, political, and economic dimensions of human security. It publishes an annual, bound volume of its articles.

Migration News

This monthly newsletter, published by the University of California Davis, concerns all manner of topics related to migration, especially how illegal immigration impacts U.S. society.

Migration World

This journal publishes articles and information about migration and refugee problems worldwide in a readable and accessible way. It is a good source for school and college reports.

National Identities

This journal is published three times annually focusing on identity/ethnicity by examining how they are shaped and changed, and on the transmission/persistence of national identities.

Patterns of Prejudice

It is a journal providing a forum for exploring the historical roots and contemporary varieties of demonizations of "the other." It probes language and construction of "race," nation, color, and ethnicity as well as the linkages between these categories. The journal also discusses issues and policy agenda, such as asylum, illegal immigration, hate crimes, Holocaust denial, and citizenship.

Policy Studies Journal

This journal of the Policy Studies Organization is produced at Iowa State University, College of Education. It is published quarterly with articles related to all issues of public policy and has occasional symposium issues and regular book reviews.

Policy Studies Review

As *Policy Studies Journal*, this journal is also a product of the Policy Studies Organization.

Political Science Quarterly

This quarterly scholarly journal discusses public and international affairs. It is nonpartisan, with scholarly reviewed articles devoted to the study and analysis of government, politics, and international affairs, with original articles and essays, review essays, and book reviews.

Race Ethnicity and Education

This interdisciplinary refereed journal publishes international scholarship, research, and debate on issues concerning the dynamics of race, racism, and ethnicity in educational policy, theory, and practice, focusing on the interconnections between race, ethnicity, and multiple forms of oppression including class, gender, sexuality, and disability.

Refugee Reports

This is a monthly report of information and documents concerning refugees and the legislation, policies, and programs affecting them. A year-end statistical issue is published every December.

Refugee Survey Quarterly

This quarterly lists abstracts of the many publications concerning refugees, including a selection of "country reports" and one on human rights–related legal documents.

Social Identities

This interdisciplinary and international journal focuses on issues addressing social identities in the context of transforming political economies and cultures of postmodern and post-colonial conditions.

Social Science Quarterly

Published for the Southwestern Social Science Association by Blackwell, this interdisciplinary quarterly has articles of original research, review essays, book reviews, and occasional symposium issues and contains articles dealing with U.S. immigration and illegal immigration policy, and issues related to the incorporation of immigrants and their children into U.S. society.

State of the World Population

This is an annual publication that covers world population growth and problems resulting from it. It includes the latest in official statistics.

Reports and Government Documents

There are innumerable government reports and studies from a variety of agencies that emphasize immigration laws, immigration policies, and their impact. This section lists some exemplary sources.

Center for Immigration Studies (CIS). 2005. "Economy Slowed but Immigration Didn't: The Foreign-Born Population, 2000–2004." Washington, DC: CIS, A Steven Camaota study and analysis.

Congressional Budget Office. 2007. "The Impact of Unauthorized Immigrants on the Budgets of State and Local Governments. http://www.cbo.gov/sites/default/files/12–6-immigration.pdf.

Department of Homeland Security. 2011. *Yearbook of Immigration Statistics, 2010.* Washington, DC: Department of Homeland Security.

Department of Homeland Security. 2013. *Characteristics of H-1B Specialty Occupation Workers, Fiscal Year 2012, Annual Report.* Washington, DC: Department of Homeland Security.

Ewing, Walter A. 2005. "The Economics of Necessity." *Immigration Policy in Focus* 4, no. 3 (May): 8. An American Immigration Law Foundation report, it can be found at http://www.ailf.org/ipc/economicsofnecessityprint.asp. Accessed on July 14, 2006.

General Accounting Office. 1990. "Immigration Reform: Employer Sanctions and the Question of Discrimination." Report to Congress. Study measuring, and finding, the increase in discrimination as a result of IRCA.

General Accounting Office. 2004. *Overstay Tracking: A Key Component of Homeland Security and a Layered Defense.* GAO-04–82. Washington, DC: U.S. Government Printing Office.

Immigration and Naturalization Service. 1992. *An Immigrant Nation: United States Regulation of Immigration, 1798–1991.* Washington, DC: U.S. Government Printing Office. It is a summary report giving the broad outline of the history of immigration regulation through the 1990 IMMACT.

Immigration and Naturalization Service. 1995. "Illegal Aliens: National Net Cost Estimates Vary Widely." Washington, DC: U.S. Government Printing Office. It is a summary of all the various studies that found pro and con measures of the net cost effect of immigration on the U.S. economy.

Immigration and Naturalization Service. 1997. "Illegal Aliens: Extent of Welfare Benefits Received on Behalf of U.S. Citizen Children." Washington, DC: U.S. Government Printing Office. It is GAO's study measuring the extent of welfare given to the children of illegal aliens.

Immigration and Naturalization Service. 1998. "Illegal Aliens: Significant Obstacles to Reducing Unauthorized Alien Employment Exists." Washington, DC: U.S. Government Printing Office.

Immigration and Naturalization Service. 1999a. "Illegal Immigration: Status of Southwest Border Strategy Implementation." Washington, DC: U.S. Government Printing Office.

Immigration and Naturalization Service. 1999b. "Welfare Reform: Many States Continued Some Federal or State Benefits for Immigrants." Washington, DC: U.S. Government Printing Office.

Immigration and Naturalization Service. 1999c. "Welfare Reform: Public Assistance Benefits Provided to Recently Naturalized Citizens." Washington, DC: U.S. Government Printing Office.

Immigration and Naturalization Service. 2000a. "Alien Smuggling: Management and Operational Improvements

Needed to Address Growing Problem." Washington, DC: U.S. Government Printing Office. It is GAO's report on alien smuggling with estimates of its extent and suggestions to curb the trend.

Immigration and Naturalization Service. 2000b. "H-1B Foreign Workers: Better Controls Needed to Help Employers and Protect Workers." Washington, DC: U.S. Government Printing Office.

Immigration and Naturalization Service. 2000c. "Illegal Aliens: Opportunities Exist to Improve the Expedited Removal Process." Washington, DC: U.S. Government Printing Office.

Immigration and Naturalization Service. 2004. "Overstay Tracking: A Key Component of Homeland Security and a Layered Defense." GAO-04082. Washington, DC: U.S. Government Printing Office.

Lee, Margaret. 2006. "U.S. Citizenship of Persons Born in the United States of Alien Parents." Congressional Service Research Report. http://www.ilw.com. Accessed on May 30, 2010.

Pew Hispanic Center. 2003. "Remittance Senders and Receivers: Tracking the Transnational Channels." Washington, DC: Pew Hispanic Center.

Select Commission on Immigration and Refugee Policy (SCIRP). 1981. *Final Report.* Washington, DC. Final report of the SCIRP, which laid the groundwork for what became the Immigration Reform and Control Act of 1986 (IRCA), with its employer sanctions and amnesty provisions as well as expanded seasonal agricultural workers provisions.

Stana, Richard M. 2003. "Homeland Security: Challenges to Implementing the Immigration Interior Enforcement Strategy." GAO-03–660T. Washington, DC: U.S. Government Printing Office.

Suro, Roberto, and Audrey Singer. 2002. "Latino Growth in Metropolitan America: Changing Patterns, New Locations." Survey Series, Census 2000. Washington, DC: Brookings Institution. http://www.brookings.edu/es/urban/publications/surosingerexsum.htm.

Suro, Roberto, and Sonya Tafoya. 2004. "Dispersal and Concentration: Patterns of Latino Residential Settlement." Washington, DC: Pew Hispanic Center.

United States Citizenship and Immigration Services (USCIS). 2014. "Consideration of Deferred Action for Childhood Arrivals by Fiscal Year, Quarter, Intake Biometrics, and Case Studies, 2012–2014. USCIS Resources/Reports. http://www.uscis.gov/default/files/uscis/resources/reports.

UN High Commission for Refugees. 2006. "The U.N. Refugee Agency." http://www.unhcr.org/cgi-bin/texis/vtx/home. Accessed on February 9, 2006.

U.S. Bureau of the Census. 2001. "The Foreign-Born Population in the United States, March 2000, Current Population Reports." Washington, DC: U.S. Government Printing Office.

U.S. Department of Health and Human Services. 2000. "Temporary Assistance for Needy Families (TANF) Program: Third Annual Report to Congress." Washington, DC: U.S. Government Printing Office.

U.S. Department of Justice. April 2002. "Follow-Up Report on INS Efforts to Improve the Control of Nonimmigrant Overstays." Report No. 1–2002–006. Washington, DC: U.S. Government Printing Office.

U.S. Department of Justice. "Undocumented Aliens in the U.S." http://www.usdoj.gov/graphics/aboutinst/statistics/illegalalien/index.htm. Accessed on November 14, 2001.

U.S. Department of Labor. 1999. "International Migration to the United States, 1999." Washington, DC: U.S. Government Printing Office.

U.S. Department of State. 1999. "U.S. Refugee Admissions for Fiscal Year 2000." Washington, DC: U.S. Government Printing Office.

U.S. Department of State. 2000. "Proposed Refugee Admissions for Fiscal Year 2001: Report to Congress." Washington, DC: U.S. Government Printing Office.

Nonprint Resources

America 101. 2005. 86 minutes, color.
Fabia Films
Two Mexican brothers get smuggled over the border to try and find their "American dream."

Angel Island: A Story of Chinese Immigration. 2002. 12 minutes, color.
Films for the Humanities and Sciences
From 1910 to 1943, Chinese immigrants passed through Angel Island in San Francisco Bay, sometimes called the Ellis Island of the West. They were legally discriminated against, and this program looks at how two women are raising funds and awareness to have the old immigration station restored. Slated for destruction, the station was spared in 1970 when a park ranger discovered, beneath layers of paint, poems written by anxious detainees over their fear of deportation.

Animas Perdidas (Lost Souls). 2010. 60 minutes, color.
ITVS/PBS
A documentary by Monica Navarro, it chronicles the emotional journey of her uncle, a U.S. military veteran deported to Mexico, and uncovers the secrets of her family's past, when they had to start over to forge new lives in an unfamiliar "homeland."

The Asianization of America. 2002. 26 minutes, color.
Films for the Humanities and Sciences

This program examines the role of Asian Americans half a century after repeal of the Chinese Exclusion Act, seeking to determine what accounts for their success in academia and the extent to which they can, should, or want to blend into the American melting pot.

Backyard (El Traspatio). 2009. 122 minutes, color.

Tarazod films, Tardon/Berman Productions

A feature film starring Jimmy Smits, it tells the true story of the border town of Juarez, Mexico, where since the mid-1990s, thousands of women have gone missing or turned up as sun-burnt corpses in the Sonora Desert.

Beyond Borders: The Debate over Human Migration. 2007. 51 minutes, color.

Brian Ging Films

The debate between Noam Chomsky and Jim Gilchrist presents both sides of the controversy over illegal immigration to the United States and what should be done about the problem.

Biomedical Weapons: A Modern Threat. 2003. 25 minutes, color.

Insight Media

This program defines biochemical weapons and discusses the manufacture of such weapons as anthrax and mustard gas. It provides simulations of biochemical attack and outlines their psychological affects. It explores the history of biochemical terrorism and addresses the likelihood of a terrorist attack.

Bioterrorism. 2001. 50 minutes, color.

Insight Media

The anthrax episode in the United States in the wake of 9/11 raised awareness of the possibility of a wide-scale bioterrorism attack in the United States. In this program, officials from the departments of state and defense and leading bioterrorism experts including several veterans of the massive Soviet bioweapons program discuss the many obstacles standing in the way of a successful attack.

Borderline. 2012. 90 minutes, color.

Tall Tale Productions

This documentary explores the aftermath of the 9/11 attacks as experienced by ordinary people living and working along the U.S.-Canada border.

Caught in the Crossfire: Arab-Americans in Wartime. 2002. 54 minutes, color.

First Run/Icarus Films

This film covers New York City's Arab population caught in the cross fire of President Bush's War on Terrorism, and the cold welcome it now experiences. CNN diplomatic correspondent for a leading independent Arab newspaper, Raghida Dergham, is featured, as are Khader El-Yateem, an Arab Christian, whose Arabic Lutheran Church serves as a haven for Brooklyn Arabs, Muslim and Christian alike; and Ahmed Nasser, a Yemen-born police officer stationed at Ground Zero after 9/11, who relates how Arab American calls for help when harassed were ignored in his precinct. Film shows how they are torn between their adopted country and their homelands as they wrestle with their place in wartime America.

Chasing the Sleeper Cell. 2003. 60 minutes, color.

Insight Media

This PBS program features a joint investigation by *Frontline* and the *New York Times* into an ongoing domestic terrorism case involving Al Qaeda operatives and the U.S. citizens they trained. It discusses FBI and CIA effectiveness in combating sleeper cells.

Conspiracy: The Anthrax Attacks. 2004. 50 minutes, color.

Insight Media

This program looks at how, less than two weeks after 9/11, news outlets and prominent senators became targets of the first biowarfare attacks in U.S. history. It investigates mysteries surrounding the strain of anthrax used, which had been under the control of the U.S. biodefense industry.

Coyote. 2007. 94 minutes, color.

Side Street Productions

Filmed in Los Angeles, this documentary directed by Brian Petersen tells the tale of two young Americans who decide to begin smuggling immigrants into Arizona for profit. In Spanish and English.

Crossing Over. 2009. 113 minutes, color.

MGM/The Weinstein Company

An independent crime film drama, this feature film starring Harrison Ford, Ashley Judd, Ray Liotta, and Jim Sturgess is a multicharacter canvas showing how immigrants of different nationalities struggle to achieve legal status in Los Angeles.

Death on a Friendly Border. 2002. 26 minutes, color.

Filmmakers Library

The border between Tijuana and San Diego is the most militarized border between "friendly" countries anywhere. Since 1994, when the United States began Operation Gatekeeper, on average one person per day dies trying to cross. This film puts a face on that daily tragedy by following the story of a young woman who makes the perilous journey, with its hardships of heat, thirst, and abusive border guards.

The Double Life of Ernesto Gomez. 2001. 54 minutes, color.

Filmmakers Library

This film focuses on 15-year-old Ernesto Gomez, who has two identities, two families, and three nations: the United States, Mexico, and Puerto Rico. It follows his journey from

Mexico to the United States to meet his Puerto Rican birth mother and to learn of his heritage. This award-winning film documents his struggle for identity.

The Dream Is Now. 2013. 31 minutes, color.

At http://www.thedreamisnow.org/

This video is a moving and thought-provoking look at the undocumented youth in America directed by Davis Guggenheim, the Academy-award-winning director of documentary films. It became a documentary important in the political and public opinion battles over the Dream Act and President Obama's DACA executive action. It is both moving and thought provoking. This short video brings the pressing issue to the nation's attention to debate, to discuss, and for viewers to decide for themselves.

Dying to Get In: Undocumented Immigration at the U.S.-Mexico Border. 2005. 40 minutes, color.

Films for the Humanities and Sciences

A documentary film by Christopher Deufert, directed by Brett Tolley, who imbedded himself with a group of Mexicans crossing the U.S.-Mexico border, it presents their story as they make the journey across the border.

The 800-Mile Wall. 2009. 90 minutes, color.

Jack Lorenz Productions/Gatekeepers Productions

An award-winning film by John Carlos Frey, it is a powerful, independent film about the border fence.

El Chogui: A Mexican Immigrant Story. 2002. 57 minutes, color.

Filmmakers Library

This film follows a young peasant, Louis Miquel, from Oaxaca, Mexico, as he tries to lift his family out of poverty by boxing. He immigrates to the United States, as did countless of his compatriots. The film follows his transition over six years, from his tension-filled, illegal border crossing with his sisters, to later when he brings his four brothers to California.

English Only in America. 2002. 25 minutes, color.

Films for the Humanities and Sciences

When California passed its "English only" law, it set off a storm of legal and social debate that continues to rage. This film interviews persons pro and con the English-only policy from social, legal, and education perspectives.

Facing Up to Illegal Immigration. 2004. 23 minutes.

Films Media Group

Discussion of the issue of whether there is a realistic way to stop illegal immigrants at America's borders. It grapples with the fact that the world's only superpower cannot seem to control its borders and cannot seem to function without illegal immigrants. An ABC News special, it offers a balanced look at the illegal immigration situation in the United States, addressing issues such as the liability of porous borders in a time of terrorism, or the need—like it or not—for illegal aliens in the workforce and whether they really take jobs away from U.S. citizens or whether they are doing work that Americans themselves are unwilling to do.

From a Different Shore: The Japanese-American Experience. 2002. 50 minutes, color.

Films for the Humanities and Sciences

Japanese Americans are often considered a "model minority." This video explores their experiences from the first immigrants, the Issei, through their children, the Nissei, who endured confinement in camps during World War II, to their grandchildren, through three families whose members span all three generations.

From the Other Side. 2002. 99 minutes, color.

Icarus Films

With technology developed by the U.S. military, the INS has stemmed the flow of illegal immigrants in San Diego. But for the desperate, there are still the dangerous deserts of Arizona, where renowned filmmaker Chantel Akerman shifts her focus. It is a multiple-award-winning documentary film.

The Golden Cage: A Story of California's Farmworkers. 1990. 29 minutes, color.

Filmmakers Library

A modern "Grapes of Wrath," this film offers a vivid and moving portrait of contemporary farmworkers using historical footage, interviews, newspaper clippings, and black-and-white stills. It traces the history of the United Farm Workers union from the 1960s to 1990, showing the tactics used by many companies to evade using union labor. It shows candid interviews with legal and illegal migrant workers, growers, doctors, and others.

Human Contraband: Selling the American Dream. 2002. 22 minutes, color.

Films for the Humanities and Sciences

This ABC news program investigates the lucrative trade in smuggling into Mexico desperate human beings from all over the world, who view that country as the back door to the United States. INS officials discuss multilateral efforts to combat illegal entry to the United States.

Illegal Americans. 2002. 45 minutes, color.

Films for the Humanities and Sciences

This CBS news documentary looks at the hazardous enterprise of immigrants coming to the United States illegally, focusing on their plight. It examines their living conditions in detention centers, the growing strains they place on the U.S. cities. It looks at those who provide assistance persons who manage to evade capture, the sweatshops that, exploit them, and the efforts of some who attempt to beat the system by using false IDs and marriages of convenience.

Immigrant Nation: The Battle for the Dream. 2010, 96 minutes, color.

A documentary from Esau Melendez, it won an award at the Oaxaca Film Fest.

The story of the modern immigrant rights movement and struggle seen through the eyes of a single mother, Elvira Arellano, who fought against her forced deportation and separation from her American-born child.

Immigration: Who Has Access to the American Dream? 2002. 28 minutes, color.

Films for the Humanities and Sciences

Program reviews how new policy directives affect the survival of new immigrants to the United States, covering a variety of questions, such as how many immigrants should be allowed in; who, if anyone, should receive preferential treatment; and how illegal immigrants should be handled. It examines those issues from various perspectives: those seeking entry and organizations that assist them; an immigration judge; an immigrant from Kenya; and a Korean immigrant owner of a New York City deli.

Inside the Terror Network. 2001. 60 minutes, color.

Insight Media

This PBS video examines three of the 9/11 hijackers for insight into the making of a radical terrorist. It traces their movements in the days, months, and years leading up to the 9/11 attacks and shows how they slipped between the cracks of U.S. law enforcement.

Interpol Investigates: One-Way Ticket. 2004. 60 minutes, color.

Insight Media

This program examines illegal immigration issues, highlighting the case in which a boat carrying more than

300 illegal Chinese immigrants ran aground in New York harbor. It shows how the case led domestic and international investigators to the gangs of Chinatown and on a seven-year hunt to find the leaders of the smuggling operation.

Legacy of Shame: Migrant Labor, an American Institution. 2002. 52 minutes, color.

Films for the Humanities and Sciences

This video is a follow-up to the 1960 award-wining *Harvest of Shame*. It documents ongoing exploitation of America's migrant labor by highlighting efforts made to protect them. It investigates pesticide risks, uneven enforcement of employment and immigration regulations, and peonage conditions. It covers efforts of rural legal services as advocates for this "silent-minority." It is a CBS news documentary.

Legal Limbo: The War on Terrorism and the Judicial Process. 2004. 23 minutes, color.

Films Media Group

It asks the question, does the war on terrorism require a fundamental shift in the U.S. judicial process? Highlighting two case studies, the program examines whether the judicial process was sidestepped by the Bush administration in the interest of combating terrorism. Cases examined are those of Zacharias Mousssauoui and his role in the attacks of 9/11; and Jose Padilla, a U.S. citizen accused of plans to use a "dirty bomb."

Liberty and Security in an Age of Terrorism. 2003. 23 minutes, color.

Films Media Group

This film grapples with the issues of balance between national security needs of the post-9/11 world and the basic civil liberty values central to our society. Using a hypothetical scenario, a panel of persons confronts the issues and wrestles with the high-stakes questions in discussing the implications of the USA Patriot Act, surveillance of suspects, closed deportation hearings, demands for student information, and just what constitutes an unaligned combatant.

Laredoans Speak: Voices on Immigration. 2011. 75 minutes, color.

Border Town Pictures

Veteran actor Pepe Serna takes viewers through the issues involved in the debate over undocumented immigration through the eyes of citizens of Laredo, Texas. The film is directed by Victor Martinez.

The Line in the Sand. 2005. 100 minutes, color.

Sun Films, Inc.

A documentary film, it deals with the illegal immigration and security on the southern border of the United States and on the Minutemen Project.

Maid in America. 2005. 60 minutes, color.

PBS/ITVS

Three undocumented workers' experiences are chronicled as they toil as cooks, housekeepers, and even surrogate mothers, often at the expense of their own families, as they attempt to nurture their American dreams.

A Nation of Immigrants: The Chinese-American Experience. 2002. 20 minutes, color.

Films for the Humanities and Sciences

This video explores the plight of Chinese immigrants, including their hard work for pitifully low wages, racial discrimination, victimization in race riots, and so forth.

The Other Side of Immigration. 2010. 55 minutes, color.

Roy Germano Films, LLC

In English and Spanish, this documentary is based on 700
   interviews and is a thought-provoking and challenging
   film for audiences of all political and ideological sides of
   the illegal immigration debate. It puts real faces on illegal
   immigrants. It garnered a place on the American Library
   Association 2011 List of Notable videos for adults.

The Patriot Act under Fire. 2003. 23 minutes, color.

Films Media Group

For many, worrying about constitutional rights seems like
   an archaic luxury in an age of international terrorism.
   The need for tighter security made civil liberties seem
   less critical when the nation confronted such terrorism
   by passing urgent measures such as the USA Patriot Act,
   designed to defend the country. Two years after its passage,
   ABC News and Ted Koppel take a hard look at the law with
   representatives from the Justice Department, the ACLU,
   and others.

Precious Knowledge. 2011. 75 minutes, color.

Dos Vatos Productions, ITVS

Disenfranchised high school seniors become academic
   warriors and community leaders in Tucson, Arizona's
   embattled ethnic studies classes while state lawmakers try to
   eliminate the program.

Sin Nombre (Without a Name). 2009. 96 minutes, color.

Creando Film, Focus Films Feature

This film won several awards at the 2009 Sundance Film
   festival. A Honduran teenager, Sayra, reunites with her
   father and tries to realize her dream of a life in the United
   States. Directed by Cary Toji Fukunaga, it is in Spanish
   with English subtitles.

The State of Arizona. 2014. 90 minutes, color.

PBS/ITVS, Latino Public Broadcasting Production

The turbulent battle over illegal immigration in Arizona that
   came to a head with passage of Arizona Senate bill 1070

frames this riveting documentary that tracks multiple perspectives as America eyes the results of its passage seen from all sides of the issue.

Stories from the Mines: How Immigrant Miners Changed America. 2002. 57 minutes, color.

Films for the Humanities and Sciences

America's rise to superpower status was fueled to a great degree by the social and industrial impact of coal-mining in northeastern Pennsylvania. This meticulously researched program uses location footage, archival film, period photos, dramatizations, and academic commentary to examine U.S. labor. It vividly captures the agitation and the often-violent suppression that characterized the times and emphasizes the precedents, including child labor laws, and the right to collective bargaining, set against the stark backdrop of immigrant miners being exploited by industrialists.

The Terrorism Alert System. 2003. 23 minutes, color.

Insight Media

This video explains the now much maligned five-level terrorism alert system developed by the DHS. It provides recommendations to government and the private sector on responses to each level of risk.

They Come to America: The Cost of Amnesty. 2012. 99 minutes, color.

Corinth Films

A film by Dennis Lynch of FAIR, it depicts the human and financial costs of illegal immigration.

Those Who Remain. 2008. 96 minutes, color.

Sombre del Guyabo Productions

A documentary film directed by Carlos Hegerman, it tells an intimate and discerning tale depicting the impact of migration on families and communities left behind by loved ones who have traveled north to find work in the United States.

Ties that Bind: Immigration Stories. 2002. 58 minutes, color.

Films for Humanities and Sciences

This film examines the human drama behind the current
immigration debate on both sides of the Texas/Mexico
border while exploring the root causes of why Mexicans
emigrate. Emphasis is on the role of transnational
corporations and their social/economic impacts on both
Mexicans and North Americans. It explores the increasingly
restrictive nature of immigration policies, as well as the
strong family values that immigrants bring with them and
their positive impact on U.S. culture.

Trafficked: Children as Sexual Slaves. 2004. 52 minutes, color.

Filmmakers Library

The trafficking of women and children for the purpose of
prostitution is a global problem. The United Nations
estimates that more than 1 million children are forced into
sexual slavery each year. This documentary follows Chris
Payne, a former police officer turned private investigator,
as he investigates this shocking crime. It focuses on the
case of "Nikkie," a young Thai girl found working in a
brothel in Sydney who is hastily deported. Payne examines
the circumstances that forced her into a brothel and what
became of her after her deportation back to Thailand. His
search leads him to Asia and the parents of another Thai
"sex slave," whose death in an immigration detention center
made the headlines. A powerful documentary, it offers
disturbing insight into the international sex trade.

The Undocumented. 2004. 90 minutes, color.

ITVS/Two Tone Production

Approximately 2,000 immigrants trying to cross the
unforgiving Sonora Desert in search of a better life have
perished trying to cross the U.S.-Mexico border. The film
gives faces to some of the dead and follows their tragic, long
journey home.

Under the Same Moon. 2007. 106 minutes, color.

Creando Films

This documentary won a Sundance Film Award, Jury Prize in 2007. Directed by Patricia Riggin, in Spanish and English, it follows a young Mexican boy who travels to the United States to find his mother after his grandmother passes away.

Wetback: The Undocumented Documentary. 2005. 96 minutes, color.

IMDb Productions

A Canadian documentary film, it chronicles the struggles and hardships of a handful of Mexicans trying to relocate to the United States.

When East Meets East. 2002. 53 minutes, color.

Films for Humanities and Sciences

This genre-breaking documentary explores the issues of ethnic and cultural identity through interviews with some of today's most prominent Asian film figures.

With Us or against Us: Afghans in America. 2002. 27 minutes, color.

Filmmakers Library

This short documentary examines the experiences of Afghan immigrants in the United States and their plight facing discrimination and hysteria after the 9/11 attacks.

iAmerica.org
iAmerica.org
READY
AMERICA
iAmerica.org
I am READY
AMERICA
erica.org
READY

Precursor Legislation: Setting the Stage for Things to Come

1790 In one of its first official actions, the U.S. Congress establishes a uniform rule of naturalization that imposes a two-year residency requirement for aliens who are "free white persons of good moral character."

1802 Congress revises the 1790 act to require a five-year residency requirement and that naturalizing citizens renounce allegiance and fidelity to foreign powers.

1819 Congress enacts law requiring shipmasters to deliver a manifest enumerating all aliens transported for immigration and requiring the secretary of state to inform Congress annually of the number of immigrants admitted. This act, for the first time, keeps count of the number of immigrants who enter "legally" for the purpose of permanent immigration. In short, it is the first official "immigration act."

1848 Treaty of Guadalupe Hidalgo guarantees citizenship to Mexicans remaining in the territory ceded by Mexico to the United States. This action sets the first base for the flow of

Community activists rally during an event on Deferred Action for Childhood Arrivals, DACA and Deferred Action for Parental Accountability, DAPA in downtown Los Angeles on February 17, 2015. The White House promised an appeal after a federal judge in Texas temporarily blocked President Barack Obama's executive action on immigration and gave a coalition of 26 states time to pursue a lawsuit aiming to permanently stop the orders. (AP Photo/Nick Ut)

Mexicans to the United States and provides for a citizen base from Mexico into which future immigrants, both legal and undocumented, can assimilate. It forges the first link into what develops as "chain migration" from Mexico and even Central America to the United States.

1855   Castle Garden becomes New York's principal port of entry for legal immigration. Its volume of immigrants sets the stage for later development of "visa overstayers" who are able to remain because such extensive numbers overwhelm the ability of immigration authorities to keep accurate track of them.

1862   Congress enacts the Homestead Act, granting acres of free land to settlers who develop the land in frontier regions and remain on it for five years, spurring heavy levels of immigration.

1868   The Fourteenth Amendment is ratified. It guarantees that all persons born or naturalized in the United States and subject to its jurisdiction are citizens and states that no state may abridge their rights without due process or deny them equal protection under the law. The amendment ensures citizenship rights of the former slaves and thereby changes the "free white persons" phrase of citizenship to include blacks. It further establishes the supremacy of federal law over actions by state governments in matters pertaining to citizenship, naturalization, and immigration.

1870   Congress enacts a law granting citizenship to persons of African descent.

1882   Congress passes the Chinese Exclusion Act, barring the immigration of Chinese laborers for 10 years and denying Chinese eligibility for naturalization. The act is reenacted and extended in 1888, 1892, and 1904. Its harsh provisions induce many Chinese immigrants to get around the law by using falsified documents—such as "paper sons and daughters." This sets a precedent for using phony documents by illegal aliens that persists to the present day.

1885   Congress passes an act making it unlawful for laborers to immigrate to the United States under contract with a U.S. employer who in any manner prepays passage to bring the laborer to the country. In some ways it serves as the precursor to employers who hire illegal aliens using fake documents: the employer simply does not verify the accuracy of the documents, in some cases knowing or suspecting that they are illegal.

1886   *Yick Wo v. Hopkins* overturns a San Francisco municipal ordinance against Chinese laundry workers as discriminatory and unconstitutional on the grounds that the Fourteenth Amendment prohibits state and local governments from depriving any person (even a noncitizen) of life, liberty, or property without due process.

1888   Congress expands the Chinese Exclusion Act by rescinding reentry permits for Chinese laborers and thus prohibiting their return (also known as the Scott Act).

1889   In the case of *Chae Chan Ping v. United States*, the Supreme Court upholds the right of Congress to repeal the certificate of reentry as contained in the 1888 act, thereby excluding ex post facto certain Chinese immigrants who had previously entered legally.

1891   Congress expands the classes of individuals excluded from admission, forbids the soliciting of immigrants, and creates the position of superintendent of immigration.

1892   Ellis Island is opened as the nation's leading port of entry. It becomes the source of many visa overstayers from European countries.

1894   Congress extends the Chinese Exclusion Act and establishes the Bureau of Immigration within the Treasury Department, the first of several such home departments to immigration services.

1897   A federal district court decides the case *In re Rodriquez*. This west-Texas case affirms the citizenship rights of Mexicans based on the 1848 Treaty of Guadalupe Hidalgo and notwithstanding that such persons may not be considered "white."

1898   In the case of *Wong Kim Ark v. United States*, the Supreme Court rules that a native-born son of Asian descent is indeed a citizen of the United States despite the fact that his parents may have been resident aliens ineligible for citizenship.

1903   Congress enacts a law making immigration the responsibility of the Department of Commerce and Labor.

1906   The Basic Naturalization Law codifies a uniform law for naturalization. With some amendments and supplements, it forms the basic naturalization law thereafter.

1907   Congress adds important regulations about issuing passports and the expatriation and marriage of U.S. women to foreigners. It continues to stir controversy until Section 3 of the act is repealed in 1922. President Theodore Roosevelt issues an executive order, known as the Gentleman's Agreement, by which Japan agrees to restrict emigration of laborers from Japan and Korea (which was then under Japanese jurisdiction). Picture brides, however, are permitted to emigrate. Congress passes the White-Slave Traffic Act forbidding importation of any woman or girl for the purpose of prostitution or similar immoral purposes.

1911   The Dillingham Commission issues its report, whose recommendations form the basis for the quota acts of the 1920s.

1915   The Americanization/100 Percentism campaign begins and is supported by both government and private enterprise. These social movements represent the first attempt at "forced assimilation" encouraging the adoption of the English language and social customs. After World War I, its perceived failure will contribute to the disillusionment that set the stage for the quota acts of the 1920s.

1917   The United States enters World War I in April. Congress enacts an immigration act that includes a literacy test and bars all immigration from a specified area known thereafter as the Asian barred zone. The Departments of State and of Labor issue a joint order requiring passports of all aliens seeking to enter the United States and requiring that the would-be entrants be issued visas by U.S. consular officers in their country of origin rather than seeking permission to enter the United States only when arriving at the port of entry. Puerto Ricans are granted U.S. citizenship.

1918 Congress gives the president sweeping powers to disallow the entrance or the departure of aliens during time of war. Similar presidential declarations are used in virtually all periods of war thereafter.

1919 Congress enacts a law granting honorably discharged Native Americans citizenship for their service during World War I. In the summer, the Red Scare following the Bolshevik revolution in Russia leads to the summary deportation of certain specified "radical" aliens deemed thereby to be a threat to U.S. security. It serves as a precursor to the USA Patriot Act in that respect.

1921 Congress passes the first Quota Act, in which immigration from a particular country is set at 3 percent of the foreign-born population from that country based on the 1910 census.

1922 Congress passes the Cable Act, stating that the right of any woman to become a naturalized citizen shall not be abridged because of her sex or because she is a married woman unless she is wed to an alien ineligible for citizenship. This latter provision is later repealed.

1923 The U.S. Supreme Court rules in *United States v. Bhagat Singh Thind* that "white person" means those persons who appear and would commonly be viewed as white. Thus, East Asian Indians, although Caucasians, are not "white" and are therefore ineligible for citizenship through naturalization.

1924 Congress enacts the Immigration Act, known as the Johnson-Reed Act, setting the national-origin quota for a particular country at 2 percent of the foreign-born population from that country as of the census of 1890. This new system drastically shifts the sources of immigration from South, Central, and Eastern Europe to Northwestern Europe. The act bars the admission of most Asians, who are thereby classified as "aliens ineligible for citizenship." Congress passes an act granting citizenship to those Native Americans who had not previously received it by allotments under the 1887 Dawes Act or by military service during World War I.

1925 Congress establishes the Border Patrol, charged with policing the U.S. borders against illegal or undocumented entrants. It is also charged with finding and deporting illegal aliens from the interior who had managed to elude apprehension at the border.

1929 President Herbert Hoover proclaims new and permanent quotas in which national-origin quotas for European immigrants are based on the proportion of those nationalities in the total population as determined by the 1920 census. The total number of such to be admitted is fixed at just over 150,000.

1929–1939 U.S. immigration levels slow dramatically in response to the worldwide Great Depression.

1940 Congress passes the Registration Law, which requires noncitizens to register their addresses every year. The process remains in effect until 1980. Millions of such forms are backlogged and "lost" in INS warehouses. The failure of this program contributes to the calls during the 1980s to crack down on illegal immigration and visa overstayers through enhanced capability of the INS, which is never achieved.

1941 President Franklin D. Roosevelt issues a proclamation to control persons entering or leaving the United States based on the first War Powers Act.

1942 Agreement entered with Mexico to allow migrant farmworkers to enter as temporary labor to satisfy wartime labor shortages in agriculture.

President issues Executive Order 9066, leading to the evacuation, relocation, and internment of Japanese and Japanese Americans into relocation camps.

1943 The Supreme Court rules, in *Hirabayashi v. United States*, that the executive orders for curfews and evacuation programs were constitutional based upon "military necessity."

1944 The Supreme Court decides *Korematsu v. United States*, again affirming the constitutionality of the executive orders excluding Japanese Americans from remaining in certain "excluded zones."

The Court also rules, in *Ex Parte Mitsuye Endo*, that the internment program was an unconstitutional violation of the habeas corpus rights of U.S. citizens—namely, the Nisei.

1949 Congress passes the Agricultural Act with provision to recruit temporary farmworkers from Mexico—the Bracero Program.

1956 President Eisenhower establishes a "parole" system for Hungarian freedom fighters. Two years later, Congress endorses the procedures to an act to admit Hungarian refugees.

1959 Congress amends the Immigration and Nationality Act of 1952 to provide for unmarried sons and daughters of U.S. citizens to enter as "nonquota" immigrants.

1960 Congress enacts a program to assist resettlement of refugees from communist countries who have been paroled by the attorney general (mostly Cubans).

President John F. Kennedy is elected.

1963 President Kennedy is assassinated.

1964 Bracero Program ends.

The Revolving-Door Era, 1965–2000

1965 Congress passes the Immigration and Nationality Act. It amends the 1954 act by ending the quota system and establishing a preference system emphasizing family reunification and meeting certain skill goals, standardizing admission procedures, and setting per-country limits of 20,000 for Eastern Hemisphere nations, with a total of 170,000. The first ceiling on Western Hemisphere immigration is set at 120,000.

1966   Congress amends the 1965 act to adjust Cuban Refugee status. This sets up the distinction between refugees based on anticommunist U.S. foreign policy goals and those based on economic refugee status.

1967   UN Convention and Protocol on Refugees; 130 nations sign the protocol accords. Refugees entering under its provisions (such as Cuban refugees) get resettlement assistance, whereas those entering based on economic grounds (Haitian refugees) are excluded.

1968   Bilingual Education Act is passed.

President Johnson issues a proclamation on the UN Protocols on the Status of Refugees, essentially endorsing the U.S. commitment to the multinational protocols.

1972   The House passes, but the Senate kills, a bill that would have made it illegal to knowingly hire an illegal alien. It becomes the first of many attempts prior to 1986 to impose what becomes known as "employer sanctions" for hiring illegal aliens.

Haitian boat influx of illegal aliens begins arriving on the East Coast, mostly in Florida. Haitian detention camps are set up in Miami.

France implements its *regularization* program.

1975   The fall of Saigon, then Vietnam along with Cambodia and Laos, precipitates a massive flight of refugees to the United States from the Indochina region. Vietnamese, Cambodians, and Laotians are classified as refugees from communist countries and are thereby assisted in resettlement and aided by "assimilation assistance" programs, many conducted by church-based organizations that assist immigrants.

President Carter establishes and Congress funds the Indo-chinese Refugee Resettlement Program.

Soviet Jews begin fleeing in large numbers. Civil war in El Salvador leads to beginning of their refugee movement. Haitians continue arriving in large numbers.

1976   Congress amends the 1965 act by extending the per-country limits of visa applicants on a first-come, first-served basis to Western Hemisphere nations as regulated by the preference system.

The U.S. Supreme Court rules, in *Matthews v. Diaz*, that an alien has no right to Social Security or Medicare benefits.

The Ford administration establishes a cabinet-level committee to study immigration options.

1978   President Carter and the Congress set up the Select Commission on Immigration and Refugee Policy (SCIRP).

1979   SCIRP begins its work.

Vietnamese and Southeast Asian boat people influx.

1980   Congress passes the Refugee Act to systematize refugee policy. It incorporates the UN definition of refugee, accepting 50,000 persons annually who have a "well-founded fear" of persecution based on race, religion, nationality, or membership in a social or political movement. Provides for admission of 5,000 "asylum seekers."

1981   Economic recession begins.

March 1: The SCIRP issues its Final Report, recommending many changes in policy that form the basis of IRCA and other subsequent reform acts, several of which underlie proposed reforms even after 2001.

President Reagan creates Task Force on Immigration and Refugee Policy, which reports in July.

France implements its second *regularization* (amnesty) program.

1982   Federal district judge rules the lockup of Haitians unconstitutional, ordering release of 1,900 detainees.

Major bill to amend the Immigration and Nationality Act is introduced into House.

1983 Immigration reform bill is reintroduced into Congress.

The Supreme Court rules, in *INS v. Chadha et al.*, that the use of the legislative veto to overturn certain INS deportation proceedings, rules, and regulations by the House of Representatives was unconstitutional.

France implements its third *regularization* program.

1984 Immigration reform bill passes in different versions in both chambers, dies in conference.

1985 Sen. Alan Simpson (R-WY) reintroduces what becomes known as the Simpson/Mazzoli/Rodino bill.

1986 The Supreme Court rules in *Jean v. Nelson* on INS denial of parole to undocumented aliens. Congress enacts IRCA's employer sanctions/legalization approach granting amnesty to about 1.5 million illegal aliens and more than 1 million special agricultural workers.

1987 In *INS v. Cardoza-Fonseca*, by a vote of 6 to 3, the Supreme Court rules that the government must relax its standards for deciding whether aliens who insist that they would be persecuted if they returned to their homelands are eligible for asylum.

1988 The Senate passes, but the House kills, the Kennedy-Simpson bill in what becomes the 1990 act.

U.S.-Canada Free Trade Implementation Act is signed.

Congress amends the 1965 Immigration Act regarding H-1 category use by nurses.

1989 Conference for Central American Refugee is held.

1990 Congress passes a major reform of the laws concerning legal immigration, setting new ceilings for worldwide immigration, redefining the preference system for family reunification and employment, and setting up a new category of preference called "the diversity immigrants." It enacts special provisions regarding Central American refugees, Filipino veterans, and persons seeking to leave Hong Kong. Significant changes were included with respect to naturalization procedures.

1993   Congress ratifies the North American Free Trade Agreement (NAFTA).

Donald Huddle issues his report, "The Cost of Immigration," setting off the decades-long debate over the relative costs and benefits of immigration and illegal immigration.

1994   California passes Proposition 187, the "Save Our State" initiative.

Congress enacts the Violent Crime Control and Law Enforcement Act, the "Smith Act," giving the attorney general more authority to issue the "S Visas."

Congress passes the Violence against Women Act with provision to grant special status through cancellation of removal and self-petitioning provisions.

1995   Federal district court for California rules, in *LULAC et al. v. Wilson et al.*, that many of Proposition 187's provisions are unconstitutional.

The General Accounting Office issues its first major and comprehensive report on the costs of illegal aliens to governments and to the overall economy.

A Human Rights Watch report is highly critical of the INS and alleged abuses.

1996   June: The Board of Immigration Appeals (in re: Fauziya Kasinga, A73479695) grants the first woman asylum on the basis of gender persecution (female genital mutilation).

Congress enacts Personal Responsibility and Work Opportunity Act (welfare reform), with numerous immigration-related provisions. Congress essentially enacts aspects of Proposition 187 regarding welfare and other public benefits that had been overturned.

Congress passes the Illegal Immigration Reform and Immigrant Responsibility Act (IIRIRA), the 60-plus immigration-related provisions of the Omnibus Spending Bill.

It removes other welfare and economic benefits to illegal aliens and to some legal resident aliens.

The Anti-terrorism and Effective Death Penalty Act of 1996 is passed. Among its provisions, it gives INS inspectors the power to make "on-the-spot credible fear" determinations involving asylum. It takes effect on April 1, 1997, as part of IIRIRA reforms beginning then.

The Central American Regional Conference on Migration is held in Puebla, Mexico.

Border Patrol makes a record 1.6 million apprehensions at the borders nationwide.

Congress authorizes the addition of 1,000 new Border Patrol agents annually.

1997   The Jordan Commission on Immigration Reform, set up by the 1996 law, recommends restructuring of the INS in its final report.

The "Expedited Enforcement Rules" of the IIRIRA of 1996 take effect at U.S. land borders, international airports, and seaports to issue and enforce expulsion orders. Some 4,500 INS officers are added at 300 ports of entry.

The General Accounting Office issues its Report on the Fiscal Impact of Newest Americans.

1998   President Clinton sends another immigration bill to Congress seeking, in part, a restructuring of the INS. It dies in committee when the Judiciary Committee begins hearings on impeachment.

The Agriculture Job Opportunity Benefits and Security Act establishes a pilot program for 20,000 to 25,000 farmworkers.

The Social Security Board of Trustees Report is issued, documenting positive effects of immigration on the status of the Social Security fund but also on the dire, long-term crisis in the Social Security account as the U.S. population ages and fewer active workers support ever-growing numbers of retirees.

Congress passes the American Competitiveness and Work-force Improvement Act, which expands the H-1B category to the computer industry.

California voters approve its Proposition 227, which ends bilingual education programs in state schools. The Children of Immigrants Longitudinal Study is issued.

France implements its latest *regularization* program.

1999   The Carnegie Endowment for International Peace presents its International Migration Policy Program.

Twenty-one nongovernmental organizations concerned with immigration call for INS restructuring, separation of enforcement from visa and naturalization functions, and the sending of some functions to the DOL and HHS. INS provides Border Patrol/adjudication.

In *INS v. Aguirre-Aguirre* (67 U.S.L.W. 4270), a unanimous Supreme Court rules that aliens who have committed serious nonpolitical crimes in their home countries are ineligible to seek asylum in the United States regardless of the risk of persecution when returned to their countries.

Rep. Christopher Smith (R-NJ) introduces the Trafficking Victims Protection Act of 1999.

With a restored economy, President Clinton's administration restores some of the benefits stripped away from legal aliens by the 1996 acts.

November 22, 1999: Elian Gonzalez is rescued off the Florida coast.

UNHCR issues guidelines related to Detention of Asylum Seekers in Geneva, Italy.

Trafficking Victims Protection Act is passed.

2000   Negotiations regarding the Elian Gonzalez case begin.

April: Attorney General Reno approves a Justice Department "raid" on the Miami home to "return Elian Gonzalez" to his father in Cuba.

May: Sen. Sam Brownback (R-KS) introduces a bill to establish "T-Visa."

June 1: In *Gonzales v. Reno*, the 11th circuit court rules that only the father of Elian Gonzalez can speak for the boy.

The Storm-Door Era: 2001–?

2001   September 11: Terrorists attack the World Trade Center's Towers in New York and the Pentagon in Washington, D.C. Immediate calls for a crackdown on terrorists begin.

October 24: Congress passes the USA Patriot Act, granting sweeping new powers to the attorney general, the FBI, and the Department of Justice regarding immigrants and the authority to detain "enemy combatants" involved in or suspected of terrorism.

American Competitiveness in 21st Century Act is approved.

"DREAM Act" bill introduced for first time. Reintroduced annually thereafter.

2002   The INS issues notice to several of the (now dead) hijackers that they are given permission to enroll in U.S. flight training programs. Immediate calls for restructuring of INS to remove Border Patrol functions result.

November: Congress establishes a cabinet-level Department of Homeland Security. The attorney general is granted sweeping new powers for expedited removal. INS is extensively restructured into the new department. As of March 2003, the INS is abolished; the undersecretary for Border and Transportation Security begins oversight of Immigration Enforcement and Citizenship and Immigration Services.

The United Nations issues its Protocols on Human Trafficking and Immigrant Smuggling in Polermo, Italy. The protocols are signed by 141 countries.

2003   January: The Terrorist Threat Integration Center is created.

2004   The 9/11 Commission issues its report detailing the intelligence failures contributing to the success of the terrorist cells and their attacks.

Congress passes the Intelligence Reform and Terrorism Prevention Act. It establishes the director of National Intelligence position. President Bush appoints John Negroponte, ambassador to Iraq, as the first DNI.

National Counterterrorism Center is created, largely housed and staffed in the CIA.

Unauthorized immigrants within the United States reach an estimated record of 11 million. The ICE reports 1.1 million apprehensions at the nation's borders.

2005   The House passes the Border Protection, Anti-terrorism and Illegal Immigration Control Act, also known as the REAL ID Act.

The state of Virginia passes a law prohibiting unauthorized immigrants from receiving state or local public benefits.

New Mexico passes a law extending state tuition to unauthorized immigrants.

Arizona enacts a measure preventing cities from constructing day labor centers if such centers serve unauthorized immigrants.

Nine states pass anti–human trafficking laws.

Nine states pass laws banning the issuing of driver's licenses (identification) to unauthorized immigrants.

Three states pass laws mandating state and local law enforcement agencies to enforce federal immigration laws against unauthorized immigrants.

The governors of Arizona and New Mexico issue "state of emergency" declarations because of the extreme adverse impacts of illegal immigration on their respective states.

The AIC launches a state-by-state campaign aimed at enacting state laws against illegal immigration.

The European Union ministers approve the use of biometric cards for immigration to EU countries.

The Netherlands enacts stricter anti–illegal immigration measures.

Hong Kong imposes the temperature screening of all incoming travelers.

England's High Court approves several measures announced by the government designed to "crack down" on illegal immigrants and ease procedures to deport them.

Japan begins fingerprinting all incoming immigrants.

France expels thousands of illegal immigrants.

Russia imposes fines for hiring illegal immigrants.

2006   Poland increases its border patrol by 50 percent.

Congress extends the USA Patriot Act. In March it renews the Uniting and Strengthening America by Providing Appropriate Tools Required to Intercept and Obstruct Terrorism Act of 2001 (the USA Patriot Act).

Congress passes Secure Fence Act and President Bush signs it into law. The act authorizes construction of a 700-mile bollard type fence along southwestern border.

Advocacy group, Border Action Network, established.

State of Colorado holds special session to pass measure imposing fines on businesses that employ unauthorized immigrants.

2008   President Obama's administration begins a surge in use of expedited removals to deport unauthorized immigrants.

2009   President Obama uses executive action to mitigate certain aspects of IIRIRA.

2010   State of Arizona enacts law mandating state and local police to demand anyone suspected of being illegal to show documents to prove their legal status.

In *Arizona v. U.S.* (132 S.Ct.2492), the Supreme Court rules Arizona law unconstitutional.

In Congress, Democrats introduce an "earned legalization" measure. Republicans block the measure.

2012   President Obama issues executive action order, DACA, granting temporary, conditional legal status to "Dreamer" children.

2013   Senate passes S.744, a comprehensive immigration reform measure in bipartisan vote. Measure is blocked in the House of Representatives and dies.

Sen. David Vitter (R-LA) and Rep. Steve King (R-IA) introduce bill to end birthright citizenship to persons born in the United States of parents who are in illegal status.

2014   President Obama issues executive order, DAPA, granting temporary, conditional legal residency to unauthorized immigrant parents of U.S. citizens and legal permanent resident aliens.

Surge of arrivals of children unaccompanied by adults from El Salvador, Guatemala, and Honduras. President Obama grants "Temporary Protected Status" to about 5,000 such children for whom it is deemed too unsafe to return to country of origin.

2015   House Republicans, Homeland Security Committee, introduce the Secure Our Borders First Act of 2015.

February 17: U.S. District Judge, Texas, Andrew Hanen, places injunction on Obama administration's implementation of executive actions of DAPA.

References

AFL-CIO, Department of Professional Employees. 2013. "Guest Worker Programs and the STEM Workforce." http://www.dpeaaflcio.org/guest-worker-programs-an d-the-science-technology-workforce. Accessed on February 20, 2015.

"Anti-Terror Law Passes Senate, Goes to House." *USA Today*, March 3, 2006: A-1.

Bean, Frank, George Vernez, and Charles B. Keely. 1989. *Opening and Closing the Doors.* Santa Monica, CA: Rand Corporation; Washington, DC: Urban Institute.

Center for Immigration Studies. 2012. http://www.cis.org/amnesty-and-the-employment-picture-for-less-educated.

Chiswick, Barry R., ed. 1988. *The Gateway: U.S. Immigration Issues and Policies.* Washington, DC: American Enterprise Institute.

Department of Homeland Security. 2002. "HR 5005: To Establish the Department of Homeland Security, and for Other Purposes." http://www.dhs/hr5005.html. Accessed on April 20, 2003.

Department of Homeland Security. 2013. *Characteristics of H-1B Specialty Occupation Workers: 2012 Annual Report.* Washington, DC: Department of Homeland Security.

Department of Justice. 2002. "Follow-Up Report on INS Efforts to Improve the Control of Nonimmigrant Overstays." Report No. 1–2002–006. Washington, DC: U.S. Government Printing Office.

Department of Justice. 2001. "Undocumented Aliens in the U.S." Available at http://www.doj.gov/graphics/Aboutins/statistics/illegalalien/index.htm. Accessed on November 14, 2001.

Erler, Edward and Margaret Stock. 2012. *The Cost to Americans and America of Ending Birthright Citizenship.* Washington, DC: National Foundation for American Policy.

Fix, Michael, ed. 1991. *The Paper Curtain: Employer Sanctions' Implementation, Impact, and Reform.* Washington, DC: Urban Institute.

General Accounting Office. 1995. *Illegal Aliens: National Cost Estimates Vary Widely.* Washington, DC: U.S. Government Printing Office.

General Accounting Office. 1998. *Illegal Aliens: Significant Obstacles to Reducing Unauthorized Alien Employment Exist.* Washington, DC: U.S. Government Printing Office.

General Accounting Office. 1999. *Illegal Immigration: Status of Southwest Border Strategy Implementation.* Washington, DC: U.S. Government Printing Office.

General Accounting Office. 2000. *Illegal Aliens: Opportunities Exist to Improve Expedited Removal Process.* Washington, DC: U.S. Government Printing Office.

General Accounting Office. 2002. *Alien Smuggling: Management and Operational Improvement Needed to Address Growing Problem.* Washington, DC: U.S. Government Printing Office.

General Accounting Office. 2004. *Overstay Tracking: A Key Component of Homeland Security and a Layered Defense.* GAO-04–82, May. Washington, DC: U.S. Government Printing Office.

Glazer, Nathan, ed. 1985. *Clamor at the Gates: The New American Immigration.* San Francisco: ICS.

Guest Worker Alliance. http://www.imigration.about.com/od/Browse-Topics/what-is-a-guest-worker-program.htm. Accessed on February 20, 2015.

Hayes, Patrick, ed. 2012. *The Making of Modern Immigration: An Encyclopedia of People and Ideas.* Santa Barbara, CA: ABC-CLIO.

Heritage Foundation. 2014. "The Dream Act in the NDAA: Wrong for National and Homeland Security." http://www.heritage.org/research/reports/2014/the-Dream-Act-in-the-NDAA. Accessed on February 20, 2015.

Hirschman, Charles, Philip Kasinitz, and Joshua DeWind, eds. 1999. *The Handbook of International Migration: The American Experience.* New York: Russell Sage.

"House Passes Patriot Act." *San Bernardino Sun*, March 8, 2006: A-3. http://www.politics.com/2013/ immigration-bill-2013-senate-pass. www.commondreams. org/ . . . /federal-judge-texas-places-injunction-obama-immigration. Accessed on February 24, 2015.

Information Plus. 2006. *Immigration and Illegal Aliens: Burden or Blessing?* Farmington Hills, MI: Thomson/Gale.

Kivisto, Peter and Thomas Faist. 2010. *Beyond a Border: The Causes and Consequences of Contemporary Immigration.* Thousand Oaks, CA: Sage Publications.

LeMay, Michael. 1987. *From Open Door to Dutch Door: An Analysis of U.S. Immigration Policy since 1820.* New York: Praeger.

LeMay, Michael. 1989. *The Gatekeepers: Comparative Immigration Policies.* New York: Praeger.

LeMay, Michael. 2004. *U.S. Immigration: A Reference Handbook.* Santa Barbara, CA: ABC-CLIO.

LeMay, Michael, ed. 2013. *Transforming America: Perspectives on Immigration, Vol. 3, Immigration and Superpower Status, 1945 to Present.* Santa Barbara, CA: ABC-CLIO.

LeMay, Michael, and Elliott Robert Barkan. 1999. *U.S. Immigration and Naturalization Law and Issues: A Documentary History.* Westport, CT: Greenwood.

Marshall, Ray. 2009. *Immigration for Shared Prosperity—A Framework for Comprehensive Reform.* Washington, DC: Economic Policy Institute.

Massey, Douglas S., et al. 1987. *Return to Aztlan: The Social Process of International Migration from Western Mexico.* Berkeley: University of California Press.

Massey, Douglas S., Jorge Durand, and Nolan J. Malone. 2002. *Beyond Smoke and Mirrors: Immigration Policy in an Era of Free Trade.* New York: Russell Sage.

Merino, Noel. 2012. *Illegal Immigration.* Boston: Cengage/ Greenhaven Press.

National Conference of State Legislatures. 2014. "Undocumented Student Tuition: State Action." Denver, National Conference of State Legislatures.

National Law Center. 2014. "Deferred Action for Parents of Americans and Lawful Permanent Residents." http://www.nlc.org/dapa&daca.html.

Nevins, Joseph. 2002. *Operation Gatekeeper: The Rise of the Illegal Aliens and the Making of the U.S.-Mexico Boundary.* New York: Routledge.

Papademetriou, Demetrios, and Mark Miller, eds. 1984. *The Unavoidable Issue.* Philadelphia: Institute for the Study of Human Issues.

Preston, Julia. 2014. "Ailing Cities Extend Hand to Immigrants, National Desk," *New York Times*, October 7: A-18.

Select Commission on Immigration and Refugee Policy. 1981. *Final Report.* Washington, DC: U.S. Government Printing Office.

Salzman, H. et al. 2013. *Guestworkers in the High Skill U.S. Labor Market: An Analysis of Supply, Employment, and Wage Trends.* Washington, DC: Economic Policy Institute.

Stana, Richard M. 2003. *Homeland Security: Challenges to Implementing the Immigration Interior Enforcement Strategy.* GAO-03–660T. Washington, DC: U.S. Government Printing Office.

Suro, Roberto. 2015. "California Dreaming: The New Dynamism in Immigration Federalism and Opportunities for Inclusion on a Variegated Landscape." *Journal of Migration and Human Security* 3, no. 1: 1–25.

Tomas Rivera Policy Institute. 2014. "New Laws Extend Privileges Regardless of Status." Los Angeles, CA: Tomas Rivera Policy Institute, University of Southern California.

U.S. Congress. Senate. *Uniting and Strengthening America by Providing Appropriate Tools Required to Intercept and*

Obstruct Terrorism (USA PATRIOT ACT) Act of 2001. HR 3162. 107th Cong., 1st sess. http://www.epic.org/privacy/terrorism/hr3162.html. Accessed on April 20, 2003.

Zuniga, Victor, and Ruben Hernandez-Leon, eds. 2005. *New Destinations: Mexican Immigration to the United States.* New York: Russell Sage.

Adjustment to Immigrant Status   a procedure whereby a nonimmigrant may apply for a change of status to lawful permanent resident if an immigrant visa is available for his or her country. The alien is counted as an immigrant as of the date of adjustment.

Alien   a person who is not a citizen or national of a given nation-state.

Amicus Curiae   a "friend of the court" legal brief submitted by a state or an interest group that is not a party to a case but that has an interest in the outcome of the case, in which it argues its legal position on the case.

Amnesty   is the legal pardoning of a person who entered the country illegally or is otherwise in nonlegal status and thereby changing his/her status to legal resident alien.

Asylee   a person in the United States who is unable or unwilling to return to his/her country of origin because of persecution or fear of persecution. The person is eligible to become a permanent resident after one year of continuous residence in the United States.

Birthright Citizenship   means that any person born within the territory of the United States is a U.S. citizen. It is guaranteed by the Fourteenth Amendment: "all persons born or naturalized in the United States and subject to the jurisdiction thereof, are citizens of the United States."

Border Card a card allowing a person living within a certain zone of the United States border to legally cross back and forth for employment purposes without a passport or visa.

Border Jumper is a slang expression indicating a person who crosses the U.S. border without documentation, such as a visa or border card.

Border Patrol the law enforcement arm of the Department of Homeland Security.

Bracero Program a temporary farmworker program that allowed immigrant farmworkers to come to the United States for up to nine months annually to work in agriculture or the railroads. The Bracero Program lasted from 1942 to 1964.

Certiorari a writ issued by the U.S. Supreme Court to send up for its review upon appeal the records of a lower court case.

Chain Migration friends and relatives of immigrants drawn to specific locations by their compatriots already living in the United States.

Civil Law regulates the relations between or among persons and corporations and the government, as distinct from criminal law, the offense against which is usually considered a misdemeanor punished by fines rather than incarceration.

Criminal Law regulates the relation between persons and the state, offenses against which may be misdemeanors or felonies and are punished by fines and incarceration of determined length.

Debarkation leaving a ship or airplane to enter the United States.

Deportation a legal process by which a nation sends individuals back to their country of origin after refusing them legal residence.

Diversity Immigrants a special category of immigrants established by the 1990 IMMACT to allow a certain number of visas to be issued to immigrants from countries that previously had low admission numbers.

DREAM Act   an acronym for Development, Relief, and Education for Alien Minors. The proposed law, if enacted, would grant relief from deportation to certain specified alien minors brought to the United States as children who meet a number of specified conditions and allow them a path to eventual citizenship.

Due Process of Law   the constitutional limitation on governmental behavior to deal with an individual according to prescribed rules and procedures.

Earned Legalization   a proposal to allow unauthorized immigrants to change their status to that of legal permanent residents by paying fines, and satisfying stipulated conditions akin to those who came as authorized permanent resident aliens.

Emigrant   an individual who voluntarily leaves his/her country of birth for permanent resettlement elsewhere.

Emigration   the act of leaving one's place of origin or birth for permanent resettlement.

Employer Sanctions   a restrictive device of IRCA, it imposes penalties (fines or imprisonment or both) for knowingly hiring an illegal immigrant.

Equal Protection of the Law   the constitutionally guaranteed right that all persons be treated the same before the law.

EWIs   entered without inspection—another term for undocumented or illegal aliens, those who came without proper documentation or visa.

Excluded Categories   a listing in immigration law of those persons denied entrance to the United States for stated reasons, for the purpose of permanent residence.

Exclusion   the denial of legal entrance to a sovereign territory.

Executive Action   is an order by the U.S. president or a state governor that stipulates certain changes in the implementation of policy prescribed by law.

Exempt   an individual or class or category of individuals to whom a certain provision of the law does not apply.

Expedited Removal   is a stipulation in law changing the procedures by which persons in the United States without legal status may be deported with fewer judicial process hurdles to do so.

Expulsion   the decision of a sovereign nation to legally compel an individual to permanently leave its territory.

Felony vs. Misdemeanor   distinctions in criminal law stipulating the severity of the breach of law and imposing certain lengths of incarceration or amounts of fines in punishment for breaking the criminal law.

Gang of Eight   groups of four Democrats and four Republicans in the U.S. House of Representatives and in the U.S. Senate who worked together informally to fashion a proposal for comprehensive immigration reform.

Gateway States   the top seven or so immigrant-receiving states to which immigrants first migrate before moving on to settle in other states.

Green Card   a document issued by the DHS (previously by INS) that certifies an individual as a legal immigrant entitled to work in the United States.

Guest-Worker Program   a program enabling the legal importation of workers for temporary labor in specified occupations.

H-1B Visa   a category of temporary visa issued to a nonimmigrant allowing employers who will employ guest-workers temporarily in a specialty occupation of field, for a stipulated period of time.

Illegal Aliens   individuals who are in a territory without documentation permitting permanent residence.

Immediate Relatives   in recent immigration law, spouses, minor children, parents (of a citizen or a resident alien over 21 years of age), and brothers or sisters of a U.S. citizen or permanent resident alien.

Immigrant   an alien admitted to the United States as a lawful permanent resident.

Intermestic Policy   blends inexorably laws or procedures of both national and international considerations.

Investor Immigrant   an individual permitted to immigrate based upon a promise to invest $1 million in an urban area or $500,000 in a rural area to create at least 10 new jobs.

Legalized Alien   an alien lawfully admitted for temporary or permanent residence under the Immigration Act of 1965 or under the Immigration Reform and Control Act of 1986.

Literacy Test   a device imposed upon immigrants by the 1917 Immigration Act to restrict immigration to persons able to read and write.

L-Visa   is one of two types of visa issued for persons employed at a managerial or executive level and is issued for a specified time of up to three years and renewable for a maximum of seven years. L-1A visas are for intracompany transferees who have specialized knowledge in the field; L-2 visas are issued to spouses of L-1 visas.

Mortgaging   the legal device to "borrow" against future fiscal year immigration quotas to allow entrance of immigrants, for refugee or humanitarian purposes, after the fiscal quota for their nation of origin had been filled. First used by President Dwight D. Eisenhower.

National Sovereignty   the traditional understanding of sovereignty as the right of a nation-state to control territory under its jurisdiction and to control entrance into that territory or to expel individuals not granted legal residency.

Naturalization   the legal act of making an individual a citizen who was not born a citizen.

Net EWIs   estimates the total number from each country who entered without inspection and established residency in the United States, a large majority of whom are from Mexico.

NGOs   nongovernmental organizations. The term is used to refer to organizations involved in immigration matters, usually advocacy or immigrant assistance, that are not government agencies.

Nonimmigrant   an alien seeking temporary entry into the United States for a specific purpose other than permanent settlement—such as a foreign government official, tourist, student, temporary worker, or cultural exchange visitor.

Nonpreference   a category of immigrant visa apart from family- and employment-based preferences that was available primarily between 1966 and 1978, but eliminated by the Immigration Act of 1990 (IMMACT).

Nonquota Immigrant   a person allowed entrance for a specific reason who is not charged against a nation's annual quota.

Optional Practical Training (OPT)   offers practical experience via temporary employment to F-1 student visa holders for up to 12 months; students working in STEM fields are eligible for a 17-month extension at the end of one year, with the option of applying for an H-1B visa.

Overstayer   an individual who enters the United States on a temporary visa who then stays beyond the time specified in the visa at which he/she is to voluntarily depart.

Parolee   an alien, appearing to be inadmissible to the inspecting officer, allowed entry to the United States under humanitarian reasons when the alien's entry is determined to be for significant public benefit. Used by President Dwight D. Eisenhower and numerous presidents subsequently.

Passport   a legal identification document issued by a sovereign nation-state attesting to the nationality of an individual for international travel purposes.

Permanent Resident   a noncitizen who is allowed to live permanently in the United States and who can travel in and out of the country without a visa and can work without restriction. This person is also allowed to accumulate time toward becoming a naturalized citizen.

Preference System   a device used in immigration law to establish rules and procedures to determine the order in which annual limits of immigration visas were to be issued, established by the Immigration Act of 1965.

Preferences   were specified categories of individuals to be awarded visas for permanent immigration.

Protocol   an international agreement governing the understanding and procedures that member states who are parties to a treaty agree upon for a given purpose, as in the UN protocols regarding the status and treatment of refugees.

Pull Factors   aspects of the receiving nation that draw immigrants for resettlement.

Push Factors   events that compel large numbers of persons to emigrate.

Quota Immigrant   an individual seeking entrance to the United States or coming under the system that fixed an annual number of visas awarded to a person from a particular nation or territory. Governed by immigration law from 1921 to 1965.

Racial Profiling   a pattern of behavior of police officers based on racial appearance.

Refugee-Parolee   a qualified applicant for conditional entry between 1970 and 1980 whose application for admission could not be approved because of an inadequate number of seventh-preference visas. The applicant was paroled into the United States under the parole authority granted to the attorney general of the United States.

Restrictionism   a social movement of the late 19th and early 20th centuries that favored and advocated outright banning or severe limits to immigration.

Sojourner   an immigrant who comes to the United States intending to stay only temporarily.

Special Agricultural Worker   aliens who performed labor in perishable agricultural crop commodities for a specified period of time and were admitted for temporary and then permanent residence under the Immigration and Control Act of 1986.

STEM Workforce   persons employed in specified fields for a special category of guest-worker—an acronym meaning science, technology, engineering, and mathematics.

Trafficking   the transportation of persons for illegal purposes involving sexual or labor exploitation of the individual.

Transit Alien   an alien in immediate and continuous transit through the United States, with or without a visa. Transit aliens are principally aliens and their family serving at the UN headquarters and foreign government officials and their family members.

Unauthorized Alien   an individual who is in a territory without documentation—an illegal immigrant.

Unauthorized Immigrants   those who come undocumented or break or overstay the conditions of their visa and become illegal immigrants without the status of permanent resident aliens.

Undocumented Alien   an individual in a sovereign territory without legal authorization to be there—an illegal alien or immigrant.

Undocumented Immigrants   individuals who enter the United States without inspection or proper documentation allowing them to enter and to reside in the United States and to legally work while doing so.

Unfunded Mandates   requirements placed by the federal government upon state or local government without offsetting funding for their implementation.

Visa   a legal document issued by a consular or similar state department official allowing a person to travel to the United States for either permanent or temporary reasons—such as immigrant, student, tourist, government representative, business, or cultural exchange.

Withdrawal   an alien's voluntary removal of an application for admission in lieu of an exclusion hearing before an immigration judge.

Xenophobia   an unfounded fear of foreigners.

About the Author

Michael C. LeMay is professor emeritus from California State University, San Bernardino, where he served as Director of the National Security Studies program, an interdisciplinary master's degree program, and as chair of the Department of Political Science and assistant dean for student affairs of the College of Social and Behavioral Sciences. He has frequently written and presented papers at professional conferences on the topic of immigration. He has also written numerous journal articles, book chapters, published essays, and book reviews. He is published in *The International Migration Review, In Defense of the Alien, Journal of American Ethnic History, Southeastern Political Science Review, Teaching Political Science*, and the *National Civic Review*. He is author of a dozen academic volumes dealing with immigration history and policy. His prior books on the subject are: *Doctors at the Borders: Immigration and the Rise of Public Health* (2015: Praeger); series editor and contributing author of the three-volume series, *Transforming America: Perspectives on Immigration* (2013: ABC-CLIO); *Illegal Immigration: A Reference Handbook*, 1st ed. (2007: ABC-CLIO); *Guarding the Gates: Immigration and National Security* (2006: Praeger Security International); *U.S. Immigration: A Reference Handbook* (2004: ABC-CLIO); *U.S. Immigration and Naturalization Laws and Issues: A Documentary History*, edited with Elliott Barkan (1999: Greenwood); *Anatomy of a Public Policy: The Reform of Contemporary Immigration Law* (1994: Praeger);

The Gatekeepers: Comparative Immigration Policy (1989: Prae-ger); *From Open Door to Dutch Door: An Analysis of U.S. Immi-gration Policy Since 1820* (1987: Praeger); and *The Struggle for Influence* (1985: University Press of America). Professor LeMay has written two textbooks that have considerable material related to these topics: *Public Administration: Clashing Values in the Administration of Public Policy*, 2nd ed. (2006: Wadsworth); and *The Perennial Struggle: Race, Ethnicity and Minority Group Relations in the United States*, 3rd ed. (2009: Prentice-Hall). He frequently lecturers on topics related to immigration history and policy.